POLITICAL PHILOSOPHY NOW

Francis Fukuyama and the End of History

Howard Williams, David Sullivan and E. Gwynn Matthews

UNIVERSITY OF WALES PRESS • CARDIFF • 1997

British Library Cataloguing-in-Publication Data
A catalogue record for this book is available from the British Library.

ISBN 0–7083–1427–9 cased
      0–7083–1428–7 paperback

Typeset at the University of Wales Press, Cardiff.
Printed in Great Britain by Dinefwr Press, Llandybïe.

For Jennifer, Jeanette and Mair

Contents

Preface by Series Editor

Each of the chapters in this book was written predominantly by one of the authors. Howard Williams provided chapters one, two and three on Kant, Hegel and Marx. Chapters three, four and five on Fukuyama were composed by David Sullivan and chapters seven and eight on Popper and religion and the end of history were written by Gwynn Matthews (who was responsible for first bringing the three authors together). The final chapter was written by Howard Williams and David Sullivan. This is the broad picture. However, substantial sections of each chapter were provided by the other authors as well. So the whole is a collaborative enterprise. For the sake of consistency the entire book was brought together by David Sullivan and then finally edited by Howard Williams.

Introduction

Does history have a meaning? As we draw to the close of a century which has known the most appalling suffering and misery, the answers to that question are far from clear. To many people the very existence of the Holocaust and the other lesser but still horrific evils of the century – a list which runs from the senseless slaughter of the First World War through the Soviet Gulags to ethnic cleansing in the Balkans and Rwanda – means that no possible meaning can be found. Others have argued that the very belief that there is a meaning to history has contributed to many of these atrocities. Hitler and Stalin both believed themselves to be the instruments of destiny and their rationale for the genocidal policies they pursued rested at least in large on the claim that they 'knew' the meaning of history.

The suspicion of those who claim that history has a meaning is often well founded, but not every claim to have discovered that meaning leads to fascism or Stalinism. Indeed, some have claimed to detect a hopeful, humane, meaning to history in the very fact that these authoritarian systems have not only collapsed politically and economically but intellectually too. There is no longer, so they argue, an intellectually plausible reason for advocating fascist or communist principles, precisely because history has shown them to be catastrophically bad.

In his article 'The End of History?' and his subsequent book *The End of History and the Last Man* Francis Fukuyama has given one of the strongest recent affirmations that history has a meaning and that the meaning is a positive and hopeful one for mankind. Indeed, Fukuyama goes even further and argues that we are approaching the end of history. This claim has been so often made by gloomy pessimists that we might be inclined to think that Fukuyama means that we are about to destroy ourselves by the misuse of our weapons of mass destruction, or by some spectacular contamination of the environment. But this is not his claim at all: he is arguing something far brighter and more optimistic. For Fukuyama, history is coming to an end in the sense that we, in the advanced industrial democracies at least, are in the process of moving into a period of unalloyed peace, prosperity and freedom.

The article 'The End of History?' was published in 1989, just as the old Soviet Empire in Eastern Europe was entering its final stage of dissolution and its welcome of these changes was seen by many at the time as affirming an excessively partisan, neo-conservative view of world events. But this view, whatever the specific political arguments about Fukuyama's role as a member of the American State Department, as an associate of the Rand Corporation and as an expert on Soviet policy in the Third World,[1] should not conceal the fact that Fukuyama was drawing on a very powerful tradition, which many of his critics, especially those on the Left, also subscribe to. Many people rejected the idea that history was coming to an end, but the underlying assumptions of Fukuyama's thesis are widely held in the modern Western world, and were indeed paid lip-service to, at least, by the ideologists of the old Soviet Union.

The tradition which Fukuyama draws upon is one which states that the human race is progressing and that it is moving towards an end point at which conflict and violence will cease. In its origins this idea is to be found in many religious systems, and in the West it is to be found in a particular form in Christianity, but in its modern version, and especially in Fukuyama's own work, the idea of the end of history makes a radical break with all theistic views of historical change. Fukuyama's ideas are deeply secular and the part of the tradition upon which he draws most closely is very much a product of modernity. This becomes increasingly clear as we trace Fukuyama's indebtedness to three of the greatest contributors to the tradition of the end of history who are also three of the most significant thinkers in the development of modernity.

A number of the key ideas which are central to the tradition are to be found in the writings of Immanuel Kant, arguably the greatest philosopher of the modern world. From Kant was derived the ideal of the autonomous human will and the moral responsibility which was an essential consequence of that. Fukuyama's writings are deeply indebted to this moral theory of Kant and to the political liberalism to which it gave rise. He is also strongly influenced by Kant's hope for a time of perpetual peace, where wars would cease and international society would be harmonious.

Although Kant looked forward to such a society he did not have a fully worked out theory of how the end of history might come about.

For that the tradition is indebted first to G. W. F. Hegel. Hegel argued strongly that there was an inner meaning to history and a pattern which was discernible to the rational mind, especially the rational *modern* mind which built upon the insights of its predecessors. For Hegel, the most important force in history is that of ideas, and he claims that the end of history must be understood first and foremost as the triumph of rational thought. In his own terminology, the societies at the end of history will be those in which that which is rational will become fully actualized in the world as a whole, and in the social and political sphere especially.

Fukuyama treats Hegel with the greatest respect, and writes of his own work as following in the footsteps of the master. This is most obvious in his wholehearted embracing of Hegel's belief in the supremacy of ideas – for Fukuyama, the end of history has arrived with the final triumph and undisputed dominance of a set of ideas which can never be improved upon. The content of these ideas owe as much to Kant's liberalism as they do to Hegel's philosophy, but in asserting the supremacy of ideas Fukuyama is indisputably an Hegelian.

The third great contributor to the tradition of the end of history is the one with whom, to judge by first appearance at least, Fukuyama has least in common. This is Karl Marx, who appears in 'The End of History?' and *The End of History and the Last Man* as the man whom history has proved to have been false. According to Fukuyama's reading of him, Marx shared Hegel's belief that history would end but made a fundamental mistake in his assessment of what this meant when he rejected the claim that ideas were the dominant force in history and made socio-economic relationships the crucial factor. This in turn led him to a materialist view of society and an excessively one-sided critical understanding of market forces. The end result was the tyranny of the communist regimes which for a time held sway over a large part of the world's population.

Given Fukuyama's detailed knowledge of the workings of the Soviet Union, and especially the ruthless imperialism of its foreign policy, it is not surprising that he is highly critical of the ideology of that regime, but in some respects it may have blinded him to a number of similarities between his position and that of Marx. To see how this may be so it is necessary to have a clear idea of what Marx, as opposed to his self-proclaimed followers in the former Soviet Union, actually thought about these questions, and we have devoted a chapter to him for this purpose, as well as allotting chapters to the more direct influence of Kant and Hegel.

Our lengthy discussion of Fukuyama's ideas in chapters 4 to 6 is intended both to situate him more fully in the tradition from which he has emerged and, as far as possible, to state his main arguments as sympathetically and as constructively as we can. Since the publication of the article and the book Fukuyama has been subjected to a great deal of hostile criticism, some of which seems to have been written without the benefit of first-hand knowledge of his texts.[2] By placing his ideas more clearly in the broader setting to which they belong we hope to show that they are far more coherent and well thought through than is often alleged.

In claiming that Fukuyama's theses fit well into a profoundly important tradition, we are primarily claiming that they deserve to be discussed seriously and in depth. Whether his arguments, and those of the writers whom he draws upon, are correct is another issue, and in the final part of the book we contrast his views with those of two other major Western traditions.

The first alternative with which we contrast Fukuyama is the anti-historicist position of Karl Popper. Popper's philosophy is important in its own right but it is all the more striking as a theory with which to oppose Fukuyama because Popper's general political stance is firmly located within the same broad liberal tradition which Fukuyama is seeking to defend. The comparative analysis of their two positions helps to clarify further Fukuyama's theory and also to indicate some of the dangers to which his theory could give rise if pushed too far in certain directions.

The second of the alternatives which we discuss we have referred to as theistic historicism. This is the belief that there is a meaning in history but that the meaning may be discerned only by those who accept that there is a transcendent being who stands outside history and controls it. In the Western tradition this view is associated most obviously with Christianity but similar ideas are to be found both in Judaism and in Islam. There are similarities between this view and the end of history tradition, and indeed we argue that earlier versions of the tradition, especially Hegel's, have not sufficiently freed themselves from the influence of Christianity for them to have fully matured as a distinct set of ideas. Nevertheless, the differences between the theistic and non-theistic approach are very considerable when the end of history tradition is more consistently worked out, as it is in Fukuyama's thought.

The idea of the end of history is a theory of considerable complexity but also of immense importance in the modern world. For too long it has been neglected, and with the political failure of one branch of the tradition, Marxism, it seemed for a moment that the whole tradition was in danger of complete collapse. Fukuyama, trenchant critic though he is of the old communist regimes of Eastern Europe and the moribund regime in China, has provided a new and stimulating restatement of the central ideas of the tradition. In what follows we explore the development of the tradition and try to show why, despite all the criticisms levelled against it, it still deserves to be treated as one of the seminal ideas of modern Western culture.

1 • Kant:

History and the Moral Imperative

Introduction: the nine propositions

Kant is one of the first modern philosophers for whom the idea of the end of history has a central place in an account of history and society. This, along with Kant's enormous influence in the development of modern philosophy generally, is a prime reason for beginning our discussion with him. Yet as soon as we begin to examine his use of the term 'the end of history' we find an important ambiguity within it. In English, the notion of the end of history is frequently used to refer to the idea of the completion of history, or of history coming to a close. This is the sense in which it is most often used in the current debate, and many commentators on Fukuyama write as if this were the only significant way in which the term can be used. There is, though, a very important second sense which the term can have. This speaks about the end of history in terms of purpose, of a significance which is immanent in the process of history and which enables human beings to find a meaning in their lives as they experience them in the present, without the necessity of waiting for an ideal future. For Kant, it is this second sense which is most important. He thinks it an open question whether or not history, in the sense of the temporal progress of human life, will ever come to an end. Indeed he claims that this question cannot be decided either by science or metaphysical speculation. However, he is in no doubt that in moral terms, or more broadly still in aesthetic terms, the actions of men within history can be made purposeful. We cannot claim empirically to have any certainty that history is developing towards a just society, but as rational, morally active beings we ought to act as if it is, and in acting this way we may well help to bring it about.

Kant deals with the idea of the end of history in a number of his shorter writings. Perhaps the most important of these are the essay completed in 1784 on the 'Idea for a Universal History with a Cosmopolitan Purpose', and the best-known of his political writings, *Perpetual Peace*, published in 1795. He also entered into a controversy with his former pupil Herder on the nature of history, and wrote two significant reviews of Herder's book *Ideas on the Philosophy of the History of Mankind*. Finally, Kant also deals with history in a systematic way in his *Critique of Judgement* published in 1790, and his final discussion, which clarifies some of his earlier views, is found in *The Contest of the Faculties* published in 1797.

Kant uses the essay on the 'Idea for a Universal History' to put forward nine propositions about the nature and objective of human history. These nine propositions, translated afresh for this book, are:

1. All the natural dispositions of a creature are destined to evolve completely and in accord with their purpose.

2. With the human individual (as the only rational creature on earth) those natural capacities which are intended for the use of his reason are to be fully developed in the race, and not in the individual.

3. Nature has wished that the human being should produce from himself everything that goes beyond the mechanical ordering of his animal existence, and that he should enjoy no other happiness or perfection than that which he himself, independently of instinct has created by his own reason.

4. The means employed by nature to bring about the development of all the capacities of human individuals is their antagonism in society in so far as this is, ultimately, the cause of a lawful order among men.

5. The greatest problem for the human species, to the solution of which nature drives the species, is the achievement of a *universal civil society* administering law.

6. This problem is the most difficult one, and the one which will be solved last by the human species. A human being is an animal who when he lives among his own species requires a master. But where does he get this master? From nowhere else other than the human species. Yet this master is just as much an animal who requires a master.

7. The problem of establishing a perfect civic constitution is dependent on the problem of a lawful external relation among states, and cannot be solved without a solution to the latter problem.

8. The history of the human species can be seen in the large as the realization of nature's secret plan to produce an internally, and

also – for this purpose – externally perfectly constituted state as the only condition in which the capacities of mankind can be fully developed.

9. A philosophical attempt to work out a universal world history according to a plan of nature directed at achieving the civic union of the human species must be regarded as possible and, indeed, as furthering this intention of nature.[1]

The nine propositions examined

It can be seen from these nine propositions that not only does Kant have very high expectations of world history, but he also has high expectations of the philosophy of history. The grounds for these high expectations are to be found in Kant's philosophy as a whole. In his general philosophy, particularly his moral and religious philosophy, Kant takes a dualistic view of the human individual whom he sees as divided between an empirical or natural part and an intellectual or intelligent part. In a sense this is the classical division between body and mind, or spirit and flesh. Yet Kant does not see this as an insoluble antagonism. He thinks body and mind can be mediated from both the standpoint of matter and the standpoint of intellect. However, this will not be an immediate process. We cannot simply bring nature and mind into harmony with each other; it is a process of mediation which will take place over time. The demands of our intelligent side and the demands of our instinctual side can be reconciled only through a process of development. This is the process of human evolution in which our talents and abilities improve from one generation to another. But this conflict between body and mind, nature and reason is not from Kant's point of view an unproductive or negative one. Indeed it is through the conflict between intellect and nature that the human individual is gradually civilized. In battling with our natural, instinctual side in our relations with others, we slowly develop the skills with which to live in peace and harmony.

The nine propositions which Kant puts forward in the idea for universal history move out from the individual to the nation and the international situation, and then back to the individual in the form of the philosopher of history. The first proposition claims that no individual on his own can fully realize the ends of history, and the second proposition argues that this naturally can only be achieved by the species as a whole. The third thesis emphasizes that this process of development of the species is not going to be an easy one. Indeed, it stresses the extent to which it will demand effort from the human individual.

> Nature does nothing in vain, and in the use of a means to a goal she is not prodigal. Her giving to man reason and freedom of will which depends upon it is a clear indication of her purpose. Man accordingly was not to be guided by instinct, nor nurtured and instructed with ready made knowledge; rather, he should bring forth everything out of his own resources.[2]

The first proposition seeks to demonstrate the extent to which man's powers are not only in conflict with nature but also in conflict with other men. According to Kant the human individual is an asocial, sociable individual.

> Man has an inclination to associate with others, because in society he feels himself to be more than a man (i.e. as more than the developed form of his natural capacities). But he also has a strong propensity to isolate himself from others, because he finds in himself at the same time the unsocial characteristics of wishing to have everything go according to his own wish.[3]

This asociability is both good and bad. It is bad in the sense that it prevents individuals from getting along with others, but it is good in the sense that it forces individuals to develop their own powers and abilities. The fifth proposition argues that this asocial sociability is best harnessed within a developed civil society, which for Kant means a society with laws enforced by a republican constitution.

But the problem of creating a perfectly just republican constitution is a very difficult one for a society to master. It is, indeed, a difficult one for the human race as a whole and Kant goes so far as to claim that it is the *most difficult* problem which humanity has to resolve. So the sixth proposition is concerned with the resolution of the problem proposed by the fifth, that is how in fact is it possible to create a society where individuals live under law? Kant thinks that this can only be achieved by human individuals first acquiring a master. We have to move from submission to a master to the creation of a civic and just constitution. We cannot expect a just constitution to evolve from the people themselves; it has to be gradually imposed upon them, perhaps partly by their own wish and partly against their wishes. The seventh thesis or proposition deals with the same problem, because Kant believes that the creation of a perfect civic constitution is not possible in isolation. One state on its own cannot hope to create a perfect civic constitution. The condition of international society for Kant mirrors that of individuals without the rule of law. They live in an antagonistic relationship with one another, and this means that a proper peaceful civic constitution is difficult to realize. The insecurity of nations threatens domestic law. This means for Kant that the legitimate domestic authority of a state cannot be achieved without there first of all being a settled and peaceful international order.

For Kant, the problem of war and the problem of domestic politics are intertwined. There is no solution to the difficulties of internal politics without there first of all being a resolution to the problems of war itself. This brings us to a crucial passage in Kant's essay on the 'Idea for a Universal History':

> All wars are accordingly so many attempts (not indeed in the intention of man, but in the intention of nature) to establish new relations among states, and through the destruction or at least the dismemberment of the old to create new political bodies, which, again, either internally or externally, cannot maintain themselves and which must in turn suffer similar revolutions; until finally, partly through the best civic constitution and partly through common agreement and legislation in external affairs, a state is created which, similar to a civic commonwealth, can like an automatic machine maintain itself.[4]

Kant here sets an extraordinarily ambitious agenda for history. Not only has history to bring to an end the divisive problems of domestic society; it has also to bring to an end the principal conflicts of international society. Kant does not see these as utopian goals – rather they are the goals which it is necessary to achieve in order for conventional or normal human society ultimately to proceed. Human individuals have to learn virtue if they are to live in peace and harmony with one another, and if they do not do it of their own natural inclination they will be brought to do it by development of human society. As Kant sees it, both the tendencies of the empirical world and those of the intelligible (or intellectual) world press in the same direction.

This brings us to Kant's eighth proposition which sees human history as a realization of a secret plan by nature to bring forth a perfectly constituted state. The disorder of international society has severe lessons to teach the human race. First of all it teaches us the futility of war itself. War brings with it such human suffering and loss of revenue and income that those who are engaged in it at present will from their own experience conclude that it was an unwise undertaking. As Kant puts it, 'in the end, war itself will be seen as not only so artificial, in outcome so uncertain for both sides, in after effects so painful in form of an ever growing war debt (a new invention) that cannot be met, that it will be regarded as a most dubious undertaking.'5 Crucially, the ninth proposition recognizes that we cannot expect to have this process occur automatically. Philosophers will have to make human beings aware of the shortcomings and the folly of war. At a factual level the relations among states will never cease to be ones of conflict and war unless the moral consciousness is awakened in us that this is a mistaken state of affairs. This is where the philosopher of history and the conception of an end of history can play a significant role. In the ebb and flow of day-to-day events the philosopher can possibly discover a tendency towards improvement. It is the task of the philosopher to point out this tendency and to encourage the political leaders and citizens to work with it rather than against it. Kant's argument is that necessity forces mankind to seek to remove war from the scene. However, the process of removing war from the scene can be greatly accelerated if humankind becomes conscious of the need to take steps in that direction. So Kant sees a harmony of purposes between the necessary development of human and international society and the role the philosopher can play. The philosopher can map out those steps towards improvement which are already occurring and possibly accelerate the process. There is no end to history in the temporal sense: humankind can continue to struggle with itself to produce wars and lead itself to the brink of disaster. However, there is an end to history from the philosophical or moral point of view in that humankind can become gradually sufficiently prudent and rational to avoid the consequences of its own shortcomings of character and behaviour.

Kant's view of history questioned

This philosophical sketch of the development of history raises some important questions. Kant's stress upon the need first of all to establish firm and lasting peaceful international relations before then turning to the domestic situation is highly problematic. To begin with, it seems to take away from the individual responsibility for bringing about progressive change in human life. Kant appears to overlook the contribution that good citizenship might play in bringing about the process he seeks to achieve. It is as if he believes that individuals within states cannot be trusted to work for a sensible civic constitution and that they have to wait upon international events before this goal can be achieved. But what if international events are always negative and prevent a favourable state of affairs coming into being? Are then citizens impotent in the face of. such hostile conditions? There is a gap in Kant's reasoning here, but it is a gap which is partially filled by the later (1795) essay on *Perpetual Peace*. In this essay, Kant puts more emphasis on the role that states themselves can play in the development of world harmony. The first definitive article of the essay on perpetual peace requires states to bring about republican constitutions. A republican constitution for Kant is founded upon three principles: 'firstly, the principle of freedom for all members of a society (as human beings); secondly, the principle of the dependence of everyone on a single common legislation (as subjects); and thirdly, the principle of legal equality for everyone (as citizens).'[6] In the essay on *Perpetual Peace* Kant seems to envisage progress occurring both at the level of the state and at the international level among states. This is a more hopeful prospect from the standpoint of individual citizens. By working towards a republican constitution within their states they can contribute to the gradual development of a peaceful world situation. And outside the state their leaders can work towards a worldwide civil society.

The other question that the idea for universal history raises is: How is it possible for international progress to be achieved? The essay on the idea of universal history seems to rely too much upon the accidental and the contingent – what Kant calls nature. Kant impresses upon his readers in the essay the dangers brought about by war and suggests that insecurity itself may lead to the development of a peaceful international order. But this does not seem to us to be sufficient. If excessive insecurity were all that was needed, then peace may well already have been instituted. Kant has to find some other mechanisms to lead to a more peaceful international order. These are nowhere to be found in the 'Idea for a Universal History', but the essay on *Perpetual Peace* seeks to fill the gap. Here we have the notion of improved civil states which are able to set an example for other states to follow. Kant sees this as coming about through a loose federation of states which have republican constitutions or are developing them.[7] In such a loose federation some states which are already well towards developing the perfect constitution can set an example. Kant may have hoped that the United States and France, with their constitutions based upon popular sovereignty, would help to set the tone for such a development.

Human societies emerge from a state of nature. In this state of nature there is no legal system or central authority of any kind and consequently our possessions are always at risk. When societies emerge from this insecure condition they do not immediately conform to what Kant calls 'the idea of the state'.[8] In early forms of human society people may be ruled arbitrarily by kings, an aristocratic caste or a military élite. Such societies have an advantage over the state of nature because in these societies some form of law prevails. These laws may be merely customary at first but gradually as they become codified they become the basis of a just system. The rule of law is therefore, for Kant, a crucial feature of the idea of the state, but there are also a number of other key factors, two of which are particularly important. The first of these is the requirement that the laws of the state should be made by the peoples' representatives. The second is that these laws should be enacted by an executive which is independent of the legislature. Kant believed that republican states based on these principles would incline towards peace with their neighbours because their citizens would no longer be subject to oppressive rule, and because their representatives would have the responsibility for considering whether or not to declare war.

As we will see in chapter 6, Kant's thought has been extremely influential on Fukuyama's thinking about international relations and the need for a 'pacific union' of liberal democratic states. Fukuyama claims that the pacific union has already been formed among the world's advanced liberal democracies and that the existence of the union has played a significant role in leading other countries to become liberal democracies.[9] He even agrees with Kant in seeing the constitutional republics created by the American and French Revolutions as providing role models for others to follow.

It is important to stress that the framework for Kant's view of the end of history does not move outside the structure of his philosophy as a whole. As we have seen, in his general philosophy there is a division between the natural side of man and the intellectual or intelligent side, and this is mirrored in the historical process itself. Kant sees this tension as possibly leading to progress but it is not clear in this dialectic of nature and reason which is to play the foremost role. Is it the difficulties of nature that are going to induce individuals and states to live in more peaceful relations with each other, or is it the intelligence and wit of man that is going to lead him to conclude that no other course other than peaceful federation is the sensible one? Kant seems to want it both ways. He wants both natural contingency to contribute towards progress and, on the other hand, he wants the intelligence and wit of the human individual to bring it about. However, is it possible for both forces to exert an influence simultaneously? If nature does not represent an obstacle then there is no place for the intelligence of man. In contrast, if the intelligence of man is strong enough then the role of nature is secondary. It seems to us that at this point Kant's account of the end of history is more inconclusive than he would wish it to be. Kant argues at the end of his essay 'A Conjectural Beginning of Human History' that we should demonstrate a 'contentment' (*Zufriedenheit*) in relation to the development of history thus far.[10] This contentment we should express at the growth of human society seems to conflict with his own view of the dialectic of history.

Kant's three views of history in the *Contest of the Faculties*

Kant returned to the topic of history in his last published work, *The Contest of the Faculties*,[11] where, in the second section of the essay, he deals expressly with the question of the 'end of human history'. When addressing this question Kant presents three possible ways of seeing the end of history and then recommends his own way of seeing historical purpose. He does so under the heading: 'A renewed attempt to answer the question: "is the human race continually improving?" '[12]

One could only genuinely foretell the future of the human race as a whole if one possessed supernatural powers. The future of the human race cannot be discovered from 'known laws of nature'. In this respect the activity of the human race is different from the movement of the planetary system, part of which it occupies. With the planetary system the 'eclipse of the sun and moon' can 'be foretold by natural means',[13] but no such certainty is possible in human affairs. Because of this difference prediction in relation to the human race has to take on the form of a prophecy. If we were able accurately to foretell our common future this would presuppose a *supernatural* power. Kant thinks we do not possess such a power, but what makes attempts to foresee the future from a human point of view sensible is the fact that we are not without the power to affect our own situation. Although we do not have the power to know the future we do have the power partially to *make* the future.

Kant poses the problem of history in this telling way:

> We are dealing with freely acting beings to whom one can *dictate* in advance what they *ought* to do, but of whom one cannot predict what they actually *will* do, and who are capable, if things go really badly and they experience evils incurred through their own actions, of regarding these evils as a greater incentive to do better then they did in the past.[14]

What makes the human future difficult to predict is the propensity toward evil present in the human soul. If we were always inclined to be good then we could predict a certain improvement in the condition of the human species, but because we are always capable of acting badly we cannot allow ourselves such unthinking optimism.

Kant believes there are three possible forms that our attempts to prophesy the future might take. First we might suppose that the human race was on a continuous backward track. We might imagine therefore the future of the human race as one of constant deterioration. Secondly, we might also prophesy the opposite, namely, that the human race was continuously *improving*. Here optimism would denote our attitude to the future with a firm expectation that tomorrow would always be better. The third possibility would be to assume that the human race was neither improving nor deteriorating. From this viewpoint, the human race would be seen to be at a *standstill*.

The purpose of human history is, as Kant sees it, the moral improvement of the human race. This is not an improvement from a bad or an original evil, to the good as human perfection, but rather an improvement from the worse to the better.

> Man's emergence from that paradise which reason represents to him as the first abode of his species was nothing other than his transition from

a rude and purely animal existence to a state of humanity, from the
leading strings of instinct to the guidance of reason – in a word, from
the guardianship of nature to the state of freedom. Whether he gained
or lost through this change is no longer a question when we consider
the destiny of his species, which consists quite simply in progress
towards perfection, however flawed his first attempts to attain this end
– even if they are followed by a long series of further attempts – may
prove to be?[15]

In his concern to show what value the philosophy of history might
have, Kant acknowledges that a philosophy of history cannot predict
the future, but it may none the less serve a moral purpose. It does this
by pointing the way forward and encouraging individuals to follow it.
But this assumes that human beings are free, and yet Kant
acknowledges that there are limits to the power which individuals can
exercise over their own affairs. The following passage is much more
restrained.

We should be content with providence and with the course of human
affairs as a whole which does not begin with good and then proceed to
evil, but develops gradually from the worse to the better; and each
individual is for his own part called upon by nature itself to contribute
towards the progress to the best of his ability.[16]

This is a much more cautious optimism – men may succeed under the
benevolent influence of nature or providence but only so far as their
ability will allow them. And the implication is that the ability is itself
seriously limited.

To understand Kant's mature position on this question more fully
we need to look more closely at the *Contest of the Faculties*. In this
work, as we have seen, Kant discusses three contemporary views of
the way in which we are to understand the appearance of historical
change. The assumption behind these views is that we have to put
forward a prophecy of some kind. But then the question is turned
around. Need this be a prophecy if we are dealing with the actions of
freely acting beings?[17]

Kant is here addressing the perennial argument over free will and
determinism, but he suggests that perhaps the reason why we find
ourselves with this deeply confusing way of looking at the problem is
that we are approaching it from the wrong perspective. We are

looking at the problem from within, as it were, and so getting a slanted or biased view. Because we are participants who experience these events as both free and determined we cannot rise above our experience in order to produce a clear-sighted answer. 'It is our misfortune,' as he put it, 'that we are unable to adopt an absolute point of view when trying to predict free actions.'[18] However, although we may be aware of our limitations in this respect there is nothing we can do to change the situation. Unlike the natural scientist who can adopt a neutral point from which to observe the physical world, no such position is even logically possible when observing the human events in which we are involved.

The key question for Kant at this point is therefore a practical one. Is there any evidence that the human race will show its capacity for free action in deciding for progress? 'If it were possible to credit human beings with even a limited will of innate and unvarying goodness, we would certainly predict a general improvement of mankind, for this would involve events which man could himself control'.[19]

As we have said, the *Contest of Faculties* was one of Kant's last published works. He was aware that in writing the essay he was tackling a controversial subject at a difficult time, in the aftermath of the French Revolution. Kant attempted to publish the first section, concerning the conflict of the philosophical faculty with the theological faculty, in 1794, but was prevented from doing so by the censors. Kant's wish to see the philosophical faculty as independent from the theological faculty, and therefore free to criticize the foundations of public religion, proved unacceptable to the authorities.

The discussion of history appears in the second section of the essay where Kant deals with the suggested conflict between the juristic (legal/political) faculty and the philosophical faculty. To understand his arguments properly, we need to look more closely at the three possible conceptions of history which Kant identifies.

The first view claims that the human race is in inevitable moral decline: progress is impossible. Kant rejects this argument on the grounds that such a decline into oblivion is not continuously possible 'for mankind would wear itself out after a certain point had been reached'. Those who stress continuous decline therefore must have in mind such fantastic rebirths of the human race in which everything will be put right. They must be dreaming, he continued, 'of a world created anew after the present world has been destroyed by fire'.[20]

Kant labels this the terroristic view of history, an indication of his deep disapproval of those who advocated acting politically as if this theory were correct.

According to the second theory the human race is constantly progressing in a virtually unhindered path upwards. Kant labels this account 'eudaemonistic'. Eudaemonistic theories are ones which make the pursuit of happiness the basis of our duty. He also says that if the end which the advocates of this theory had in mind were nearer it could be termed chiliastic, a reference to the theological idea of a golden age at the end of time. Kant rejects this theory because he does not believe that human beings who, after all, choose to be evil, can be expected to give up that possibility automatically. The Enlightenment thinkers who claim that human individuals will morally improve as society develops overlook the point that if we possessed an innate capacity for moral betterment then that should have made us wholly moral already.

This might seem to lead Kant to accept the third theory, which states that the human race is neither improving nor deteriorating but is at a permanent standstill. Indeed, Kant does believe that this is the standard which most people would support. But he rejects this hypothesis just as firmly as the other two. The term he uses to designate the theory, 'abderite', is indicative of the contempt in which he holds it. The term is derived from a novel popular in Kant's own day, *The Story of the Abderites*, part of the genre of eighteenth-century novels in which human frailties were lampooned. In the novel, the Abderans were a people particularly noted for their foolishness and Kant is clearly implying that those who hold to this third view of history are especially foolish. The grounds for Kant's strident opposition to the hypothesis that the human race neither progresses nor regresses lie in his belief that the cycle of endless repetition which this theory pictures is ultimately destructive of human life and values. We construct only in order to destroy. We destroy only in order once again to construct. We push up the stone of Sisyphus only to let it later fall back again. The principles of good and evil in the human race destroy themselves. 'And in the eyes of reason, this cannot give any higher value to mankind than to the other animal species, whose interaction takes place at less cost and without any conscious understanding.'

Here, as in his earlier works, Kant argues that the problem of progress cannot be solved directly from experience. Experience is based on observation and the senses, and the data which they provide can never be conclusive. As Kant puts it, 'we are dealing with freely acting beings to whom one can dictate in advance what they ought to do, but of whom one cannot predict what they actually *will* do.'[21] Our freedom as human individuals presents both the possibility of advance and the possibility of reverse. Thus the issue as to whether history has, from a moral point of view, come to an end is permanently undecided and undecidable.

Kant's account of the end of history is first and foremost moral and political rather than metaphysical in that it relates primarily to our motives in acting. As far as Kant is concerned, there can be no doctrine of first principles which encompass both what we know (the natural universe) and what we ought to do (the social universe). He urges his readers to follow the moral imperative to act justly and to work towards a more just society, but there is no underpinning metaphysical guarantee that a wholly just society will ever be established. We have always to act on faith.

But this does not complete the picture, because Kant's account of morality itself may be taken in one of two ways. In the first place, it is possible to interpret it pessimistically. From Kant's premise that we are all dual and, therefore, flawed beings, who have a foothold in the rational and natural world, we can conclude that we shall never fully attain the goal set by the categorical imperative. Not fully equal to the task set for us by the demands of morality we must, it seems, resign ourselves to the way of the world and seek simply to do our best to improve our personal conduct. But, in the second place, it is possible, starting from the same premises, to interpret Kant's account of morality optimistically. This optimistic view accepts that at present, because of man's flawed nature, we might not be able to attain the ideal of the highest good envisaged by Kant in the 'kingdom of ends'. However, stress is placed here on the hope that we may, as time passes, approximate more and more to the goal.

Conclusion

This optimistic reading of Kant's ethics is developed by Yirmiahu Yovel in one of the most important and influential books on Kant's philosophy of history.[22] The idea of the highest good (*summum bonum*), which plays such a significant role in the *Critique of*

Practical Reason is, on Yovel's interpretation of Kant, a realizable goal. It would be realized in a perfectly just community based upon the laws of virtue. Thus, for Yovel, the proper focus of attention in the study of Kant's practical philosophy, including the philosophy of history, ought to be both the individual and the community.

In keeping with this view Yovel suggests that 'Kant scholars have not yet given the concept of the highest good all the attention it deserves'.[23] Although this claim may involve a slight exaggeration, we agree with Yovel's suggestion that the more usual interpretation of the concept has tended to restrict its relevance to the sphere of personal morality. And in drawing attention to the importance of the concept for Kant in the far wider spheres of society and history he carries out a very valuable task. He tackles the problem of showing the wider significance of the concept on two fronts. He devotes a good deal of his argument to showing how the idea of the highest good with its historical connotations, frequently occurs in the critical and systematic writings, in particular the second and third *Critique*, and to demonstrating that where it occurs it does so as one of the main themes of Kant's system. As Yovel puts it, for Kant, 'the highest good becomes an ideal of a co-ordination between the natural order and moral legislation'.[24] According to this view the concept of the *summum bonum* is the most important link between Kant's theoretical and practical philosophy.

In developing this systematic view of the role of history in Kant's writings, Yovel makes much of the contrast in Kant's philosophy between what he calls 'rational history' and 'natural dialectic'. In the essay on 'Idea for an Universal History' Kant suggests we might usefully regard human society as having within it a natural dialectic which works through man's unsociable-sociability to produce progress. Yovel argues that this view is superseded by Kant's suggestion in the *Critique of Judgement* that we regard teleology in history as a reflective principle of reason.[25] The first claim implies for Yovel a concrete historical assertion, whereas the second simply implies a way of comprehending history so as to provide a basis for moral intervention. We would argue the contrast is not as sharp as Yovel suggests it is. Kant is at pains in the essay to show that he understands the idea of progress through the beneficent intervention of nature as simply a hypothesis. Understood in this way there is a close and mutually supporting link between the *Critique of Judgement* and the earlier essays on history.

So far Yovel's argument seems to us to be correct but his interpretation runs into difficulties when he addresses the thorny problem of the role which Kant attributes to politics in attaining the highest good.[26] Yovel takes an important first step by distinguishing between the broader concept of the highest moral good and the narrower concept of the highest political good. The highest political good for Kant is the condition of perpetual peace which might, on the face of it, be brought about by the creation of one world-state. However, this is a solution Kant rejects in favour of a solution which requires that we attain the highest moral good at the same time as attaining the highest political good. Yovel does not believe that in Kant's opinion the two objectives can be realized at one and the same time.[27] In saying this Yovel mistakenly identifies Kant's solution to the problem of politics at the national level with his solution at an international level. At a national level, Kant argues that peace and order can be brought about even for a race of devils, providing they possess understanding; however, at the international level he believes that peace can only be brought about by the long-term change in the moral proficiency of human individuals. Good political leadership, education and religion can all play their part in this secular change. What Kant rules out is that such a change can be brought about by creating an international state through force. It is wrong to suggest that the long-term objectives of politics and morality diverge for Kant. A Kantian moral politician can unite the objectives of politics with those of morality. Kant expresses his hope for the convergence of moral and political goals in *Religion within the Limits of Reason Alone* where he says:

> Such, therefore, is the activity of the good principle, unnoticed by human eyes but ever continuing – erecting for itself in the human race, regarding as a common-wealth under laws of virtue, a power and kingdom which sustains the victory over evil, and under its own dominion, assures the world of eternal peace.[28]

Although politics cannot assure us of the long-term victory of morality, sound moral behaviour can help assure us of the long-term victory of politics in achieving perpetual peace.

One other aspect of Yovel's important and influential book is of particular relevance to our present purposes. This concerns Yovel's reading of Kant through the eyes of other writers within the end of history tradition. Yovel seeks to justify a Hegelian reading of Kant, and to a certain extent he also anticipates Fukuyama by hinting at a Marxist reading of Kant. In making these claims he focuses especially on the areas of the history of religion and the history of philosophy. Kant's view of the development of reason has, he suggests, a great deal in common with Hegel's idea of the development of spirit. Here Yovel makes some interesting comparisons between Hegel and Kant, but, on the whole, he fails to convince that there is a significant overlap in their positions. Moreover, in stressing Kant's role as a critic of the Christian religion[29] he exaggerates the distance between Kantian and Christian ideals. Kant's aim in his philosophy of religion is to show how the main principles at the core of Christianity are fully expressed in his own philosophy. Some of Kant's shocked contemporaries may have regarded him as an atheist, but this is certainly not how he saw himself.

Kant saw many other philosophers and philosophical systems as aiming at the same kind of synthesis as he achieves in the critical philosophy, but he does not go so far as to suggest, as Hegel was to, that his philosophy is the rational point of culmination of all previous philosophy. Kant sees other philosophical systems as more in competition with his own, and all equally necessary to the attaining of the truth.

Thus, from his standpoint it is important that the one system should not fully encompass the other. Each philosopher wants to philosophize on his or her own. As Yovel suggests, the major difference between Kant's and Hegel's ontology is the latter's complete rejection of Kant's dualism.[30] Hegel believes that at certain levels of experience there is bifurcation between nature and intelligence, arbitrary will and rational will, but the whole thrust of his philosophy is to refute this bifurcation at the level of reason. Kant does not share this view. Rather, as Yovel notes, he thinks nature and reason can only be brought into harmony through gradual progress, but the antithesis between nature and reason is never entirely overcome. Thus, although there is some similarity in the long-term objectives of Hegel and Kant, they diverge markedly in their assessment of the possibilities of achieving their goal. Hegel has a fundamentally different ontology from Kant's. Hegel's stress upon the role of spirit in experience makes him a monist, whereas there are strong dualist features to Kant's ontology. But despite their ontological differences, Hegel shares with Kant a belief in the importance of the philosophy of history.

Taking his argument a stage further, Yovel suggests that 'the closer Kant anticipates Hegel, the more antinomic his own position becomes'.[31] But this brings out a weakness in Yovel's interpretation of Kant. Interesting as the suggestion is, this is the wrong way of putting the relationship of these philosophers to each other. Kant is Hegel's forerunner, not his follower, and as Karl Popper stresses in his *Poverty of Historicism*, no one can possibly anticipate new developments in knowledge.[32] The better position to adopt is, perhaps, to try to show how Hegel builds on Kant's system to bring into being his own. And in this respect there is no doubt that Hegel seized on some of Kant's more radical claims, not only in the philosophy of religion and the philosophy of history, but in all branches of philosophy, to develop his own dialectical system. We shall see throughout our discussion of the end of history tradition, not least when we come to discuss in detail the work of Fukuyama, that there is a recurring tendency to read into particular philosophers ideas that they did not ever entertain. Imputing the ideas of later writers to earlier ones is only the most glaring example of this.

It is important to stress the essential difference between Kant and Hegel at this point before we move to discuss Hegel's contribution to the end of history tradition in the next chapter. Kant's account of the end of history is first and foremost moral and political rather than metaphysical. The account which he gives urges his readers to follow the moral imperative to act justly and to work towards a more just society. But there is no underlying certainty that a wholly just society will ever be established. We have always to act on faith. In this respect he differs greatly from Hegel who, as we shall see, claims that the end of history will definitely come to pass because of the outworking of Spirit (*Geist*) in history.

2 • Hegel:
Spirit and State

Philosophy and history

Fukuyama regards Hegel, rather than Kant, as the greatest of modern philosophers, and claims that both 'The End of History?' and *The End of History and the Last Man* are Hegelian in their inspiration and orientation. This high view of Hegel's importance is not universally shared. The eminent historian Hugh Brogan wrote a highly critical review of *The End of History and the Last Man* in which he referred to 'Hegelian mumbo-jumbo', and claimed that Fukuyama's expertise as a foreign policy analyst 'can hardly benefit from the wholesale adoption of a never-plausible and now quite absurdly outdated philosophical fantasy'.[1] But to write of Hegel in this way is, as Brogan wrote about Fukuyama's dismissive comments on Popper's view of Hegel, naïve. Brogan's conviction that Hegel is no longer to be taken seriously as a philosopher is wrong, and betrays an ignorance of the revival of interest in Hegel's work amongst contemporary philosophers, but it is certainly true that Hegel's work is not as well known to non-philosophers as it ought to be. Gertrude Himmelfarb and Irving Kristol, in their considerably more measured responses to 'The End of History?', both acknowledge that discussing Hegel in serious journals in contemporary America is unusual, though much to be welcomed. This is all the more remarkable given that, in Kristol's words, 'Hegel is . . . along with Kant, the greatest philosopher of modernity'.[2]

Part of the reason for the widespread ignorance of Hegel amongst many contemporaries lies in Hegel's own writing style, which is far from clear. Kristol is probably right when he says that Hegel is 'the most *unreadable* of our great philosophers'.[3] More to the point, though, is the fact that Hegel's philosophy is both systematic and wide-ranging. Reading Hegel on almost any of the many subjects which he wrote about can be enormously rewarding even if (as with Himmelfarb and Kristol) the reader disagrees fundamentally with Hegel's conclusions. But reading him properly requires seeing him in the round, and in particular it necessitates understanding the underpinning metaphysics which are at the heart of his system. This is as much true when attempting to understand Hegel's account of the end of history as anything else. Hegel regards history as it is ordinarily understood as the outward manifestation of a deeper metaphysical process, which he refers to as the development of *Geist* or Spirit:

> History is a conscious, self-mediating process – Spirit emptied out into time . . . The goal, absolute knowledge, or spirit that knows itself as spirit, has for its path the recollection of the spirits as they are in themselves and as they accomplish the organisation of their realm. Their preservation, regarded from the side of their free existence appearing in the form of contingency, is history; but regarded from the side of their comprehended organisation, it is the science of knowing in the sphere of appearance: the two together, comprehended history, form alike the inwardizing and the Calvary of absolute spirit, the actuality, truth, and certainty of his throne, without which he would be lifeless and alone. Only
>
> > from the chalice of this realm of spirits
> > foams forth for him his own infinitude.[4]

It will be seen from this passage that theology also comes into Hegel's general philosophical vision of the realization of spirit. True philosophy for Hegel comprises within it the most important teachings of the Christian religion, and an understanding of this interplay between religion and philosophy is essential in order to understand the idea of *Geist* which is the key concept in Hegel's philosophy. The concept of *Geist* states in the shortest form possible Hegel's philosophical idealism. Hegel is not an idealist in the everyday moral sense that he expects well of other individuals and the world in general, but in the deeper philosophical sense that he thinks that reality is ultimately thought or idea. Most philosophers may broadly be categorized as either idealists or materialists, categories which Hegel himself accepted and did much to foster. Philosophical materialists believe that matter is more fundamental than ideas, because ideas are determined by material conditions, whereas philosophical idealists believe that ideas are more fundamental than matter, because material conditions can be determined by ideas. Some philosophers try to bridge the two standpoints and others try to

ignore it altogether, but even with these types of philosopher some
materialist or idealist tendencies can be read into their writings. Hegel
would argue that all genuine philosophers have to take a stand on this
issue, and he would go further to suggest that all true philosophy is
idealism.

Commentators on Hegel tend to differ in their reading of his
concept of *Geist*.[5] At one end of the spectrum Hegel's concept of
Geist may be seen as broadly equivalent with the Christian's idea of
God, and at the other end of the spectrum the concept is seen as a
kind of secularized social mind, which is Fukuyama's view.[6] It is
arguable, however, that Hegel wishes to see spirit as a wholly
comprehensive concept which includes within it both the Christian
view of deity (spirit in a pictorial or representational form) and the
more secularized notion of a human collective consciousness. As
Hegel sees it, each individual mind is both part of and distinct from
this greater mind. In other words, as individuals we can both be at one
with mind in general but also at odds with it in our behaviour and
action.

For Hegel, the world is a product of spirit, but not in the sense that
each individual person knows what spirit is. Each individual has the
task of acquainting himself or herself with spirit. Spirit can only be
known in its entirety through philosophy. But this does not mean that
those who have not read philosophy will be permanently estranged
from spirit. Living in the world and being part of society each
individual comes partially to know spirit.

Hegel's philosophical idealism is highly concrete and social in
character. He does not, for example, accept the biblical account of
creation as empirically correct. For him this is not how spirit comes
down to earth. Hegel preferred to accept the latest scientific accounts
of the origins of the universe. He was deeply impressed by natural
science and he devoted a volume of his major philosophical work the
Encyclopaedia to the *Philosophy of Nature*, a book which many
Hegel scholars regard as highly as any other of Hegel's principal
publications. But for all this realistic acceptance of scientific
knowledge, Hegel still regarded nature as ideal. He sees nature as the
other of spirit which demonstrates itself in the end to be a part of
Spirit. Another way of putting this for Hegel is to say that nature
represents the idea in its alienation or externalization. The great
achievement of natural science is to reduce the mass of external data
on nature to a comprehensible totality in the scientific law. As laws are

the product of thought Hegel takes this to imply that nature is ultimately thought. So Hegel presents the philosophy of nature as the overcoming of the alienation of spirit, or the alienated relation which we initially have with nature.

This brief summary illustrates how with Hegel nothing can resist the philosophical power of spirit. Materialists who see the existence of nature as the refutation of idealism are for Hegel shown to be wrong by the science of nature. Hegel approaches history in much the same frame of mind. He is convinced it has to be reduced to a pattern that is compatible with the intellect. History is therefore another respect in which Spirit steps into the world. For many people the writing of history is a way of bringing order to what in itself is diverse and confused. To them the philosophy of history should be seen as another way of bringing shape to an immense variety of individual historical works. For Hegel in contrast the task of the historian, and subsequently the philosopher of history, is to bring out the order that is already present in history through the activity of spirit.

The impression that Hegel gives that history has come to an end in his time gains weight from the more marked impression that Hegel gives that philosophy has reached its highest point in his time. Hegel's key thesis about the end of history is most fundamentally about the end of philosophy. Here the evidence seems indisputable:

A new epoch has arisen in the world. It would appear as if the world-spirit had at last succeeded in stripping off from itself all alien objective being, and apprehending itself at last as absolute spirit, in developing from itself what for it is objective, and keeping it in its power, yet remaining at rest. The strife of the finite self-consciousness with the absolute self-consciousness which seemed to the former to lie outside itself, now ceases. Finite self-consciousness has ceased to be finite; and in this way absolute self-consciousness has, on the other hand, acquired the actuality which it lacked before. This is the whole history of the world in general up to the present, and the history of philosophy in particular, which only depicts this strife. Now it seems to have reached its goal, when this absolute self-consciousness, which it had the work of representing, has ceased to be alien, and when spirit is thus actualised as spirit.[7]

Hegel's idea of the end of history rests upon a cumulative view of the history of philosophy. This in turn influences Hegel's view of

contemporary philosophy and his own philosophy within that contemporary picture. In essence Hegel attempts the impossible with his
philosophy. He would like to regard his philosophical system as the
logical culmination of all previous philosophy as well as the summa-
tion of the key debates in philosophy in his own time. Hegel wants to
take on all-comers, not simply by defeating them in a head-to-head
confrontation, but rather by including what is true in their ideas
within his own philosophy. Hegel's philosophy aims at totality, a
totality which reduces all other points of view into moments in his
own thinking.

This is a vigorous and extraordinarily ambitious approach, but
how far can it be accepted? So far as the history of philosophy is
concerned, Hegel was widely and deeply read in the philosophers of
the past and he gives a plausible account of the development of the
history of philosophy as the development of the one philosophy. Even
his estimation of his own system as the culmination of all other
philosophy did not seem obviously wrong to many of his contemporaries, and by the end of his intellectual career at Berlin
University in 1831 he was regarded as pre-eminent amongst German
philosophers. However, if Hegel's philosophy is to be regarded
critically we cannot take it at his own evaluation. Despite the fact that
he was an impressively well-read and successful philosopher Hegel
cannot be said to have brought philosophy to a close. At best we can
regard him as bringing to a close one particular, albeit very
important, episode in the development of philosophy.

It must be said that Hegel's own account of philosophy does not
entirely rule out this last possibility, though he puts very little
emphasis on it. His vocabulary in describing the conclusions and
implications of his own philosophical idealism is almost entirely
triumphalist and celebratory. In the early *Phenomenology of Spirit* we
are told about the emergence of Absolute Spirit from its conflicts with
all forms of finite spirit, in the *Science of Logic* the Absolute Idea
emerges from the labyrinth of forms of logical concepts, and in the
Philosophy of Right the state in its fully accomplished form is
deduced from modern civil society. Hegel presents his philosophy as
the truth revealing itself. Although Hegel does not rule out the
possibility that his own philosophy is just one shape the absolute
philosophy takes on, the whole thrust of his approach tends to create
the opposite impression. In philosophical terms Hegel takes on the
appearance of being at the top of the evolutionary scale. But an

alternative view of philosophy might simply regard him as representing one peak in a large vista of similar peaks.

In trying simultaneously to scale all the philosophical heights Hegel, if we are to see him as successful, would rob others of the autonomy of thought. His approach in this respect contrasts markedly with Kant who is anxious to encourage everyone to think for themselves. Kant is conscious that every philosopher wants to create his own system and desires not to be bound by the conclusions of others. Hegel seems to want all his contemporary philosophers, and possibly all future philosophers, to give up the search for originality by accepting the truth of his system. Hegel does not entirely rule out philosophical pluralism but his approach does not invite or encourage it.

Hegel's vision of the end of history emerges from this comprehensive, totalizing engagement with philosophy. Since absolute spirit has unveiled itself in philosophy it has now to be shown to have realized itself in the social world. Hegel's synthesizing efforts are not without their parallel in the history of philosophy. Aristotle in a similar way studied the history of Greek philosophy and sought to draw from it insights that informed his own philosophy. In attempting to answer Plato Aristotle drew heavily upon the work of the pre-Socratic philosophers. Hegel seems to have followed this lead in trying to answer Kant. Hegel is also inspired by Aristotle in the way in which he looks upon nature and society functionally. Aristotle believed that objects and institutions had an immanent *telos* (or purpose) which it was the job of the philosopher to discover and outline. Hegel takes this approach to history and the history of philosophy. Schools of thoughts, institutions and political leaders are seen as part of one purposeful picture leading towards a successful present.

The philosophy of history follows on from and is subordinate to Hegel's general philosophy. The philosophy of history outlines the outward development of the process of evolution which has already been observed within philosophy itself. World history is the way in which spirit manifests itself in the world:

> That the history of the world, with all the changing scenes which its annals present, is this process of development and realisation of spirit – this is the true Theodicaea, the justification of God in history. Only this insight can reconcile spirit with the history of the world – viz. that what has happened, and is happening every day, is not only not 'without God', but is essentially his work.[8]

Spirit does not manifest itself immediately in its complete form. The spirit of the world gradually reveals itself in a number of ascending forms, leading finally to freedom: 'Universal history exhibits the gradation in the development of that principle whose substantial purport is the consciousness of freedom.'[9]

As Hegel sees it, these ascending forms are implicit in spirit from the beginning:

> Here we have only to indicate that spirit begins with a germ of infinite possibility, but only possibility – containing its substantial existence in an undeveloped form, as the object and goal which it reaches only in its resultant – full reality.[10]

The development of spirit begins in the orient. Here human history dawns: 'In Asia arose the light of spirit, and therefore the history of the world.'[11] But it receives its completion only in the west: 'The history of the world travels from east to west, for Europe is absolutely the end of history, Asia the beginning.'[12] Like the physical sun, the sun of self-consciousness first arises in the east, but it reaches its greatest brilliance in the west. Freedom is the goal:

> The question of the means by which freedom develops itself to a world, conducts us to the phenomenon of history itself. Although freedom is primarily an undeveloped idea, the means it uses are external and phenomenal; presenting themselves in history to our sensuous vision.[13]

The outer development of world history is evidence of the inner essence. The whole process is teleological:

> The history of the world begins with its general aim – the realization of the idea of spirit – only in its implicit form that is, as nature; a hidden, most profoundly hidden, unconscious instinct; and the whole process of history (as already observed) is directed to rendering this unconscious impulse a conscious one.[14]

An end point is certainly reached, but this end point is itself a process: 'Thought is the grade to which spirit has now advanced. It involves the harmony of being in its purest essence, challenging the external world to exhibit the same reason which the individual I possesses.'[15]

We have seen with Hegel that history culminates in the Germanic or Protestant European-style state. The internal logic of history leads it to produce freedom in this completed form. We need now to look at this completed form of human development since this is crucial both for Marx's interpretation of history and the account of history put forward by Fukuyama.

The end of history and *The Philosophy of Right*

Hegel presents his account of the completed historical condition in his *Philosophy of Right*, which was published in Berlin in 1821. It represented a compendium of Hegel's lectures on the philosophy of natural law and public right and was intended to be a guide to his students in the subject. The *Philosophy of Right* develops Hegel's final systematic position on politics and law which he first put forward in outline in the third volume of his *Encyclopaedia of the Philosophical Sciences* published in 1817.

At the centre of Hegel's account of the completed human condition is his notion of civil society. Hegel drew the term civil society (*bürgerliche Gesellschaft*) from the work of the Scottish political economists of the eighteenth century, particularly from the writings of Adam Ferguson, James Steuart and Adam Smith. Adam Ferguson and James Steuart belonged to the historical school of Scottish political economy and were responsible for developing the notion of a progressive market economic order which formed the basis of modern civil society. Steuart was the author of *An Inquiry into the Principle of Political Economy* (1767). Hegel is known to have studied Steuart's work in detail whilst he was a private tutor in Bern in the 1790s, and he is thought to have studied Ferguson's *Essay on the History of Civil Society* (1767) when he became professor of Philosophy at Berlin in 1818. Adam Smith's *Wealth of Nations* (1776) is the classic text of political economy which puts forward the striking idea that the market economy works spontaneously in such a successful and effective way that it might almost be regarded as being guided by a 'hidden hand'. Hegel was particularly impressed by these writers' understanding of the modern economy and their suggestion that such an economy had its own internal coherence. Hegel believed, as they did, that the system of free labour, unhindered exchange of contracts and open markets for goods and services led to the possibility of prosperity for the majority of the populations of those states which adopted it.

The commercial society described by political economists provided the basis for the satisfaction of the individual's needs, and in so doing provided the foundation for an effective community. Hegel acknowledged that at a surface level commercial society was a confusion of networks of requirements and needs. Some needs remained unfulfilled because individuals did not have the necessary means to satisfy them and some services and goods remained unused because the necessary demand was absent. However, on the whole the workings of the crisscross network of requirements and needs produced remarkable results. Hegel saw it as similar to the apparently chaotic movement of the planets in space, which to the naked eye seemed to possess no order, but once examined in detail and made subject to laws by scientists demonstrated a striking coherence.[16]

Whilst not wholly endorsing Adam Smith's notion of the 'hidden hand' working in an undisclosed way to produce the best effect for the society as a whole, Hegel none the less extols the virtues of the free market economy. He speaks appreciatively of the way in which a commercial society seemingly allows everyone simply to pursue their own narrow interests at the same time as bringing about the advantage of the whole. On these grounds Hegel sees civil society as an ethical sphere. The beauty of the commercial economy is that it allows everyone to place personal gain at the forefront of their minds without at the same time wholly submerging the moral. Thus indirectly, in the commercial sphere, material interests are rendered virtuous.

Hegel argues that the pursuit of personal interest in civil society is not wholly unstructured. The surface impression of unbridled individuality and material advantage is very much an appearance. In practice self-interest is pursued within a social framework drawn together by social classes and corporations. Essentially Hegel believes that three classes are to be found in civil society. These classes are: the substantial or immediate class; the reflective or business class; and the universal class. Those belonging to the substantial or immediate class are all those who work in the agricultural sphere. And just as with the reflective or business class, Hegel does not distinguish in the agricultural estate between those who have a controlling interest, such as the landowners, and those are subordinate in the group, such as peasants or agricultural workers. The business class is for Hegel the general group to which all those working in manufacturing, commerce and finance belong. Hegel makes no attempt here to distinguish, as Marx does crucially, between employers and employees. Hegel's final and central class, the universal class, is the bureaucracy, made up primarily of civil servants. The universal class has the particular role of overseeing civil society to ensure that its spontaneous harmony is maintained and also safeguarded where it looks endangered.

Hegel's class system plays a highly significant role in his account of freedom. He believes that the fluid, open class system of modern civil society is what provides the context for human freedom. Without the existence of such classes and our belonging to one of them our freedom would be empty. Self-direction and the development of a fulfilling life presuppose a settled social and economic order. Part of this is that freedom is not the same for everyone. Each individual is born into one class in civil society, displays specific physical and mental characteristics, and enjoys a certain standard of life. The choice and freedom is to be found in the individual's ability to move amongst the various classes to find the niche which best suits his taste and capacities. It is this ability to choose one's career (albeit hemmed in by inherited advantages and disadvantages) that, in Hegel's view, raises modern society vastly above the society of Ancient Greece as depicted by Plato. In Plato's *Republic* no one gets to choose the class to which he or she may belong. Freedom is extinguished through the apportionment of roles by the Guardians. The potential for each individual to both fail or succeed is the glory of modern civil society. It is, in a sense, the secular realization of the Protestant Ethic.

The final, and very important, feature of Hegel's civil society to stress is the role played by corporations in mediating between the individual and the state. Hegel sees the various groups of civil society as forming corporations to advance their interests. These are not corporations in today's sense of large-scale business enterprises (although they might well be included within this Hegelian framework) but rather corporations in the sense of civil institutions such as architects' organizations, solicitors' and barristers' associations and district council associations. Today's political scientist might describe such associations as interest or pressure groups. For Hegel, they also play a part in the realization of freedom because they provide the individual with a 'second home' within civil society through which they can pursue their personal interests. From the point of view of the society as a whole they also perform the valuable role of aggregating interests and so allowing the state to oversee and direct them better.

We will see later in the book that Fukuyama regards such institutions as of great importance, and that they play a central part in his theory of liberal democracy. Indeed, they help to provide Fukuyama with an alternative, and in his view superior, account of liberal democracy to that offered by writers such John Locke, John Stuart Mill and John Rawls, all of whom Fukuyama regards as laying far too much stress on the concept of the individual.

The state which represents both the realization of spirit and the realization of human freedom emerges from civil society. Hegel does not see the final form of the state as something which is imposed upon society but rather he sees it as growing organically from the day-to-day relationships of individuals. Just as civil society emerges from the outgrowing of the family, so the state emerges from the limitations of civil society. Despite all its extraordinary advantages over all previous forms of society, civil society is not sufficient in itself. The pursuit of self-interest, which is given full rein in civil society, must be framed within a wider community context.

As we saw earlier, Hegel does not wholly accept the *laissez-faire* account of commercial society. In his view, Adam Smith's 'hidden hand' does not work with perfection and the spontaneous workings of the commercial economy have to be supplemented by the activity of the state. Not only has the state to provide public goods, such as roads, street lighting and harbours; it has also to attempt to meliorate the effect of commercial crises.[17] Hegel recognizes that the market is to some extent self-regulating and that after periods of crises normality may soon follow. However, he does not believe that society is required always to wait for this process to occur. Public agencies may mediate to accelerate the process.

Hegel believes that in economic terms the state has also to take important responsibilities in relation to the growth of poverty. The public authorities cannot sit idly to one side and watch large sections of the population sink into poverty. Because the growth of the commercial society has undermined family and local ties individuals cannot now wholly look to those nearest to them to support them in times of crisis and so state therefore has an important welfare role. As Hegel sees it, 'the individual becomes a son of civil society, which has as many claims upon him as he has rights in relation to it.'[18] Although the state has obligations in relation to the impoverished sections of society, Hegel is not entirely sure how it can best discharge this obligation. Partly the obligation can be fulfilled by allowing a measure of poor relief, partly some regular employment can be offered through the encouragement of public works and partly the problem might be dealt with through allowing emigration. But these problems of poverty, of economic dislocation and economic management demonstrate how of itself civil society brings into being the state.

For Hegel, the state that emerges at the end of the historical process and adequately allows the modern individual freedom is a constitutional monarchy.[19] Hegel will not allow that the relevant way in which to discuss the appropriate forms of constitution is in terms of Aristotle's three-sided distinction between monarch (or autocracy), aristocracy (or oligarchy) and democracy. In his view, a properly developed constitutional monarchy contains within itself all that is valuable in three types of constitution.[20] The democratic moment is contained within a constitutional monarchy in so far as it is appropriate, just as the aristocratic element has its place. Equally, the monarch is not simply imposed as the contrary of these two other moments but rather as their synthesis.

It is difficult to deny that there is a slightly authoritarian tinge to the state which with Hegel emerges at the end of history. Some commentators have seen evidence of this in Hegel's claim that it is important that there should be one individual will at the head of the state. Nevertheless, this issue must not be pushed too far. Hegel does not want the constitutional monarch to exercise this power in an arbitrary way. Shlomo Avineri, one of the most prominent amongst a number of modern commentators on Hegel who regard Hegel's theory of the state as compatible with liberalism, argues that the monarch's power is one of last resort.[21] Most political issues are decided beforehand by open discussion in corporations, parliamentary institutions, and, above all, by civil servants (the universal class). Fukuyama also reads Hegel in a liberal way, arguing that for Hegel, 'the embodiment of human freedom was the modern constitutional state, or, again, what we have called liberal democracy'.[22] Significantly, though, Fukuyama, as we noted earlier, emphasizes the importance of membership of smaller communities, and the importance of civil society rather than individualism, as the core of Hegel's (and Fukuyama's own) defence of liberal democracy.[23]

While it is certainly possible to overestimate Hegel's leanings towards authoritarianism, there is also a danger of laying too much emphasis on his commitment to democracy. Fukuyama certainly puts too positive a gloss on this aspect of Hegel's thought. The illiberal element in Hegel's thinking can be seen particularly clearly in his desire to rule out popular democracy within the state which emerges at the end of history. Hegel regards the French Revolution as a frightening example of what can happen when the principle of popular sovereignty is carried through and so he would not allow a form of political representation in his realized state which put power in the hands of the people or their representatives. The political representatives he *is* prepared to countenance perform their appropriate constitutional role when they provide information with which legislation can be framed and when their criticisms anticipate possible objections which might be raised by the population at large.

The final form of the state which Hegel envisages is very much in the hands of the civil service. This is because Hegel thinks that the civil service forms part of the only class in civil society which has the well-being of the whole as its particular interest. Members of the civil service, particularly those in its higher echelons, are the only people who have the specialist information and insight with which to deal with the society's problem. Furthermore, as modern civil society is already an accomplished fact, there are no new vast tasks to be undertaken. Hegel has in mind a continuous process of adjustment and tinkering rather than any kind of complete overhaul.

This last point is related to Hegel's claim that the end of history must be seen first and foremost as being characterized by the end of philosophy. The state which emerges at the end of history will be the highest expression of spirit, and therefore of reason, in history. The rational will have become fully actual. So just as the end of philosophy will mean that there are no revolutionary new ideas to be thought, so in the state at the end of history there will be no revolutionary decisions – much less actions – to be taken. It is the fear that such a state will be a dull, even stagnant, place which lies behind the much-quoted passage from 'The End of History?' in which Fukuyama warns that 'the end of history will be a very sad time'.

> The struggle for recognition, the willingness to risk one's life for a purely abstract goal, the world-wide ideological struggle that called forth daring, courage, imagination, and idealism, will be replaced by economic calculation, the endless solving of technical problems, environmental concerns, and the satisfaction of sophisticated consumer demands. In the post-historical period there will be neither

art nor philosophy, just the perpetual caretaking of the museum of human history.[24]

Such a society brings grave risks. As Fukuyama puts it, men in such a world would be in danger of lapsing back from good citizens into 'mere *bourgeoisie*'[25] – a significantly unHegelian phrase but one which is sufficiently close to point us in the right direction. What Hegel really fears is that such a society would be in danger of becoming weak and unhealthy.[26] To understand what he means by this, and how he believes that it can be avoided, we need to turn to his account of international relations at the end of history.

International relations at the end of history

In Hegel's philosophy of history there is a significant difference between life within the state and the relationship between states. Whereas progress towards freedom seems to appear assured within states, it encounters limits in the international sphere. This is because Hegel does not envisage the realized international condition as an entirely peaceful one. The international situation at the end of history is unresolved in the sense that war is an ever-present possibility. This is not to say that Hegel envisages continual warfare as inevitable, but he does claim that the absence of war cannot be counted upon. Indeed for Hegel it would not be desirable for war totally to disappear at the end of history, and he rejects Kant's idea of perpetual peace.[27]

Hegel's arguments in support of this position are almost wholly opposite to those which Kant deploys in defence of perpetual peace. Whereas Kant argues that justice within states will only truly become possible when there is justice in the international community, Hegel believes that justice is only truly possible within the state. A key element in Hegel's argument at this point is his account of patriotism, which he sees in exclusivist terms and which he considers to be a key element in the working of modern society. Patriotism is primarily an emotional rather than a rational commitment to the state (though it is in no sense irrational), and it provides the force that binds the members of the state together. Hegel argues that patriotism is most often so deeply a part of the life of the community that it is usually unremarked and simply taken for granted, but there are times when it suddenly becomes a burning issue.

Patriotism is often understood to mean only a readiness for exceptional sacrifices and actions. Essentially, however, it is the sentiment which, in the relationships of our daily lives and ordinary conditions, habitually recognises that the community is one's substantive groundwork and end. It is out of this consciousness, which during life's daily round stands the test in all circumstances, that there subsequently also arises the readiness for extraordinary exertions.[28]

It is because patriotic members of a state are so deeply imbued with the values and ethos of the state that they are ready to rise to the challenge to fight for it in time of war. But the occasional foreign conflict also has the effect of reinforcing in the minds, and hearts, of the subjects of a state the importance of governmental institutions. That is to say, the act of being involved in war, of realizing that the life of the state is itself at risk and in need of defence, deepens a person's commitment to the state.

So it is because people are members of a specific state and identify closely with it that they are ready to go to war in its defence. But why should this remain the case at the end of history, when we might expect, as Kant does, a more cosmopolitan world view to prevail? Some commentators have indeed claimed that Hegel was either an advocate of an eventual pacific union of states under whose auspices war would be abolished or that the logic of his major principles inexorably lead to such a conclusion. Alexandre Kojève stands out as one of the most important advocates of this view, not only because of his intellectual influence on a generation of European thinkers but also due to his considerable power in the bureaucracy of the newly emerging European Economic Community in the late 1940s and early 1950s.[29] More recently, Andrew Vincent has also argued that the logic of Hegel's position ultimately leads him to conclude that wars will cease.[30] Such a reading of Hegel gains most plausibility when it is argued in the context of his account of the end of history, which has been the subject of a considerable amount of recent discussion. If the world is becoming progressively more rational then it would seem logical to suppose that war, which most people would see to be deeply irrational, would eventually cease in the new international order brought about by reason.

For Kojève, striking evidence of the emergence of the end of history was to be seen in the coming together of the states of Western Europe into what he believed would eventually become a single federal state.

This idea that wars should cease and that the states of Europe should come together in a peaceful union to guarantee this is by no means new in Western culture. William Penn's *An Essay Towards the Present and Future Peace of Europe* (1693), the Abbé St Pierre's *Plan for a Perpetual Peace in Europe* (1713), and Immanuel Kant's *Perpetual Peace* (1795) all claimed that perpetual peace would be possible only if the states of Europe were confederated together in a single union.

It was not only in the realm of ideas that such unions have existed in the past. Hegel himself refers to the Holy Alliance, formed by the kings of Prussia, Austria and Russia in the aftermath of the defeat of France in 1815, as a serious attempt to introduce perpetual peace into Europe and in the Addition to section 324 of the *Philosophy of Right*, he explicitly links Kant's discussion with the Holy Alliance.

> Perpetual Peace is often advocated as an ideal to which humanity should strive. With that end in view, Kant proposed a league of monarchs to adjust differences between states, and the Holy Alliance was meant to be a league of much the same kind. But the state is an individual, and individuality essentially implies negation. Hence, even if a number of states make themselves into a family, this group as an individual must engender an opposite and create an enemy.[31]

The juxtaposition of Kant's ideal of a league of enlightened Republican states with the autocratic Holy Alliance is an odd one at first reading. Certainly, the Holy Alliance was never meant to form a single union in the form which Kant and earlier writers had envisaged for a pacific union. But that is precisely Hegel's point, and the main thrust of his argument is very powerful. He is claiming that any attempt to curtail the independent sovereignty of the state is doomed to failure. Even if successful, it will only succeed in creating a new state which will act in just the same way as its previously independent component parts had done and find enemies to fight. Even a union based on Enlightened, republican principles would deteriorate into the authoritarian and intolerant force which the Holy Alliance had, in Hegel's view, been from the beginning.

Hegel, then, explicitly rejected the idea of perpetual peace and the concept of a pacific union which would guarantee it. But what are we to make of this explicit rejection? Might it be that the fundamental principles of his political philosophy actually lead, as Kojève and Vincent suggest, to a position which he consciously, but inconsistently, rejected? Or might it even be, as Fred R. Dallmayr has suggested,[32] that as states increasingly gain substantial recognition from each other, wars will cease between them, even though there is no overarching authority to impose the peace? To put it plainly, does the inner logic of Hegel's thought about war lead the Hegelian to pacifist conclusions? It does not, but in order to see why this is so we have to examine what Hegel has to say about warfare. Hegel's rejection of pacific unions is also, and consciously, an acceptance that war is an inevitable part of any international system in which states are independent and sovereign.

One of the most important modern attempts to claim that Hegel was opposed to war is that of Shlomo Avineri. In his article 'The Problem of War in Hegel's Thought' and his justly acclaimed book, *Hegel's Theory of the Modern State*,[33] Avineri has argued against the views of Karl Popper and other mid-century critics and sought to reinstate Hegel as a serious and respectable philosopher. In this, as in so much else of his contribution to Hegel scholarship, Avineri's work has been of immense importance. But the very effectiveness of his work, and the fact that *Hegel and the Modern State* is still widely read in English-speaking countries as an essential introduction to Hegel's political thought,[34] means that his account must be discussed at some length.

Earlier in the passage from *Philosophy of Right* 324A which was quoted above, Hegel uses the metaphor of a healthy body to explain his view of war.

> In peace civil life continually expands; all its departments wall themselves in, and in the long run men stagnate. Their idiosyncracies become continually more fixed and ossified. But for health the unity of the body is required and if its parts harden themselves into an exclusiveness, that is death.[35]

This choice of metaphor has caused great difficulties for liberal defenders of Hegel, and Avineri's comment on it in *Hegel and the Modern State* represents a major attempt to tone down its impact. 'This has to be read very carefully,' he argues, 'just as a situation of stress − like a plague − brings out the solidarity of a family, so a situation of warfare brings out the ability of men to transcend their self-centred interests. From this there follows no glorification of the plague − or war.'[36]

Avineri's introduction of a new metaphor – that of the plague – unfortunately obscures the issue. There is a significant difference between a plague and war, which is that, in Hegel's view at least, states sometimes seek war, or at least eagerly embrace it when it comes along – especially after long periods of peace. *Philosophy of Right* 334 is very important in this connection because in this section Hegel argues very strongly that the decision to go to war will be decided not just, not even primarily, on the basis of the external conditions but on its own internal needs and interests. Indeed, he could hardly be more explicit about the way in which the internal interests of the state may very well lead to war

> . . . a state may regard its infinity and honour as at stake in each of its concerns, however minute, and it is all the more inclined to susceptibility to injury the more its strong individuality is impelled as a result of long domestic peace, to seek and create a sphere of activity abroad.[37]

This is very different from the metaphor of the plague, which by definition is not sought after.

The reference to the plague seems all the more important in the context of *Philosophy Of Right* 324 because Hegel explicitly – and, in the view of many commentators, notoriously – ascribes the illness not to warfare but to perpetual peace. Even in the very passage Avineri quotes, Hegel (quoting in turn from his own earlier work *Natural Law*) asserts that 'the ethical health of peoples is preserved in their indifference to the stabilisation of finite institutions. . .'[38]

Stephen Walt puts the point very well when he says that in Hegel's view, war is an ethical necessity because without it states would become fatally diseased. The following comment, directed against Avineri, is apposite:

> . . . for Hegel, then, war is not just a disease which, by attacking the body of the state and the ethical health of its citizens, maintains or tests that health. War is also a vaccination which, by generating antibodies, strengthens the body of the state and improves the ethical health of its citizens.[39]

Avineri argues that as the single acceptable purpose of war, according to Hegel, is to shake people out of their comfortable lethargy, Hegel did not regard war as glorious, or see it in any sense in imperialistic terms. He refers to the passage in the *Phenomenology of Spirit* in which Hegel makes what Avineri describes as

> the extreme suggestion that 'in order not to let [the particular ends] get rooted in and settled in their isolation and thus break up the whole into fragments and let the common spirit evaporate, governments have from time to time to shake them to their very core by war.'

Avineri then comments on this:

> . . . War is the power of negativity, and this is significant, since even if one rejects Hegel's reasoning altogether, one should bear in mind that the ends of the initiated war are not political, that its aim is not the aggrandisement of states or princes, but rather the bringing out of the relativity of human existence. Furthermore, there is no glory in such a war.[40]

There are two things about the claim which Avineri makes in this passage that are contestable. First, it is odd to say, as Avineri does, that the purpose of war as Hegel sees it – the bringing out a sense of shared identity and unity among members of a state – is not political. It is surely highly political, not least because it is strengthening the state against not only external aggression but also internal divisions. This is an extremely important point to emphasize – for Hegel it is the well-being of the state which is at issue and therefore going to war on these grounds is highly political. It is analogous to the bloody fight for survival of the first man at the dawn of history in the *Phenomenology of Spirit*, where in order to gain recognition he is willing to put his life at risk. The state goes to war, putting its life at risk, in order to gain recognition as a state, that is to say as a political entity whose members are not weak and self-centred individuals but a body of people who gladly subordinate themselves, their property and their families to the greater good of the state. Recognition of that fact is what is sought in going to war, and it may be all the more important after a long period of peace both because it forces people within the state to act in this way and because it forces other states to take due notice that peace has not weakened the resolve. For Hegel, war is not an aberration to be avoided where at all possible (let alone at all costs) but a necessary feature of the life of the state. War is essential both for the internal health of the state and the external respect which it gains from other states.

The second part of Avineri's claim which is contestable is the argument that war is not about 'the aggrandisement of states or princes, but rather the bringing out of the relativity of human existence'. And because of this it is not about glory. But this is equally contentious. It may be that the real purpose of going to war is to improve the ethical health of the nation, but that does not mean that war should be treated in a clinical fashion. How could it be? War is by its nature violent and aggressive. Encouraging soldiers to meditate on the relativity of human existence would have one of two consequences. It would either make them deeply dispirited and fearful or it would make them fanatical, as with the Islamic warriors of Iran in the Iran–Iraq war, in quest of the glories of martyrdom. It is highly likely that wars will sometimes involve extending the territory, or at least the political and economic influence, of the attacking state. It is certain that Hegel envisages it being presented as a matter of honour and the interests of the state. The passage quoted above from *Philosophy of Right* 334 makes this very clear. It is also inherent in the very idea of recognition, which as we have seen, plays such an important part in Hegel's account of war. For recognition is, in part at least, about forcing the other person, or the other state, to acknowledge your worth. And because the relationship between states, especially states at war with each other, is far less amenable to subtle nuances than the relationship between individuals is, the way in which recognition will be gained from an enemy state will frequently involve an acknowledgement of the glory of the victor.

This argument is linked to Hegel's particular view of the state as having a personality. As the realized state possesses a personality it has to assert this personality in relation to other states. 'Sovereignty, at first simply the universal thought of this ideality, comes into existence only as subjectivity sure of itself . . .'[41] Each particular state has to express this independence through its actions, and in doing so it will receive the recognition it deserves from other states. '. . . every state is sovereign and autonomous against its neighbours. It is entitled in the first place and without qualification to be sovereign from their point of view, i.e., to be recognised by them as sovereign.'[42]

Recognition is not something that is given casually; it has to be earned and consequently conflict always hovers in the background. Because of the personality of each state, 'if states disagree and their particular wills cannot be harmonised, the matter can only be settled by war'.[43] International law can provide a framework within which to resolve disputes, but of itself can produce no binding resolution.

It is important to stress that going to war is the only ultimately reliable means of testing the state because a number of critics have suggested that other means might be found through which states could assert themselves and gain recognition.[44] To see why this should be so we need to examine the relationship between the two benefits which Hegel draws from a state's going to war, the internal cohesion which it encourages and the external recognition which it earns. Stephen Walt has argued[45] that the two ideas are wholly unrelated, and if this is so then it may well be possible that external recognition, which only affects a state's relationship with other states, not its internal life, can be achieved by peaceful means. This is to read Hegel as if he were a classical realist, for whom matters of foreign policy are to be decided solely on the basis of self-interest. But Hegel's position is quite different from this: it is based on a passionate commitment to the moral well-being of the state and the external affairs of the state must be judged primarily in those terms. It is for this reason that the internal cohesion which war encourages and the external recognition which it brings to a state are inextricably combined.

A crucial passage for understanding the relationship between the two aspects of Hegel's theory of international relations is *Philosophy of Right* 322–323. In 323 he argues that the individuality of the state, its true character, we might say, is expressed most fully in its relationship to other states. It is precisely because of this that the idea of a union between states is based on a fundamental misunderstanding of the nature of the state – those who advocate such a union 'have very little knowledge of the nature of a totality or of the feeling of selfhood which a nation possesses in its independence'.[46]

In 323 he takes the argument a stage further. It might appear that the relationship which states have to each other, and their quest for recognition from each other, is not of any special importance to life within the state, as if the relationship with other states was purely an external matter which had no bearing on the inner life of the state. In fact, says Hegel, the opposite is the case. It is only in the pressures of conflict with other states that the willingness of individuals to sacrifice their lives, property and so on, is given full significance.

Here it must be stressed that, for Hegel, the state's struggle for recognition is simultaneously the struggle of the individuals who

make up that state for recognition. Even this puts it too indi-
vidualistically. In participating wholly in the state's struggle for
recognition the individuals find that their personal struggle for recognition has become inextricably bound up with the state's struggle.
This is why Hegel argues in 324, and the Remark to it, that it is so
profoundly wrong to identify the state with civil society in this
context. People do not fight primarily in order to safeguard their
property or their lives – if that was the only motivation then they
would rarely have a real motivation to go to war. Except in cases
where your own country is invaded and your life and property are
directly in danger there is little point in putting your life in jeopardy in
order to defend it. Indeed, in most cases it would be much more
sensible, if this were the motivation, to negotiate a peace deal which
would leave your individual life and property intact. In fact that is an
argument which many pacifists would find compelling – better to
negotiate away some of the rights and privileges of your state than to
risk your life, and the lives of others. The point of this argument is
that the pacifist, of this type anyway, sees the state as something
external to him or her self. Indeed, the attitude of such a person to the
state may be deeply ambiguous to begin with: the state may well pose
a significant threat in its own terms to the freedom and well being of
the pacifist. Why defend leviathan? Hegel's point is completely the
opposite of this – you defend the state because it alone can provide
the context in which you can lead a meaningful and purposeful life.
An attack on your state is not an attack on an external, brooding
monster but on something of which you are a part and which, just as
importantly, is a vital part of you.

It is for this reason that a pacific union, whether its form be a
Republican Confederation or a Holy Alliance, cannot be a proper
kind of political order. Each state has its own unique personality
which would have to be sacrificed to the greater interests of the larger,
and this Hegel thinks is simply not acceptable.

But why is this not acceptable? After all, this is precisely what Hegel
advocates in the case of the individual in relation to the state. Why
could it not happen in the case of states?

Andrew Vincent argues for this position. Just as the individual
person at the level of subjective spirit is incomplete and needs to pass
through objective spirit to absolute spirit, so the state has to pass from
its subjective phase, where it sees itself as a single entity in isolation
from other states, through the objective phase to the absolute. This

last point leads Vincent to some rather fanciful speculations about
what this end condition might be: 'One might even hazard the
speculation that the kind of world order that Hegel could have
formulated, or expected, would be a virtually anarchical community
of artists, Christians and Hegelian philosophers.'[47]

Vincent's extrapolation of Hegel's theory of international relations
is certainly plausible. Unfortunately, while being plausible it is not
accurate. In seeking to find the real internationalist Hegel beneath the
shell of the obstinately nationalist it is reminiscent of those Young
Hegelians of the Left who claimed to have found a revolutionary
beneath the state philosopher. It may well be that Vincent's Hegel
offers a more palatable view of international relations, but he is not
the Hegel of the *Philosophy of Right*.

Vincent's argument echoes Kojève's in positing a rational and
political end of history. And like Kojève, Vincent emphasizes that
Hegel is not a relativist who claims that all states are equally worthy.
There are objective criteria which Hegel posits by which we can assess
the worth of states,[48] and these criteria are best exemplified in the
contemporary Protestant states of Hegel's own day, including – but by
no means exclusively – Prussia.

> This might lead one to draw the logical inference that there are good
> and bad states, or at least states with less reality than others. This is
> exactly the step that Hegel takes when he argues that a bad state, that
> is to say, one which does not fulfil the formal and substantive
> requirements, has no 'genuine actuality'. This is a deeply puzzling
> remark by one who is supposed [by many commentators] to accept a
> plurality of distinct nation states.[49]

Yet the remark is only puzzling if we assume that Hegel is claiming
that there is no way of assessing the relative worth of different states.
There is nothing inconsistent in claiming both that some states are
more advanced than others – a point which Hegel makes frequently –
and saying that each of these states is distinct. The puzzlement only
arises if we look at what Hegel is saying from the perspective of
someone who already accepts the claim that some international order
is highly desirable. In fact, far from claiming on the basis of this
argument that history is moving towards some benevolent
international order, let alone a European (super)state, Hegel claims
quite the opposite. He asserts, quite aggressively, that states and

peoples which are weaker, which do not conform to the norm, will perish.[50]

However, it is important not to paint Hegel in excessively militaristic colours. He does not regard war as a ceaseless or constantly threatening condition, as the following passage makes clear.

> The fact that states reciprocally recognise each other as states remains, even in war – the state of affairs when rights disappear and force and chance hold sway – a bond wherein each counts to the rest as something absolute. Hence in war, war itself is characterised as something which ought to pass away. It implies, therefore, the proviso of the jus gentium that the possibility of peace be retained (and so, for example, that envoys must be respected) and, in general, that war not be waged against domestic institutions, against the peace of family and private life, or against persons in their private capacity.[51]

Hegel seems to be advocating here a kind of culture of limited war in which restrictions are placed upon the kinds of painful methods that are employed. Hegel's view of war seems to be that of killing with rules.

> Modern wars are therefore humanely waged, and a person is not set over against another person in hatred. At most, personal enmities appear in the vanguard, but in the main body of the army hostility is something vague and gives place to each side's respect for the duty of the other.[52]

This notion of the moral limitation upon legitimate means of war may appear somewhat hollow at the end of the twentieth century. A century of total war seems to have undermined any conception of compassion, reasonableness and moderation applying to the circumstances of conflict. Twentieth-century wars have not been fought in the gentlemanly manner Hegel seemed to envisage. The striking feature of modern war seems to be the precise opposite of the Hegelian concept because families, civil life and property have been comprehensively drawn into military campaigns. The Second World War put all three constantly at risk and the bombings of civilian populations, as occurred in Dresden and Coventry, as well as at Hiroshima and Nagasaki, among many other places, were carried out in order to cause the greatest possible damage to civil life, property and families.

There is a peculiar irony to this since for Hegel limited war is not a universal phenomenon but something uniquely European. European culture has created a sense of identity amongst the peoples of that continent. 'The European peoples form a family in accordance with the universal underlying their legal codes, their customs, and their civilization. This principle has modified their international conduct in a state of affairs otherwise dominated by the mutual infliction of evils.'[53] In this respect Hegel might feel badly let down by the European spirit, which far from bringing about a relatively stable end to history, has continuously prolonged humankind's learning process.

Hegel might respond to this criticism by arguing that the realized European state does not lead to an absolute justice. Justice in Hegel's system is never fully or finally embodied. World spirit is always ready to move on. There is an ambivalence here. We take this ambivalence to be between the finest present condition of the human race, which is the norm that all existing society should seek to adopt, and the ideal which is encompassed in world history. Not even the most advanced human state can realize the whole of the human species' potential for freedom. The 'highest right of all' therefore is to be found not in any existing condition (even civil society) but in 'the history of the world which is the world's court of judgement'.[54]

Fukuyama has sometimes been criticized for playing down the importance of war in Hegel's thought and for following Kojève's approach, here as elsewhere, too closely. In fact the opposite is the case and Fukuyama argues that Hegel's account of the inevitability of war has to be taken with the utmost seriousness. He is especially critical of Kojève's claim that wars will inevitably cease at the end of history: '. . . Kojève suggests that the end of history will mean the end of all large disputes, and hence the elimination of the need for struggle. Why Kojève chooses to make this very un-Hegelian position is not at all clear.'[55]

Unlike Hegel, Fukuyama does believe that there is at least the possibility that wars will one day cease. His arguments are explicitly Kantian, and he does believe that there may be occasions when the peace will have to be enforced through the threat of arms. But for Fukuyama there is always the possibility, even in a democratic world order, of wars occurring as states retain their need to struggle for self-identity.

The argument that states have conflicting values which mean that they can never be fully reconciled to each other might seem to imply that Hegel is a relativist. That is to say, that he believes that there is no one, absolute truth but that each succeeding epoch of history brings forward new truths which are accepted as such because they are the truths for this period. Hegel rejects this view. In his philosophy there is ultimately one truth, the truth which will be (or, in his view, has been) discovered at the end of history. This follows from his view of the history of philosophy, in which the doctrines of each philosophical school are taken up by its successor, and its valid principles incorporated. In this account, what is valuable in each tradition, or in each historical period, is preserved in the later, higher stages of the evolution of human thought. When the highest stage is reached, at the end of history, truth is seen in its totality.

Fukuyama claims that Hegel's thought provides a great service in undermining the radical relativism which is widespread in modern Western society. In particular, he contrasts Hegel's position with that of Nietzsche, for whom the process of 'unmasking' dominant beliefs and ideologies is never-ending, and which always threatens to lead either to nihilism or to the dominance of the strong few over the weak and helpless many.[56]

Hegel's end of history is, then, a reaffirmation of the possibility of absolute truth, and a rejection both of pessimism and relativism. But not everyone was enthusiastic about the kind of society which Hegel sought to describe, and shortly after his death an alternative vision of the end of history emerged which was almost completely to overshadow it. This was the theory of Karl Marx.

3 • Marx:

Communism and the End of Prehistory

The answer to the 'riddle of history'

When Hegel died in 1831 his fame and influence were enormous, especially in the German states. Yet despite this there was considerable debate about both the meaning and the significance of his work. Many academic German philosophers regarded Hegel as having provided a more or less complete account of reality and saw their task as simply being that of filling in the few gaps which remained, and then propagating the master's system as widely as possible. To adapt a phrase of Fukuyama's, they were engaged in caretaking Hegel's legacy.

Others were not so convinced that this was all that was left for philosophers to do, and an increasing number of thinkers began to challenge the orthodox view. These critics, who subsequently became known as the Young Hegelians of the Left, argued that while there were elements of Hegel's system which remained valuable much of his philosophy was erroneous. At the core of this error, they claimed, was Hegel's idealism. Increasingly, his critics came to regard themselves as philosophical materialists, and in doing so they frequently expressed their opposition to Hegel's idealism by attacking Christianity, which they saw as having been given a spurious justification by idealist metaphysics.

The most important of these critics was Ludwig Feuerbach, whose book *The Essence of Christianity*[1] offered a fundamental attack on all religious belief. According to Feuerbach, religion can be explained in purely natural terms as the expression of mankind's desire for a better life beyond the grave. The true philosophy exposes the falseness of all such hopes and explains such beliefs in terms of the material conditions from which they emerge. 'Man is what he eats', Feuerbach claimed, in his most memorable phrase, and by way of application of this insight sought to offer a wholly physical and causal explanation for all ideas, philosophical as well as religious.

Marx always held himself aloof from many of the Young Hegelians of the Left – indeed he attacked some of their ideas in trenchant terms in a number of his early works such as *The Holy Family*[2] and *The German Ideology*[3]. Despite this, his thinking was influenced by Feuerbach, and he held him in some regard. In particular Marx approved of Feuerbach's materialism, but with significant reservations because he believed that this brand of materialism was insufficiently far-reaching. In a short series of comments on Feuerbach, first written in an attempt to clarify his own thoughts and only later published by Engels, Marx attacked what he took to be the cardinal error of Feuerbach's position.

> The chief defect of all hitherto existing materialism (that of Feuerbach included) is that the thing, reality, sensuousness, is conceived only in the form of the *object or of contemplation*, but not as a *sensuous human activity, practice*, not subjectively. Hence, in contradistinction to materialism, the *active* side was developed abstractly by idealism – which, of course, does not know real, sensuous activity as such. Feuerbach wants sensuous objects, really distinct from the thought objects, but he does not conceive human activity as *objective* activity. Hence in *Das Wesen des Christentums* [*The Essence of Christianity*], he regards the theoretical attitude as the only genuinely human attitude, while practice is conceived and fixed only in its dirty-judaical manifestation. Hence he does not grasp the significance of 'revolutionary', of 'practical critical' activity.[4]

The problem with Feuerbach's materialism, in Marx's estimation, is that it is static. It completely fails to take into account the fact of historical development, and in particular the profoundly conflicting forces which are at work at the heart of human affairs. Feuerbach was right to reject Hegel's belief that ideas form the basis of reality, but he went too far when he also, effectively, rejected Hegel's dialectical method. In this respect Marx's philosophy represents a synthesis of Hegel's dialectic with the materialism of Feuerbach and his fellow Left Hegelians. Such a synthesis leads to a revolutionary consequence – literally so, Marx hoped. Once Marx's approach has been grasped it is no longer sufficient to criticize an idea in the abstract. All ideas, even the most apparently abstract and remote metaphysics, must be tested against the practical world. Marx is not here naïvely contrasting the practical and the theoretical in the manner of the 'practical man of the world'. Quite the opposite, in fact. He is claiming that theory and practice must always be seen as intimately connected and as enjoying what amounts to a symbiotic relationship. An advance in theory must be tested in practice, but that practice throws new light on the theory, which must be modified and in turn tested against new practical constraints. The process is unending, but it is also constructive – the more that ideas are thought through and tested by practice the clearer and more advanced both become. This provides the inner dialectic of history, and it shows that for Marx any understanding of history must take full cognisance of this dynamism.

Such an account of history is, of course, deeply Hegelian in method, and Marx, like Hegel, believed in an end to human history as it has hitherto developed. But there are radical differences in their respective metaphysical assumptions which lead to very different conclusions about what this end will be. Unlike Hegel, Marx claimed that the end to be sought would bring about such a revolutionary change in the nature of society that it would be tantamount to a new beginning in human affairs. Marx underlined what he saw to be the fundamental nature of this change when he described all events preceding this revolutionary change as belonging to 'prehistory'. Truly human history – the history of free people in control of their own destiny – would only begin with the collapse of capitalism and the emergence of communism.[5]

> Communism as the positive transcendence of private property, as human self-estrangement, and therefore as the real appropriation of the human essence by and for man; communism therefore as the complete return of man to himself as a social (i.e. human) being – a return become conscious, and accomplished within the entire wealth of previous development. This communism, as fully developed naturalism, equals humanism, and as fully developed humanism equals naturalism; it is the genuine resolution of the conflict between man and man – the true resolution of the strife between existence and essence, between objectification and self-confirmation, between freedom and necessity, between the individual and the species. *Communism is the riddle of history solved, and it knows itself to be this solution.*
>
> The entire movement of history is, therefore, both its actual act of genesis (the birth act of its empirical existence) and also for its thinking consciousness the comprehended and known process of its becoming.[6]

Marx makes clear, in this passage from the *Economic and Philosophic Manuscripts of 1844*, that the end to history is implicit within history itself, and that the end is communism. As Marx sees it, history is the unfolding of a progressive development of society towards an ideal. He suggests we should therefore read history backwards from the standpoint of the realization of communism.

This brings us to a peculiar feature of Marx's thought that has been the subject of considerable debate amongst Marx scholars. There is a curious blend in much of Marx's writings of the apocalyptic and the coldly factual. Both here in the *Economic and Philosophic Manuscripts of 1844* and in his later writings Marx frequently refers to his work as scientific, and often draws a close analogy with the natural sciences. For Marx, it is scientifically demonstrable that communism represents the coming together of all the diverse strands of human historical development. Yet at the same time, his announcement that communism is 'the riddle of history solved' takes on a miraculous air, and the mundane processes of everyday life are transformed into activities of a semi-divine significance. This second strand in Marx's thought is not unusual in the writings of philosophers of history, who often see an important aspect of their work as providing a method of giving significance and meaning to social and individual activities. Philosophies of history attempt to situate individual and social events within a wider context and may also regard those events as part of a narrative affecting the human race as a whole. This is the approach to the philosophy of history which Marx would be aware of from Hegel and Kant. Also, Marx's religious background as part of a Jewish family converted to Protestantism would have made him conscious of historical narratives, like that of the history of the Jews and the life of Christ, with a universal significance. However, Marx takes this broad framework of the philosophy of history and gives it an entirely new application. With Marx the philosophy of history is given an acute actuality in the present, and in this way he attempts to bring together the speculative and the scientific elements of his thought. The present with him may not only be understood as part of a process leading to a greater goal, but also *is* the process of realizing that greater goal. 'Communism is for us not a state of affairs still to be established, not an ideal to which reality has to adjust. We call communism the real movement which abolishes the present state of affairs.'[7]

As Marx sees it, the material process of production of human society unavoidably leads in the direction of communism. The pattern of history is dictated not so much by a goal which is merely intellectually conceived but rather by a necessary process internal to economic development and human society. Individual and social purposes are structured by economic needs and these needs and the forces to which they give rise are directly amenable to scientific investigation. Marx regards this as an entirely new insight he and Engels have brought to the study of history:

> In the whole conception of history up to the present this actual basis of history has been either totally neglected or considered as a minor matter irrelevant to the course of history. Thus history must always be written according to an extraneous standard. The actual production of life appears as something unhistorical, while the historical appears as something separated from ordinary life, something extra-superterrestrial. Thus the relation of man to nature is excluded from history and the antithesis of nature and history is created.[8]

Marx believes that Hegel can be included amongst those philosophers who fail to take into account 'real interests' in presenting a view of history. Perhaps for Marx Hegel is also the model representative of the view of history as subject to 'extra-superterrestrial' guidance. But Marx seems to misread Hegel here. Hegel's superterrestrial spirit may indeed have transcendent qualities but for Hegel it is supposed to emerge in the immanent working of social and political processes. A Hegelian might well say that spirit is no more appended to actual history than Marx's conception of communism. Marx's account of the necessary economic development of the human race is as much dependent on non-empirical assumptions as is Hegel's with its account of the evolution of spirit.

But Marx is very good at making his account of history sound like the real thing.

> . . . since for the socialist man the entire so-called history of the world is nothing but the creation of man through human labour, nothing but the emergence of nature for man, so he has the visible, irrefutable proof of his birth through himself, of the process of his creation.[9]

Yet despite the plausibility, the same problem recurs – Marx's assessment of the historical process confuses the moral and the empirical. Marx seems to be running together in this instance his desire to see the path of human events as following a progressive pattern with the observed course of events. Many observers may wish to see events in a different light from Marx or indeed they may wish to see events separately from any pattern. Indeed, this argument is, as we will see later, at the heart of Karl Popper's criticism of Marx's philosophy of history. Marx's supposition about history has, of course, been extremely influential but it suffers from the fact that Marx wants to see it as something more than a supposition. Marx shares with Hegel the desire to see his philosophy of history as reality itself. As he and Engels put it in *The German Ideology*:

> The premises from which we start are not arbitrary ones, not dogmas, but real premises from which abstraction can only be made in the imagination. They are real individuals, their activity and the material conditions under which they live, both those which they already find existing and those produced by their activity. These premises can thus be verified in a purely empirical way.[10]

In their view of history Marx and Engels are both monists and dogmatists. They are monists in that they believe that one principle can be seen as underlying human history, namely, material production, and they are dogmatists in believing that they solely give the correct outline of that principle. Marx's genius led him to an intellectual arrogance, an arrogance which he shared with Hegel. Neither is prepared to see their point of view as one possible interpretation of the world. They like to appropriate all points of view within their own. Ultimately such philosophical imperialism is a sure recipe for intellectual stagnation.

Fukuyama also sees Marx as beguiled by the Kantian and Hegelian idea of a universal history. According to Fukuyama, Marx

> appropriated large parts of the Hegelian system for his own purposes. Marx accepted from Hegel a view of the fundamental historicity of human affairs, the notion that human society evolved over the course of time from primitive social structures to more complex and highly developed ones. He agreed as well that the historical process is fundamentally dialectical, that is, that earlier forms of political and social organisation contained internal 'contradictions' that become evident over time and led to their downfall and replacement by something higher.[11]

But the question can be raised as to whether or not Fukuyama is correct in suggesting that 'Marx shared Hegel's belief in the possibility of an end of history'. It is doubtful that Marx 'foresaw a final form of society that was free from contradictions, and whose achievement would terminate the historical process'.[12] Marx does seem to envisage an end to history in the sense that history, as Fukuyama notes, may have some immanent purpose but Marx does not seem to think that realizing this purpose brings an end to history. Rather, as we have seen, he believes that the emergence of communist society will usher in the end of pre-history and the beginning of history proper, when human beings will, for the first time, be able to control their own destiny. In some respects, as we will see in our detailed discussion of Fukuyama later, Fukuyama and Marx are much closer than Fukuyama realizes at this point.

In the *Economic and Philosophic Manuscripts of 1844* Marx claims that 'communism is the necessary pattern and the dynamic principle of the immediate future, but communism as such is not the goal of human development.'[13] In writing this he seems to envisage human history developing a purpose taking it beyond communism, so communism represents the object of history for now – but only for now. The Preface to *A Contribution to the Critique of Political Economy* seems to corroborate this view:

> No social order is ever destroyed before all the productive forces for which it is sufficient have been developed, and new superior relations of production never replace older ones before the material conditions for their existence have matured within the framework of the old society. Mankind thus inevitably sets itself only such tasks as it is able to solve, since closer examination will always show that the problem itself arises only when the material conditions for its solution are already present.[14]

Something decidedly new happens with the end of the capitalist era and the transition to communism. But this decisive break does not represent the end of history:

> The bourgeois mode of production is the last antagonistic form of the social process of production – antagonistic not in the sense of individual antagonism but of an antagonism that emanates from the individuals' social conditions of existence – but the productive forces developing within bourgeois society create also the material conditions for a solution of this antagonism. The prehistory of human society accordingly closes with this social formation.[15]

Marx seems to regard human history up to the present as a kind of collective nursery ground for humanity. It is a period of our enforced immaturity, leading up to the point where we can finally break free of our domination by economic forces. Unlike Kant, who sees an element of choice in our previous immaturity and lack of independence, Marx tends to see it as almost wholly externally enforced. According to Marx the immanent purpose of history is to change the human individual from the object of development into its subject.

> In a higher phase of communist society, after the enslaving subordination of the individual to the division of labour, and therewith the antithesis between mental and physical labour, has vanished; after labour has become not only a means of life but life's prime want; after the productive forces have also increased with the all-round development of the individual, and all the springs of co-operative wealth flow more abundantly – only then can the narrow horizon of bourgeois right be crossed in its entirety and society inscribe on its banners: From each according to his ability, to each according to his needs![16]

As with Hegel, human freedom is the inner objective of history. Unlike Hegel, though, Marx does not equate this freedom with the enjoyment of liberal rights within a free market economy but rather with their transcendence. And unlike Kant, Marx does not identify freedom with our moral potential.

The engine of progress

What are we to make of Marx's idea that human society attains higher standards of morality only when the material conditions are present for the resolution of such problems? As we have seen, improvement for Marx is not an abstract ideal which we project and imagine as lying outside society; rather it is one which has to be realized within the present social, cultural and economic context. For example, there is very little point in arguing for a free press in an agricultural society where the printed word has not yet gained a foothold. Equally, in countries where there is a high infant mortality rate it is understandable that better health care for the newborn will take precedence over nursery school places for the under-fives. Marx regards human history as an unfolding drama, but his teleological account of it focuses first on the stage, the setting and the props against which the drama is played out. It is only at a secondary level that Marx goes on to discuss the cast and the plot that draws them together. The plot Marx sees as very much dictated by the stage upon which the drama is set. As he puts it in the essay *The Eighteenth Brumaire of Louis Bonaparte*: 'Men make their own history but they do not make it under circumstances chosen by themselves, but under circumstances directly encountered, given and transmitted from the past. The tradition of all the dead generations weighs like a nightmare on the brain of the living.'[17] Thus, the room for manœuvre in leading the human race on to a new stage in human history is not very great. Successful initiatives will probably depend on working with the grain, rather than against it. In the Preface to the German edition of Volume One of *Capital*, Marx puts the same point very graphically:

> Intrinsically, it is not a question of the higher or lower degree of development of the social antagonisms that result from the natural laws of Capitalist production. It is a question of these laws themselves, of these tendencies working with iron necessity towards inevitable results. The country that is more developed industrially only shows, to the less developed, the image of its own future.
>
> . . . even when a society has got upon the right track for the discovery of the natural laws of its movement – and it is the ultimate aim of this work to lay bare the economic law of motion of modern society – it can neither clear by bold leaps, nor remove by legal enactments, the obstacles offered by the successive phases of its normal development. But it can shorten and lessen the birth-pangs.[18]

Progress is inevitable, 'the natural laws of capitalist production . . . working with iron necessity' will ensure that. But what are these laws which play such a crucial role in Marx's theory of history? Social orders for Marx rest upon a definite type of economic structure which is forged first of all by what he calls 'the mode of production'. A mode of production is defined by considerations of time and space and more particularly by the technical level of production. The nature of a mode of production will differ according to whether it is set in the country or the town, and naturally according to the nation, continent and point in time where it is found. At the core of this variation in the mode of production is the technique employed. For

Marx, for instance, it makes a crucial difference whether or not the method of propulsion of a machine is water- or steam-power. Clearly a flour mill powered by steam will be a great deal more productive (efficient) than one powered by water. Technique is, of course, dictated by past technique but also by the power of human invention. A technique of production can be transformed beyond all imagination by innovation. To take an example from our time, in the late twentieth century the microchip has brought about extraordinary changes in business, comparable perhaps to the effects of the introduction of steam propulsion in Marx's day. Our remarkable inventiveness in the economic sphere leads Marx to the optimistic, if somewhat disputable, conclusion that 'mankind thus inevitably sets itself only such tasks as it is able to solve, since close examination will always show that the problem itself arises only when the material conditions for its solution are already present'.[19]

This strong element of determinism in his account of historical change led some of Marx's contemporaries to charge him with being too reticent about encouraging change where it did not seem absolutely inevitable. He was even accused by some socialists of not being sufficiently revolutionary![20] It might also appear to be the case that there is far more to be said for Marx's standpoint the nearer you are to the top of the tree in the process of human development. The implication of Marx's argument is that, if the time is ripe, your cause may well be a successful one. However, if you are much lower down in the order of human development, say, a Third World country with enormous external debts, then your situation in the short term may be extremely bleak.

In this respect, Marx's account of history leads to a kind of ethical relativism. His political theory does favour the oppressed but only particular kinds of oppressed persons – those who, because of favourable economic circumstances, are in a position to transform their condition. Marx thus seems to abandon any attempt at an ethical universalism with his privileging of the proletariat – or the next group up, so to speak – in the historical process. The cause of the proletariat gains precedence over perhaps, more underprivileged individuals – particularly in agricultural societies – who may be suffering greater deprivation.

Marx did indeed regard other underprivileged classes in capitalist society as being potentially dangerous to the cause of socialist revolution. In one of his most significant works of contemporary history, *The Class Struggles in France 1848–1850*, for example, Marx referred to the French peasantry as a reactionary and counter-revolutionary force. The language he used to describe their participation in the French presidential election of December 1848, which resulted in the election of Louis Napoleon (later Napoleon III) is scathing.

> 10 December 1848 was the day of the *peasant insurrection*. The symbol that expressed their entry into the revolutionary movement, clumsy but cunning, rascally but naïve, oafish but sublime, a calculated superstition, a pathetic burlesque, an inspired but stupid anachronism, a momentous, historic piece of buffoonery, an undecipherable hieroglyph for the understanding of the civilised – this symbol bore unmistakably the physiognomy of the class which represents barbarism within civilisation.[21]

Marx believed that because the proletariat was the most advanced class in the most advanced economies of the world, its emancipation would lead to an emancipation of the whole of humankind. But this claim is highly contentious, especially so in the light of the way in which those who have attempted to put Marx's ideas into practice this century have acted. A large proportion of the world's population is indeed working class, but it is far from being the majority. And even if the working class was the majority it is, morally speaking, highly debatable to say that the needs of other groups should be sacrificed for the good of the majority, as happened with the treatment of the peasants in the Soviet Union in the 1930s or to those labelled reactionaries in the Cultural Revolution in China, to take two of the most notorious examples. The tendency of socialists to argue that the interests of the majority should have priority over those of minority groups was strongly criticized in Marx's own lifetime by Alexis de Tocqueville and John Stuart Mill, and we will see that the danger of the 'tyranny of the majority', a term first used by Tocqueville, is something which figures prominently in Fukuyama's account of democracy.

This is not to suggest that Marx himself would have countenanced the abuses which took place in his name in the Stalinist Soviet Union or Mao's China. But there is a significant theoretical problem for Marx in explaining why such abuses are morally wrong. Marx's difficulty is that he requires an ethical standard of judgement which lies outside the historical process he describes. It is very reasonable to accept that the advance of the working-class movement is good in so far as it advances certain universal human aims but the advance of the movement cannot be assumed to encompass all that is good. Such an assumption, excluding as it does all other claims to know what is good, might breed fanaticism – as, of course, it has done in our century.

There is a marked social and political realism in the ethical standpoint Marx adopts. His philosophy of history allows him to recommend one group rather than the other as the embodiment of all human aspirations. Marx's choice of group is partly conditioned by ethical considerations, but also partly by the consideration of what group is most likely to alter the present status quo. Marx's theory of history does not then promise to eliminate deprivation and pain, not even in the long run. What he offers to do is to decrease the misery and exploitation of the working class without promising anything other than some positive side-effects for the worst-off social groups. With the working class in charge socialist countries might well take advantage in their external relations of the relatively poorer underdeveloped countries where there is no working class near taking power. Because the working class is designated as what is progressive and ethically good the ethical claims of others are in danger of being belittled or even totally disregarded.

Marx's purpose was to be universalist. He wished to see the working class as the majority group for the whole of mankind, but that never was a likelihood in his day. Today, as the technology of advanced capitalism makes more and more direct producers redundant, the chances of this happening are becoming even more remote. So Marx's theory of history needs to do more to draw in the non-working-class underprivileged, but it is doubtful whether it can do so without endangering the theory as a whole. To draw in the underprivileged others Marx would have to consider the claims of groups that might not wish immediately to overthrow capitalism (indeed who might even want more of the system!). Marx might also have to consider using the existing capitalist political and economic structure to help those worst-off individuals.

A point to consider is that Marx's dialectical view of history may itself have untoward implications and consequences which set it off track. For instance, the growth in the use of domestic appliances has considerably lessened the amount of labour time which has to be devoted to domestic chores. The freeing of domestic labour time might help to account for the desire of women to emerge from the household economy and make their presence felt in the wider market and economy. The equality of women with men is potentially much more realizable now in capitalist societies than ever before. There might therefore be a case for the question of the condition of women to be placed at the top of the political agenda from Marx's point of view. But his general outlook makes this doubtful. First the working class as a whole holds pride of place, and the women's cause can only ever be a part of this. Secondly, although women make up one-half of humankind, their emancipation without regard to the interests of men would not realize the universal objectives of Marxism. Thus, Marx's ethical relativism and social realism might lead one to adopt feminism as the cause of human emancipation, whereas his universalist or near-universalist aspirations and his desire to encompass the traditional ethical goals of philosophy might lead him to subordinate the feminist movement to wider political goals.

The women's issue provides an example of how Marx's theory accounts well for certain concerns moving to the top of the political agenda but does not of itself demonstrate why that concern should be sustained at the top of the agenda. Marx is in danger of having his moral and political priorities being decided by non-moral developments. This is a sure path to ethical and political chaos. Immediate political goals should be dictated by the long-term (universal) ethical standpoint, and not vice versa. In this respect, we believe that Kant, because of his wholly consistent universalization, is a better guide to political action than Marx.

Hegel's highest form of human society, the Protestant state founded upon a civil society, is not for Marx the end point of human history. The main reason why Marx does not regard the Protestant state as the final complete form is because it rests upon a capitalist society. That very civil society about which Hegel was so enthusiastic, a civil society whose nature Hegel had learned about by reading the Scottish political economists, disenchanted Marx. Instead of integrating all classes into one community, Marx regarded capitalism as dividing society into two hostile camps – the bourgeoisie and the proletariat. As far as Marx was concerned, the modern working class was not a class within society, but a class outside it. The working class constitutes 'a sphere of society having a universal character because of its universal suffering and claiming no particular right because no particular wrong but unqualified wrong is perpetrated upon it.'[22] Marx believes that the modern working class in its desire for recognition will lead human society beyond a wholly market economy based on a division of classes. From a Hegelian dialectical perspective, Marx sees history as having one more twist in its tail before a period of sustained freedom and prosperity can be attained.

For Fukuyama, the economy provides one certain guarantor of the forward movement of history. Fukuyama believes we cannot fully unlearn the lessons of the past, so that the most advanced technology will always be accessible to us and since we are desiring creatures we will choose to use it. For Marx, the economy is also the guarantor of progress, but in a more complex sense. Marx thinks that the collapse of capitalism, brought about by its own internal contradictions, although not wholly inevitable, is highly probable. Furthermore, because Marx sees capitalism as an exploitative economic system, he also thinks its collapse is *morally* necessary. Progress for Marx, then, comes about only through the demise of the very economic system upon which Fukuyama bases his optimistic account of the future.

The story of the possible and morally necessary collapse of capitalism is told in *Capital*. Marx thinks that the inherent difficulties of a capitalist economic system begin with its basic unit, the commodity. The commodity is both an object of use and an object of exchange. But a commodity cannot be used until it is exchanged, and it cannot be exchanged if it is not needed in use. So there is the constant possibility present in capitalist production that goods can be manufactured that no one will buy and the goods individuals want to buy might not necessarily be in sufficient quantity. Capitalist production is subject to supply and demand. Supply and demand in other words always ultimately balance but often at great cost to consumers and producers. Although the vagaries of supply and demand may not of themselves lead to the demise of capitalism, Marx does believe that the sudden collapse of trade brings about great suffering amongst direct producers and manufacturers. Unemployment and loss of income always seem to loom on the horizon for the capitalist employees and the continued existence of capitalism on its present scale is threatened by the imbalances of supply and demand.

However, it is probably true to say that the greatest threat to the continuation of the capitalist system is caused by the problems of its *extended* reproduction. This is reproduction at a more advanced level. Here economic growth is taken into account. Now, although economic growth is one of the most remarkable features of a market economy it is also (according to Marx) where its greatest vulnerability lies. Capitalist economies have the potential to become wealthier and wealthier. Instead of economic activity taking place at an even pace under capitalism it may expand dramatically from decade to decade and from generation to generation. Marx describes this as the 'Historical Tendency of Capitalist Production'. Accelerated economic development leads to two remarkable processes – the centralization and concentration of production. Capitalism begins with individual production, from small parcels of land or small-scale workshops and business premises. But gradually production loses its individual character and takes on a social form. The modern factory replaces the specialist workshop and the large corporation replaces the individual employer.

Marx argues that this centralization and concentration of production both greatly strengthens and greatly weakens the capitalist system. It greatly strengthens the capitalist economy by increasing its productivity enormously. The larger the units of production, the more costs can be shared and the more efficient they can be. Less efficient producers are driven out of the market by the more efficient units, and eventually one national economy might be dominated by only (say) three companies in one line of production. We can now, perhaps, see the same process taking place at a continental and, even a world level where, for example, the number of large aircraft manufacturers can be no more than six, and the number of large motor car producers is no greater than twelve. For Marx, this concentration is the positive side of capitalist development. Markets are dominated by a handful of large, efficient producers. But the negative side is that all this concentration of economic power is attained at the expense of the direct producers. Marx puts it very graphically in *Capital*:

> Along with the constantly diminishing number of the magnates of capital, who usurp and monopolise all advantages of this process of transformation, grows the mass of misery, oppression, slavery degradation, exploitation; but with this too grows the revolt of the working class, a class always increasing in numbers, and disciplined, united, organised by the very mechanism of the process of capitalist production itself.[23]

The concentration and centralization of capital also leads to the concentration and the centralization of the working class, which now too finds itself in place to transform the economic system. The demand for socialism grows out of the economic considerations of the working class. The conditions for the realization of a planned socialist economy are, however, provided by capitalism itself.

Conclusion

Despite many differences of detail and their fundamental metaphysical clash about idealism and materialism there are many similarities between Hegel's and Marx's views of history and it will be useful at this point to summarize these before turning to our discussion of Fukuyama.

The assumptions they have in common are:

1.   The development of human history falls into distinct stages or epochs.
2.   These stages represent a change in gravity in the location of historical development from East to West.
3.   World history is progressive. There is an improvement from the more primitive condition of mankind to the more advanced.
4.   This is not just a material improvement; there is also a cultural and moral improvement.
5.   Human freedom represents one of the main goals of this progressive development.
6.   There is a distinct point of culmination where the higher level of society is achieved. For Hegel, this point of culmination is in the Germanic Protestant world; for Marx, it is communist society.
7.   This end point is dynamic. There is a high point reached, but the high point is a continuous process.
8.   Both Hegel and Marx therefore take a teleological view of history. They believe there is a pattern underlying the unfolding of events in world history. Another way of expressing this is to say that Hegel and Marx both believe that the course followed by world history is a necessary one.

There is one fundamental point of difference that stands out in Hegel and Marx's appreciation of history. This difference is to be found in their choices of agency in bringing about the necessary steps forward. Ultimately Hegel has the one agent who is both worldly and otherworldly, namely *Geist* or Spirit. Spirit for Hegel calls the tune in the unfolding of history. Human individuals are the agents of the one higher agent. Marx rejects this metaphysical standpoint. His agents are, in contrast, social classes and the forces of production. Amongst these agents there is one candidate for the heroic role. With Marx the proletariat or the working class steps on the scene as the agent which can complete the task of world history.

4 • Fukuyama I:
Reinventing Optimism

Intellectual influences: from Kant to Kojève

Turning from a discussion of Kant, Hegel and Marx to a consideration of Fukuyama requires a number of changes of approach. Most
obviously, Fukuyama is a contemporary writer whose work is still in
the process of developing. This is a practical problem which arises
from the fortunate fact that the author is still alive and may well
produce further works of perhaps greater significance. At a more
philosophical level, there is the problem that it is not possible to look
at his work with the benefit of historical perspective.

In this respect Fukuyama's ideas are more immediate to us than are
those of Kant, Hegel or Marx – we engage with him directly because
he speaks from and to our immediate situation. This is not to claim,
of course, that his ideas are intrinsically more important than those of
Kant or Hegel or Marx, nor is it to say that their thinking is no longer
relevant to us. Quite the opposite is the case, and Fukuyama's
discussion of these three thinkers, along with his use of other great
philosophers from the past, especially Plato and Nietzsche, is an
indication not only of their continuing importance but also of the
way in which their central ideas are appropriated and reinterpreted in
the present. Our reading of past philosophers always takes the form
of a dialogue. We do not passively receive their wisdom; rather, we
enter into debate with them, rejecting some of their ideas but taking
others and moulding them to the particular purposes and preoccupations of our own time. According to Hegel, this is the only way it is
possible to engage seriously with earlier thinkers, and as we shall see,
Fukuyama's approach is very much in the spirit of Hegel.

There is another way in which reading Fukuyama differs from
reading earlier philosophers. With earlier writers what primarily
interests us in them, certainly if we are studying them as philosophers
or political theorists rather than as historians, is the general principles
which they propound rather than the answers which they give to the
specific political problems of their own day. There has rightly been an

increasing emphasis, through the work of Quentin Skinner, John Dunn and others, on the need to understand the context in which past thinkers thought and wrote, and this has been of considerable help to philosophers in interpreting the works of the great thinkers of the past. Peter Laslett's work on Locke's *Two Treatises of Government*, for example, has immeasurably furthered our understanding of Locke's motives and purposes in writing and has provided a deeper appreciation of the nuances of his thought, but we read Laslett to understand Locke better as a political philosopher, not because Locke's role in the Exclusion Crisis holds any practical interest for us today. Equally, the emphasis which a follower of Leo Strauss will lay on the importance of reading a text in its historical context has great value in allowing us to reach a deeper appreciation of the ideas contained within it. Alan Bloom's commentary on Plato's *Republic*, for example, provides many illuminating insights into the nature of Athenian politics and Plato's relationship to it which deepen our understanding of the text, but we read Plato – as Bloom and Strauss do, and, indeed, as Fukuyama does in following them – in great measure for the profound insights which it offers to us in the world of the late twentieth century.

Reading Fukuyama, by contrast, we cannot avoid being deeply interested and involved in the specific political context in which he writes because we share that context. The outcome of the political conflicts in ancient Athens have little direct political relevance to us, nor do the far more recent but still remote events of late Restoration England. But the end of the Cold War, the rise of aggressive nationalism and the dangers posed by the proliferation of weapons of mass destruction, are of the utmost concern to us. If we are at all politically aware, we cannot fail to be engaged with the issues which preoccupy Fukuyama, and whether we agree or profoundly disagree with his analysis of them our appreciation of his more abstract theories is coloured by our response to those events.

It is for this reason that Fukuyama's dual role as a political actor and a political philosopher must be borne in mind in any serious discussion of his work, even though the separation is not always clear-cut and the two aspects of his work often interact, as indeed is only to be expected. Failure to properly appreciate both elements has sometimes led to serious misunderstandings of his work. Some critics have seen him as a naïve optimist who has simply ignored the reality of international politics, while others have claimed that he is, in effect, little more than a spokesman for the American foreign policy establishment.

The widely differing interpretations to which Fukuyama's work has given rise is related to a further way in which he differs from the earlier thinkers we have been discussing, which is related to his writing style. Not even their staunchest supporters have ever claimed that Kant and Hegel wrote in clear and lucid prose. Some of Marx's writings, particularly his journalism, are eminently readable but a considerable part of his most important work, including *The Paris Manuscripts*, the *Grundrisse* and *Capital*, make very considerable demands upon the reader. Reading Fukuyama is quite different. He writes in a very accessible and fluent manner, with dramatic and appealing chapter titles and frequent use of illustrative examples. This style has many advantages, but it does suffer from one serious drawback. Kant, Hegel and Marx justified their technical styles because such styles allowed them to be rigorous and precise in the ways in which they expressed themselves. However difficult it might be to read a work such as Kant's *Critique of Pure Reason*, the attentive reader quickly becomes aware that Kant is using his key terms in a clear and unambiguous way. By contrast, in choosing to write in a more popular style Fukuyama has had to forgo some of this rigour and this has meant that a number of central ideas and the terms in 'The End of History?' and *The End of History and the Last Man* are expressed more ambiguously than they ought to be.

This popular style has, unfortunately, led some critics to under-estimate the value of *The End of History and the Last Man*, and several, such as Stephen Holmes, John Dunn and Joseph McCarney,[1] have claimed that the book is confused and ill-thought out. In particular, they have pointed to the perceived conflict between the positive message signalled by the first part of the title – the triumph of liberal democracy at the end of history – and the pessimism which is held to pervade the last part of the book, which is summed up in the Nietzschean idea of the last man. It is true that the book, which is long in words and broad in scope, does contain some inconsistencies, but they are relatively minor ones. We shall be arguing that the allegations of confusion are ill-founded and that the central themes of the book are coherent and well developed.

Nevertheless, although there is no central confusion in the book, there are ideas which need to be drawn out in more detail, and connections between concepts which need to be made more explicit.

In some respects, and despite its length, the book might best be seen as part of a larger project. Some parts of the project, such as testing the principles of the book against more recent events in world politics, still need to be developed, and Fukuyama himself has already contributed to this in subsequent articles.[2] But the project has been ongoing for many years and *The End of History and the Last Man* draws on earlier phases of it, notably the work of Leo Strauss and his followers such as Allan Bloom, and on the writings of Alexandre Kojève. We shall be discussing these earlier writers, and Fukuyama's relationship to them, in the course of the next three chapters.

Mention of the influence of twentieth-century philosophers on Fukuyama brings us to one further general point about his relationship with Kant, Hegel and Marx. This is the fact that Fukuyama's use of their works is selective. There is, of course, a sense in which everyone's use of other writers is selective, but Fukuyama's is self-consciously so. When he uses the writings of Hegel, for instance, he is quite clear that he is using them as tools to help interpret the modern world. He is not primarily interested in Hegel as a historical philosopher, nor is the accuracy of his detailed interpretation of Hegel of overriding importance to him. It is a dialogue carried out with only half an ear to what the other is saying. Fukuyama has been heavily criticized by Hegelian scholars[3] for what they have argued are quite serious misunderstandings of Hegel, but such criticisms, although valid, are not as grave for Fukuyama as some have taken them to be. Indeed, paradoxically, they may even work to his ultimate advantage.

The reason for this lies in the particular way in which Fukuyama uses Hegel's writings. He is not, as some hostile critics have maintained, simply and naïvely trying to force Hegel's analysis of nineteenth-century political and intellectual life onto the very different world of the late twentieth century. Rather, he is looking to what is alive in Hegel and offering suggestions as to how that may be applied to the contemporary situation. This is an example of the importance of keeping Fukuyama's two roles as a political philosopher and an observer of the contemporary world clearly in mind. His starting-point is the work he carries out as an analyst of contemporary international relations, and he turns to Hegel for philosophical tools to help him in that analysis. But Fukuyama is deeply immersed in the events of current world politics, as *The End of History and the Last Man* abundantly demonstrates, and he reads Hegel in the light of contemporary history, not vice versa.

There is, though, a further way in which Fukuyama's reading of Hegel is less than straightforward. His understanding of Hegel is shaped, as he makes very clear, by the Russian-French writer Alexandre Kojève. During the years 1933–9 Kojève conducted a series of seminars at the École des Hautes Études in Paris on Hegel's *Phenomenology of Spirit*.[4] These lectures had a dramatic impact on those who attended them, including such future luminaries as Raymond Aron, Maurice Merleau-Ponty and Jacques Lacan, and through their own subsequent publications, they exerted a powerful influence both on interpretations of the *Phenomenology of Spirit* and much more widely on French and European intellectual life. Fukuyama regards Kojève very highly indeed as a commentator on Hegel, referring to him as Hegel's 'greatest interpreter in the twentieth century'.[5] For much of the book he treats the views of Kojève and Hegel as the same. His concern, he says, is with the ideas rather than the philosophers who originally articulated them, and consequently he is interested 'not in Hegel *per se* but in Hegel-as-interpreted-by-Kojève, or perhaps a new, systematic philosopher named Hegel-Kojève'.[6]

Kojève's reading of Hegel is not uncontroversial, and there are aspects to his life and work which at first sight fit rather oddly with Fukuyama's proclamation that the triumph of Western liberalism was made manifest by the collapse of communism. Most problematic is the fact that Kojève was a communist. The following passage bears quoting at length because it conveys the flavour of Fukuyama's relationship to Kojève.

At the centre of Kojève's teaching was the startling assertion that Hegel had been essentially right, and that world history, for all the twists and turns it had taken in subsequent years, had effectively ended in the year 1806 . . . [B]ehind this seemingly odd conclusion is the thought that the principles of liberty and equality that emerged from the French Revolution, embodied in what Kojève called the modern 'universal and homogeneous state,' represented the end point of human ideological evolution beyond which it was impossible to progress further. Kojève was of course aware that there had been many bloody wars and revolutions in the years since 1806, but these he regarded as essentially an 'alignment of the provinces.' In other words, communism did not represent a higher stage than liberal democracy, it was part of the same stage of history that would eventually universalise the spread of liberty and equality to all parts of the world.[7]

This is indeed problematic. Fukuyama is not a Marxist. Quite the opposite, he regards Marxism, which he largely identifies with the communist regimes of the Soviet Union, Eastern Europe and China, as having been comprehensively defeated. It is not that Marxism has triumphed over liberalism but rather the opposite. Because of this he has to argue that 'really' Kojève was a liberal rather than a Marxist, but, as even he acknowledges, this presents considerable difficulties.

In a long footnote to the page which has just been quoted, Fukuyama acknowledges that 'there are certain problems in seeing Kojève himself as a liberal, insofar as he frequently professed an ardent admiration for Stalin and asserted that there was no essential difference between the United States, the Soviet Union, and China of the 1950s . . .'[8]

This seems a pretty damning admission and critics of Fukuyama such as Stephen Holmes have seen it as evidence of confusion on his part.[9] Fukuyama goes on to claim in the same footnote that Kojève's thinking developed and that Marxism was not central to his belief in the end of history. After the Second World War, Kojève became a senior bureaucrat of the European Community and in a footnote to his *Introduction to the Reading of Hegel* referred to the United States as having 'already attained the final stage of Marxist "communism" '.[10]

Even though the difficulties are greater than Fukuyama acknowledges, there is a very real sense in which both Marxism and liberalism share crucial assumptions. They are both part of modernity, and looked at from that perspective the conflict between them is not quite so great. Certainly liberals and humanistic Marxists have many beliefs in common, such as a faith in the power of reason, a conviction that progress is possible and a disapproval of the evils of unbridled capitalism.

Most significantly, Fukuyama's optimism is predicated on the same principle which underlies the optimism of Hegel and Marx – that there is an inexorable process at work in history which has led, in the case of Hegel, or will lead, as Marx confidently predicted, to the end of what he called 'prehistory' and to the dawn of a new age. In terms of the kind of society which he believes is in the process of emerging at the end of history, Fukuyama is much closer to Hegel than he is to Marx. Although Fukuyama's relationship to Hegel is a critical one, and mediated in part through the work of Kojève, Fukuyama does offer the most self-conscious recent attempt to carry forward the idea of the end of history in the Hegelian tradition.

The idea of progress

The central, dominating theme concerning the end of history which Fukuyama shares with Kant, Hegel and Marx is a belief in progress. Although they have rather different ideas of progress, and certainly different visions of the society which progress will bring at the end of history, Kant, Hegel and Marx all share this central conviction. The belief in progress is, indeed, a powerful motif in a much broader swathe of modern Western culture. The very idea of modernity itself incorporates a conviction that what is most recent – most modern – is, in some important senses, an improvement on what preceded it.

Yet despite the abiding power of the belief in progress it seems, as we said in the Introduction, almost impossible for someone writing at the end of the twentieth century to recapture the optimism that was so marked a feature of the writings of Kant, Hegel and Marx. Much that has happened in the intervening years has forced us to rethink our belief that we have progressed and that we will continue to progress. And a great deal is happening at the present time which prompts us to consider whether we might yet regress further. From the Holocaust and the Gulag to the ominous resurgence of an aggressive and militaristic nationalism and anti-Semitism in Eastern Europe and the Balkans, Europe's hope in its own future, let alone that of the rest of the world, has been severely tested.

It is often said that defenders of the idea of progress are naïve and impractical. They simply do not understand the dark forces at work in the real world and turn their eyes away from the depths of the misery and suffering that are always present in human affairs. Such charges are often made by those who regard themselves as realists, as being able to face up to the darkness and learn to accommodate to it. Reaching such an accommodation is presented as the most rational way of dealing with the harshness of life, of controlling the forces that would otherwise overwhelm us. But there is a fine line to be drawn between exercising control and being controlled, and realism itself is often charged with reaching an overindulgent *rapprochement* with corruption and injustice.

Partly because of such fears about realism, the belief in progress has not been entirely without supporters. Fukuyama, both in his article 'The End of History?' and in his book *The End of History and the Last Man*,[11] has argued forcefully that the idea of progress is central to our understanding of the modern world. To reject the idea of progress is, he claims, to jettison any realistic hope of understanding our present situation. Moreover, realism, far from offering the 'only plausible way to act in the world, in fact enters into a fatal compromise with forces which are already in decline. Realism is not the way of the future; rather, it offers only a forlorn link with a discredited past.

Fukuyama is optimistic, but he is far from being naïve. He acknowledges that the horrifying events of the twentieth century such as the Gulags and the Holocaust have 'made all of us into deep historical pessimists'.[12] These cannot be ignored, but nor should they be allowed to dominate our thinking to the exclusion of anything positive. In fact, when we consider the long-term implications of these events we find that what stands out most dramatically is that those who perpetrated them, and the systems in whose names they were carried out, failed in their ultimate objectives. What is most striking is not the power and dominance but rather the weakness of allegedly strong states.[13]

During their times of political and military success, Nazi Germany and the Soviet Union appeared to their contemporaries, especially in the liberal democracies, to be invincible. Even after the collapse of fascism as an ideology at the end of the Second World War, many people continued to see communism as a permanent force in world affairs. Yet communism, like fascism, collapsed in the First World and is now largely discredited as a political ideology.

The demise of these systems came about for different reasons. Nazi Germany was defeated in war, by the Soviet Union in alliance with the Western liberal democracies, whereas the collapse of communism in the Soviet Union came about through internal dissent and change. But the underlying reason in both cases was the loss of legitimacy, a loss of faith both in the ideology and in the political leaders who attempted, with more or less genuine enthusiasm, to carry it out.

Legitimacy is a crucial idea for Fukuyama. Ultimately, he argues, all governments depend for their existence on being recognized as having a legitimate right to rule. This does not mean that the right must be acknowledged by all those they rule: if it did, only democratic governments could rule with any form of stability. What it does mean is that those who rule must have the support of at least the most powerful members of society. Hitler's rule over Germany was based in part on terror, but his ability to exercise control over millions of people was possible only because it was seen as legitimate by the Nazi party, the army and other important institutions in the state.

The same held true for the Communist Party in the Soviet Union and for the continuing rule of the Chinese Communist Party.

Such legitimacy may keep rulers in power for a considerable time, but there is a fatal weakness. A government whose legitimacy is based on an ideology which effectively excludes the great majority of its citizens from decision-making is inherently unstable. For as long as its policies are successful such a government may retain power, but when those policies fail, there is no reservoir of public support from which it can draw. The internal contradictions which Fukuyama claims are always present in such political systems will become so powerful that they will bring about its downfall.

In the case of fascism, the internal contradictions arose from the defeat of the German armies by allegedly inferior races. Even if Germany had won the Second World War, Fukuyama argues, 'fascism would nonetheless have lost its inner *raison d'être* in the peace of a universal empire where German nationhood could no longer be asserted through war and conquest'.[14]

Leaving aside the details of Fukuyama's assessment of the failure of German fascism, whose conclusions are far from obvious, what is most significant here is the method which he applies in analysing this and the large number of other cases which he discusses. It is the method of the dialectic, already familiar from our discussions of Hegel and Marx.

Fukuyama's argument is that non-democratic states will eventually collapse under their own internal contradictions. Sometimes external forces will contribute to the collapse, but it is the internal pressures which will always be decisive. The defeat of Germany at the end of the Second World War was the immediate cause of the demise of fascism, but it was the internal necessity within fascist ideology to continually extend the power of the state through war which led it into conflict with the Western powers and the Soviet Union in the first place. Equally, the economic competition with the United States and Western Europe weakened the USSR, but that only served to propel the Soviet economic and political system more quickly along the path to failure which its own internal structures had already laid out. By contrast, Fukuyama argues, liberal democracy has no internal contradictions of this kind and so whatever the short-term difficulties, its ultimate success, as well as the failure of all possible alternatives, is assured.

'The End of History?' and the triumph of liberalism

The central thesis of both 'The End of History?' and *The End of History and the Last Man* is, then, that history is not only coming to an end but that the end is a positive one. This is a striking claim, and one that needs to be explained in detail before we can properly assess its validity. In saying that the end of history is upon us, Fukuyama is arguing that the human race is moving beyond the conflicts and oppression of the past into an era of peace and freedom. He claims that a 'remarkable consensus' has emerged over 'the past few years' that liberal democracy as a system of government has 'conquered rival ideologies like hereditary monarchies, fascism and more recently communism'.[15] But it is not merely a practical political triumph which Fukuyama is arguing for. His argument is deeper, in a way that has important implications for his general perspective. At the heart of the triumph of liberal democracy is an intellectual success. Liberal democracy has emerged as the dominant ideology of the modern world. Even more than that, it has come to be recognized as the final ideology, the one that has ultimately triumphed. Because of this, no further development in political ideology is desirable or even possible. Any new political ideology which emerged as a rival to liberal democracy would inevitably be false. This is not to say that all modern states are, or soon will become, democratic, nor is it to deny that some countries which achieve a liberal democratic form of government might not, as he puts it, 'lapse back into other, more primitive forms of rule like theocracy or military dictatorship'.[16] What is central to his argument is that 'the *ideal* of liberal democracy' cannot be improved upon.

It is best to begin our account of Fukuyama's analysis of the current situation where he does, with his now famous article 'The End of History?', which in many ways sparked off the current widespread debate about the end of history.

The article 'The End of History?' was very much a product of its particular time. Published in the summer of 1989, it gave voice to a powerful feeling that the momentous events of the late 1980s in world politics had some inner meaning, and that some deeper explanation should be sought which would make sense of them. The timing of the article's publication was all the more fortuitous in that the fall of the Berlin Wall occurred almost immediately after 'The End of History?' was published. The response to the fall and to its accompanying and succeeding events was in many cases one of uncertainty. The belief that Fukuyama's analysis made sense of these events provided a receptive audience whose members were initially very responsive to the solution he offered.

The article had two pronounced central themes – the victory of liberalism and the power of Hegel's philosophy to provide an explanatory framework in which to explain its ascendancy. With one very important exception, the tone of the article was positive if not triumphalist, celebrating the demise of communism as the removal of the last great obstacle to the success of liberalism.

The end of history, in Fukuyama's understanding of the term, refers to the decline of totalitarian political regimes and the triumph of liberal politics and liberal economic policies as the only viable social system. This is a process which began in the eighteenth century with the American and French revolutions, but the collapse of communism in Eastern Europe and the Soviet Union marked a great step forward in bringing history to an end. Fukuyama is unashamedly bullish about this triumph of Western liberalism over its international enemies, a feature of the article which perhaps contributed to its initial widespread success:

> . . . the century that began full of self-confidence in the triumph of Western liberal democracy seems at its close to be returning full circle to where it started: not to an 'end of ideology' or a convergence between capitalism and socialism, as earlier predicted, but to an unabashed victory of economic and political liberalism.[17]

Liberalism has defeated its great enemy, socialism, and Fukuyama is celebrating that victory. But what precisely does this mean? In particular, what is Fukuyama referring to when he discusses liberalism? As the passage just quoted indicates, he has in mind two related but quite distinct phenomena – political liberalism and economic liberalism.

Fukuyama is careful in *The End of History and the Last Man* to differentiate between liberalism and democracy,[18] but in 'The End of History?' he offers a definition of liberal democracy which neatly sums up his view of the relationship between the two, and of why they have triumphed at the end of history.

> The state that emerges at the end of history is liberal insofar as it recognises and protects through a system of law man's universal right

to freedom, and democratic insofar as it exists only with the consent of the governed.[19]

We will discuss Fukuyama's account of democracy later, but for the present we will focus on his account of liberalism. In the above definition, liberalism is defined primarily in terms of individual rights. In *The End of History and the Last Man* Fukuyama adds to the definition the provision that the system of law protects not only certain individual rights but also freedom from government control. He then goes on to list what he takes to be the three basic rights, a list which he borrows from James Bryce's *Modern Democracies*, first published in 1931. The first of these is civil rights, by which he means absence of control over a person and his property by the state. The second is religious rights, which effectively means the guarantee of religious toleration. The third is political rights, which are rights enabling people to participate freely in the political process. These include the right to free speech and the closely related right of press freedom.[20]

Religious rights are straightforward – the wish to practice any or no religion is a matter of private conscience and is of no concern to the state. The first and third rights are more problematic. It is far from clear how they differ significantly from each other. Both emphasize the freedom of the individual in relation to the state and therefore both seek to limit the role of the state. One feature which Fukuyama is seeking to underline with both of them is that neither civil nor political rights justify a welfarist approach to society. In the same paragraph he dismisses what he refers to as the practice of socialist countries 'to press for the recognition of various second- and third-generation economic rights, such as the right to employment, housing, or health care'.[21] These, he argues, often come into conflict with other, presumably first-order rights, such as the right to property, and therefore ought to be rejected.

The theory of liberalism which emerges is therefore couched in terms of what Isaiah Berlin first referred to as 'negative' liberty,[22] a concept which emphasizes individual freedom and seeks to limit the role of the state. Such a definition has frequently been closely identified with capitalism and an emphasis on the importance of the free market.

In accepting this terminology and the thinking which underlies it, Fukuyama claims that political liberalism and economic liberalism reinforce each other. He defines economic liberalism specifically in terms of the ideas of the market economy. These ideas in turn underpin both the general intellectual defence of capitalism, and the practical economic policies favoured by governments in capitalist societies. The effect of such policies, he argues, are seen in what he refers to as 'the ineluctable spread of consumerist Western culture', which he claims can be observed,

> in such diverse contexts as the peasants' markets and colour television sets now omnipresent throughout China, the co-operative restaurants and clothing stores opened in the past year in Moscow [the process of privatization has since gone much further in the Soviet Union], the Beethoven piped into Japanese department stores, and the Rock music enjoyed alike in Prague, Rangoon and Tehran.[23]

There are two important consequences of the close identification of political and economic liberalism. The first is that it leads Fukuyama to see oppressive societies such as China as having significant liberal elements in them. The peasants' markets help to chip away at China's illiberal political system, and in doing so they make it less viable as a system. Secondly, it emphasizes consumerism as an important part of the liberalizing process. The 'omnipresent colour television sets' in China and the rock music enjoyed around the world spread the values of Western consumerist culture, which in turn reinforces the demand for a market economy which can supply the consumers. This, in its turn, leads to demands for political liberalism.

It may appear strange that Fukuyama gives such importance to consumer culture, which is so often dismissed in the West because it is superficial and empty of real value. There is a very important part of Fukuyama which agrees with this disdain for at least some aspects of the consumer culture – though the real significance of this did not become fully apparent until the publication of *The End of History and the Last Man*, a point to which we will return later. But there is an equally important sense in which Fukuyama sees the values which are associated with a consumer culture as being of cardinal importance in the acceptance of the market economy. This brings us back to his utilization of Hegel.

The Hegelian idea which Fukuyama most wishes to focus upon is that of the primacy of consciousness in history, the fundamental importance of ideas and values in determining the way in which history develops, which has already been discussed in the chapter on Hegel.

Fukuyama's account of this theory of history in 'The End of History?' is brief and succinct, though it masks a number of problems which become distinctly troublesome in *The End of History and the Last Man.*

> For Hegel, all human behaviour in the material world, and hence all human history, is rooted in a prior state of consciousness . . . This consciousness may not be explicit and self-aware, as are modern political doctrines, but may rather take the form of religion or simple cultural or moral habits. And yet this realm of consciousness in the long run necessarily becomes manifest in the real world, indeed creates the material world in its own image.[24]

Fukuyama is highly critical of all attempts to give a purely materialistic account of the world, in which economic or other material forces are the ultimate driving force. In this respect he is highly critical of Marx, as one might expect from Fukuyama's own political and economic theories, but also of non-Marxists such as Paul Kennedy whose *The Rise and Fall of the Great Powers* owed much of its success, in Fukuyama's eyes, to being based on a type of economic determinism.[25]

Fukuyama's invocation of the Hegelian analysis of the end of history was central to the argument of the article, and initially it was accepted with enthusiasm. But criticisms soon began to emerge. As we have seen, a number of Hegel scholars claimed that Fukuyama's reading of Hegel was seriously flawed, and they argued that his attempt to develop a Hegelian perspective on the end of the Cold War was not helped by the fact that his interpretation of Hegel was derived in large part from the work of Kojève. What, they asked, was genuinely Hegelian in Fukuyama's argument, and how much were these really the ideas of Kojève? Even more damning, how far did Fukuyama himself know where the debt to Hegel ended and that to Kojève started?

These two central themes of the article are explored in more detail in Fukuyama's subsequent book, *The End of History and the Last Man*, which also takes up and elaborates upon a third theme introduced only in the last paragraph of the article, that the end of history will be 'a very sad time':

The struggle for recognition, the willingness to risk one's life for a purely abstract goal, the world-wide ideological struggle that called forth daring, courage, imagination, and idealism, will be replaced by economic calculation. The endless solving of technical problems, environmental concerns, and the satisfaction of sophisticated consumer demands. In the post-historical period there will be neither art nor philosophy, just the perpetual caretaking of the museum of human history.[26]

The appearance of this paragraph at the close of the article struck many readers as being distinctly odd. As we have seen, the bulk of the article is extremely positive in the way in which it presents the triumph of liberalism, and the ever increasing rationality of the modern world. It is all the more surprising, then, that Fukuyama admits, in the same last paragraph, to 'a powerful nostalgia for the time when history existed'. Even more striking are the final words of the article. 'Perhaps this very prospect of centuries of boredom at the lack of history will serve to get history started once again.'[27]

In a subsequent reply to his critics in *The National Interest*,[28] Fukuyama noted that this passage had often been quoted with surprise, as if it was impossible to see how someone who was an advocate of liberalism could nevertheless recognize 'fundamental tensions and weaknesses'[29] within it. Nevertheless this is precisely his position. The most acute problem for liberal democracy, in Fukuyama's view, is that while liberal states provide a framework of security from internal and external dangers they are constitutionally incapable of offering guidance on what counts as a good life, let alone how to achieve such a life. As a consequence there is a vacuum in liberal societies which can be filled with all manner of things, some of which are very far from being good or desirable. These include 'sloth and self-indulgence as well as moderation and courage, desire for wealth and preoccupation with commercial gain as well as love of reflection and pursuit of beauty, banality alongside spirituality'.[30] Liberal societies, he argues, still have contradictions within them which 'could yet result in their undoing'. He makes a further claim which seems even more radical: 'These problems are perennial and deserve to be studied by every generation that enjoys the benefit of our modern democratic-egalitarian society.'[31]

In addressing this issue Fukuyama is raising what was to become a dominant theme in his book, the problem of the last man. We will discuss this issue at length in the next chapter, but it is very important to underline here that in raising this issue, at the end of 'The End of History?' and again in 'A Reply to my Critics', Fukuyama is signalling that his understanding of liberal democracy, and his belief that it represents the highest stage of political ideology, is far from naïve or simplistic. Quite to the contrary, and despite his critics, his analysis of the idea is subtle and complex.

Unfortunately, before the book was published, many critics had already made up their minds that Fukuyama's ideas could be dismissed as naïve. Many believed that their reluctance to accept his ideas was justified by subsequent events. Almost immediately after the article had been published, the belief that liberalism had triumphed in the old Eastern bloc and that mankind was entering a time of peace and international harmony was dashed by the emergence of violent civil wars in Yugoslavia and other parts of the old communist world. Such ethnic conflict along with the resurgence of what appeared to many Westerners to be the irrational force of militant Islamic fundamentalism seemed to undermine the optimistic claim that history was coming to an end.

These criticisms misinterpreted an essential part of Fukuyama's theory. They failed to see that the core of his argument lay in the claim that the end of history was to be understood in terms of the victory of the *idea* of liberal democracy, and that such a victory did not mean that wars and other conflicts would immediately cease. In 'A Reply to my Critics' Fukuyama reiterated this argument and illustrated it by acknowledging the possibility of a counter-revolution in the Soviet Union which would bring to power a fascist regime in that country[32] and by suggesting that nationalist conflicts will increase on the European continent over the next two decades.[33] As an avowed Hegelian, Fukuyama argues that ideas ultimately determine the way in which events will unfold – but the truth of the ideas cannot be judged simply by reference to short-term events.

We suggested earlier in the chapter that Fukuyama's writing style sometimes had the effect of concealing the depth and sophistication of his thought. In the case of 'The End of History?' that is compounded by the shortness of space in which he is forced to present his ideas. They are, as we have seen, highly complex, so complex, indeed, that it required a 400-page book to spell them out properly.

5 • Fukuyama II:
Recognition and Liberal Democracy

Before considering the arguments of *The End of History and the Last Man* in detail it is as well to recap on Fukuyama's central thesis. In saying that the end of history is upon us, Fukuyama is advancing two quite distinct arguments.

First, he is arguing that the human race is moving beyond the conflicts and oppression of the past into an era of peace and freedom. As we have already seen, this was taken by most readers to be the dominant theme in his article 'The End of History?', but while it is of considerable importance it is in fact secondary to his main argument. It plays a similar role in *The End of History and the Last Man*, where Fukuyama develops it by drawing heavily on Kant's liberal inter-nationalism. We will return to this argument and discuss it in more detail in the next chapter.

The second, more fundamental, argument is concerned not with political practice but with political ideas. At the heart of the triumph of liberal democracy, according to Fukuyama, is an intellectual success. Liberal democracy has emerged as the dominant ideology of the modern world. Even more than that, it has come to be recognized as the final ideology, the one that has ultimately triumphed. Any new political ideology which emerged as a rival to liberal democracy would inevitably be false. It is very important to stress again here, against some of Fukuyama's critics, that he is not claiming that all modern states are, or soon will become, democratic, nor is he denying that some countries which achieve a liberal democratic form of government are incapable of falling back into non-democratic ways of government. What is central to his argument is that 'the *ideal* of liberal democracy' cannot be improved upon.

Although the initial interest in 'The End of History?' centred on his comments on contemporary international politics, there is a very important sense in which the intellectual triumph of liberalism is the only really complete and unalloyed success which Fukuyama recognizes and seeks to defend. Practical consequences have already flowed from this intellectual triumph and will continue to do so, but his central position is deeply Hegelian: the role of ideas is primary in history and material events, including political, scientific and military events, follow in the wake of the ideas. Ideas are the dominant force in the world which give order to social and political structures. What has come to an end is the history of political philosophy as a live issue. In this sense – for a Hegelian, the most important sense – history has come to an end.

Science, economics and the nature of democracy

The contrast between the end of the history of philosophy and the process of non-intellectual history is made very clear in Fukuyama's discussion of scientific development and its attendant forces. In some ways the development of science goes hand in hand with the development of philosophy – the most abstract and theoretical aspects of the sciences are rooted in philosophical theories. But the application of science, the development of workable technologies and their economic application, are far more firmly part of the material world, and as such they are still struggling to reach the end of history.

Fukuyama offers two reasons for stressing the centrality of science. The first is that science, and the technology which it produces, gives decisive military advantage to those states which possess it. It might seem that such a view is hardly progressive. Indeed, many critics would argue that the development of modern science has been bad for humanity, not least *because* it has placed such powerful destructive forces in the hands of governments and the military. Fukuyama does not disagree fundamentally with this. He is not defending war but simply arguing that the impetus of modern science is so great that governments cannot afford to ignore it, not least because potential enemy states will embrace the technology. So governments continue to finance scientific research which in turn leads to further scientific progress.

The second reason for emphasizing the beneficial and progressive nature of science is more positive. This is that the products of modern science and technology make people's lives more comfortable and more secure. Those who live in the scientifically advanced societies of the Western liberal democracies have more than ample food and clothing, good medical care: in essence, all that is needed, and more, to secure the basic necessities of life. And they have the added advantage of being able to pursue intellectual and cultural activities. Scientific progress leads to the good life.

In making this claim, Fukuyama is clearly assuming that there is a close relationship between scientific development and economic change. Indeed, he makes this point explicitly when he traces a close connection between advanced industrialization, which he understands to have been created by modern natural science, and capitalism. In other words, scientific progress brings capitalism.

This much is clear and straightforward for Fukuyama. But while that relationship is clear the connection between capitalism and democracy is more problematic.

> . . . [T]he relationship between economic development and democracy is far from accidental, but the motives behind the choice of democracy are not fundamentally economic. They have another source and are facilitated, but not made necessary, by industrialisation.[1]

There are issues here which we touched upon in the last chapter when we discussed Fukuyama's account of liberalism and the relationship of political liberalism to economic liberalism. As in that discussion it is important to be clear about Fukuyama's definition of the key terms he is using, specifically here about the terms 'capitalism' and 'democracy'.

The form of capitalism which Fukuyama seeks to defend is decidedly closer to one in which the market is largely free and unfettered than to anything approaching a managed or welfarist version. We saw in the last chapter that in the economic sphere Fukuyama seeks to defend a theory of 'negative' freedom in which liberalism is defined primarily in terms of individual rights, and that he sees such freedoms as being sustained by a free market economy. Indeed so important does he see the relationship to be between the free market and political freedom that he claims that the growth of even a limited market economy in China is a powerful force propelling China towards an eventual acceptance of democracy. The function of the system of law in Fukuyama's vision of a liberal society is to protect individual rights and to ensure the greatest possible freedom from government control by limiting the power of the state: it does not have a major role in ensuring the economic or social well-being of its members.

The emphasis on negative liberty, then, leads Fukuyama to reject the social democratic and welfarist strands in liberalism – such as John Rawls' account in A Theory of Justice – and to embrace a

standard *laissez-faire* account of capitalism. When we turn to Fukuyama's account of democracy on the other hand, we find a rather
more complicated theory. By democracy he understands primarily a
set of ideas and secondarily the institutions which embody them. In
developing his theory of democracy, Fukuyama traces a close
connection between democracy and culture and this leads him to
argue that what he refers to as Anglo-Saxon liberal democratic theory
has been deficient because it places reason and calculation over less
tangible but more important forces such as passion and emotional
commitment.

This leads Fukuyama to the somewhat unusual view that Hegel is
more important as a theorist of liberalism than Locke or Hobbes (he
follows Leo Strauss in seeing Hobbes as a founding father of
liberalism). He argues that this is the case because whereas the Anglo-
Saxons see liberty in selfish terms, summed up in the phrase
'enlightened self-interest', Hegel sees it in unselfish terms. Locke and
Hobbes defended bourgeois society, something which, Fukuyama
claims, has often been a source of persistent unease amongst their
critics.

> In short, the *bourgeois* is selfish; and the selfishness of the private
> individual has been at the core of critiques of liberal society both on
> the part of the Marxist Left and the aristocratic-republican Right.
> Hegel, in contrast to Hobbes and Locke, provides us with an
> understanding of liberal society which is based on the non-selfish part
> of the human personality, and seeks to preserve that part as the core of
> the modern political project. Whether he ultimately succeeds in this
> remains to be seen: the latter question will be the subject of the final
> part of this book.[2]

This is an extremely important passage because in it Fukuyama
rejects the Lockean idea of liberalism as being radically incomplete
and offers in its place a modified Hegelianism. Locke argues, in his
Two Treatises of Civil Government[3] that men first lived in a state of
nature, a society in which there was no state and in which each person
had virtually limitless freedom. The most natural condition of
mankind is one in which there is no coercion and in which everyone
recognizes each others' natural rights. Over a period of time people
agreed to give up some of their freedoms and to create a state. The
state would be governed by a ruler who would be obliged to respect

the extensive natural rights which the people brought with them from the state of nature. The relationship between ruler and ruled was based on a social contract. The contract was central to Locke's political theory because it embodied the idea that both sides had rights and that if the contract was to be binding all the parties had to consent freely to its terms.

Fukuyama sees the idea of the contract as being far too limited a metaphor to form the basis of political life. His immediate criticism here is that the idea of the contract is based on a narrowly selfish concept of human nature and human society. People enter the contract, and hence agree to live together in a state, because they believe it is in their own best interest to do so. The metaphor of the contract fits very well with the idea of a bourgeois society – the most usual use of contracts is in business transactions and seeing political life in such terms is indicative of a narrowness of attitude to oneself and other members of one's political community.

Hegel was highly critical of social contract theory because it led to an excessively individualistic understanding of society. In his view, society was held together not by the choice of its individual members but by the far deeper communal values which those members all inherited from their common past. In this respect Fukuyama is following Hegel, but his slighting reference to the bourgeois mentality owes a good deal to later writers. In part it is indebted to Kojève, and particularly to Kojève's Marxism, but more importantly it draws on Nietzsche's attack on the bourgeoisie, whom Nietzsche dismissed contemptuously as the last men.

We will return to Nietzsche and his influence on Fukuyama later, but for the moment we need to complete our discussion of Fukuyama's interpretation of democracy. It is apparent in what way his theory is different from the theory of democracy which is dominant in current British and American thought. He takes this argument a stage further by contrasting the individualism of the Anglo-Saxons with what he takes to be the superior idea of a moral community.

> In place of an organic moral community with its own language of 'good and evil,' [members of the Lockean state] had to learn a new set of democratic values to be 'participant,' 'rational,' 'secular,' 'mobile,' 'empathetic' and 'tolerant.' These new democratic values were initially not values at all in the sense of defining the final human virtue or

good. They were conceived as having a purely instrumental function, habits that one had to acquire if one was to live successfully in a peaceful and prosperous liberal society.[4]

Fukuyama derives the term 'organic moral community' most directly from Nietzsche, for whom the state is 'the coldest of cold monsters'[5] precisely because it is rational and calculating. The concept of an organic moral community is also central to Hegel's political theory, and that of other German idealists such as Fichte, where the primacy of cultural traditions over conscious rational decisions in the development of political life is stressed.

> For democracy to work . . . citizens of democratic states must forget the instrumental roots of their values, and develop a certain irrational thymotic pride in their political system and a way of life. That is, they must come to love democracy not because it is necessarily better than the alternatives, but because it is *theirs*.[6]

Fukuyama argues that there are four cultural conditions which help to support a stable democracy. The first is a fairly homogeneous national, ethnic and racial consciousness. He means by this that democracy cannot function well in a society which lacks a sense of national unity. If people have a stronger allegiance to their tribe or nationality than they do to the larger community, democracy will be undermined.

Secondly, there must not be an exclusivist state religion. In other words, religion must be a private matter and tolerance must be exercised about religious beliefs (and the absence of them). Democracy cannot function where people's primary social allegiance is to their religion.

Thirdly, there is a need for a relatively equal society before democracy emerges. He refers approvingly to Alexis de Tocqueville's argument in *Democracy in America* that American democracy emerged in a society where there was no native aristocracy and which practised a fair measure of social equality.

The fourth condition is the need for a healthy civil society. The concept of civil society has an important role in Hegel's political thought, but Fukuyama refers at this point to Tocqueville, who argued that democracy works best when developed from the bottom up rather than being imposed from the top down. Tocqueville laid a great emphasis on the local governments of the New England townships as places where citizens could learn to practise the art of government.

Fukuyama does not claim that where these conditions occur democracies will inevitably emerge. They are not sufficient conditions; what they do provide is an institutional framework in which democratic practices and ways of thinking can take root. In addition to these there must also be a political will to ensure that the state is governed in a democratic way and he points out that the Weimar Republic met all the above requirements but it still fell victim to Nazism.

This brings us back to our earlier comment that in Fukuyama's account of democracy ideas are of the greatest importance and the institutions which come to embody them are only of secondary concern. Because of his Hegelian belief in the primacy of ideology, Fukuyama is concerned to stress that democracy, which is primarily about ideas, cannot be explained exclusively in economic, and hence material, terms. Indeed, he spends considerable time considering and rejecting three arguments which purport to show that the motives behind the choice of democracy are fundamentally economic. It will be helpful to look at these in some detail because they illustrate a good deal about his central thesis.

The first attempt to explain democracy in terms of the rise of capitalism is a functional (or pragmatic) argument. On this view, democracy has emerged because it alone is capable of mediating the complex web of conflicting interests that are created by a modern economy. The examples which are often referred to here are those such as conflicts of interest between the working class and the middle class or the difficulties raised by new groups of people claiming economic and political rights such as women or racial minorities.

Fukuyama rejects this interpretation and argues that while democracy is best at settling disputes when there is a large measure of consensus already present within a society, it is much less successful at resolving disputes where there are deep-seated sectional differences. In particular, democracy is poorly equipped to settle disputes between different ethnic or national groups. He points to a number of examples which he thinks illustrate his point, such as the problem of fully integrating Blacks into American society.

So he rejects the argument that democracy has arisen simply as a pragmatic means of mediating between competing interest groups. The second argument which he considers and rejects shares important features with the first. This is the argument that the highly complex nature of the capitalist system makes it impossible to control other than by democratic means.

The difficulty with this view, says Fukuyama, is that it does not explain what he takes to be a central feature of history, namely that there is a universal evolution in the desire for liberal democracy.

> For by this account, democracy is not the *preferred outcome* of any of the groups struggling for leadership in the country. Democracy becomes instead a kind of truce between warring factions, and is vulnerable to a shift in the balance of power between them that would allow one particular group or elite to re-emerge triumphant.[7] (Italics in the original.)

In other words, this interpretation makes democracy a by-product of economic development and not an end to be desired for its own sake.

The third and, in Fukuyama's view, the most powerful line of argument linking economic development with liberal democracy is the claim that successful industrialization produces an educated middle class whose members demand political participation. Because industrially advanced societies need these skilled and educated workers their views have to be taken into consideration and society gradually liberalizes.

This argument assumes that education leads to the inculcation of liberal values. Fukuyama seeks to rebut this by pointing out that there is no necessary connection between education and liberalism. As in the first two arguments, democracy is not something which emerges as a by-product of some other force. However, he does not push this counter-argument very strongly, partly because he recognizes considerable value in the claim that education can be a very important force in helping democracy to emerge. In so far as education is understood as an economic force – workers have to be educated to a high level in order for capitalism to function efficiently – Fukuyama cannot accept that it is an explanation for the emergence of democracy. However, seen as a means of enabling people to use reason more effectively, and to articulate their values and desires more cogently, education is very much a contributory factor in the development of democracy.

Fukuyama's crucial point is that democracy is not explicable as the by-product of economic forces; rather it is sought for its own sake, because it embodies values which men and women aspire to. This explains why liberal democracy has succeeded, not only as the most successful political system in the modern world but also, and more importantly, as the dominant political ideal. If it were merely the pragmatic by-product of economic forces there would be no guarantee that its success would be anything more than transitory. It would be quite plausible to assume that as economic conditions change democracy would cease to be useful and its place could be taken by some other political system more suited to the needs of the economy. For Fukuyama, democracy has to be desired (and be desirable) for its own sake. More than that, it not only has to embody values which people aspire to, it has to do so better than any other possible political system or theory.

Fukuyama's argument is, then, strongly Hegelian in its emphasis on the primacy of ideas over material forces, specifically in the discussion of capitalism and democracy in the emphasis of ideas over economic forces. This being the case, the next question which arises is: what are the fundamental ideas which underpin democracy and which motivate people in their struggle for a democratic society?

The struggle for recognition

For Fukuyama, the most important concept to understand when seeking to explain the rise of democracy is that of recognition. By recognition, he means the need which human beings have to be acknowledged and respected by others. In political terms, this can be seen in the striving for liberty and democratic rights. People whose rights are denied remain unsatisfied and frustrated even though they may enjoy economic prosperity. What they lack, and what drives them to work for a democratic government, is dignity.

Fukuyama begins his account of recognition by referring to a key passage in the *Phenomenology of Spirit*, where Hegel introduces the idea of a primitive first man at the dawn of history. This first man shares with the animals certain basic natural desires such as the desire for food, sleep, shelter and, above all, for the preservation of his own life. But the first man is radically different from the animals in two ways. The first is that unlike the animals he is able to rise above his natural instincts and drives and to act freely. It is through this capacity that he is able to act as a moral agent. But his moral agency does not take place in a vacuum, nor is he to be understood primarily as an isolated and autonomous individual, he is also a social being who needs to be respected by other people. His own sense of self-worth and identity is intimately connected with the value that other people place upon him, upon their willingness to appreciate him as a human being, and this is the second way in which he differs from the animals and is truly a human being. Recognition involves both these elements – the ability to act freely, and thus be a responsible moral agent, and the need to gain the respect of others for having chosen to act in a way that is honourable.

The struggle for recognition should not be equated with popular movements in contemporary culture which emphasize the idea of self-esteem, or feeling good about oneself. Fukuyama is scathing about such movements, and argues that they are destructive of the possibility of true recognition. This is because they are unable, or unwilling, to differentiate between the worth of different actions, whether they are the most insignificant or, by contrast, call for great boldness of spirit or physical courage. The recognition of others is of value only if it is hard won, something which is prized as an acknowledgement of special, personal worth. The giving of recognition has to be the considered and genuine respect for another person, not simply the repeating of a glib platitude. If it is not genuine in this way, it ceases to have any value beyond the superficial. Fukuyama cites examples drawn from what he sees to be the fashionable but ultimately vacuous practice of counselling. Constantly comforting people and seeking to shield them from the harmful consequences of their own actions may have a short-term beneficial effect on the recipient, but ultimately it is counter-productive; 'in the end, the mother will know if she has neglected her child, the father will know if he has gone back to drinking . . .'[8] By contrast, the mother who struggles and sacrifices her own happiness for the good of her children, or the father who fights down the temptation to return to drinking, and so brings happiness to his wife and children, is entitled to a proper sense of self-respect through the recognition they have gained for what they have achieved.

Hegel also claimed that the search for genuine, worthwhile recognition is hard and difficult. For this reason he claimed that the most fundamental way in which a man can assert his own value, and be recognized as a man by others, is through risking his life. Thus the encounter of the first man with other men leads to a violent struggle in which each seeks to make the other recognize him by risking his own life. It is the most basic but also the most human of responses.

This confrontation can lead to one of three results. First, it can lead to the death of both of the combatants, in which case, obviously, neither succeeds in being recognized. Secondly, it can lead to the death of one of the combatants. This is an undesirable outcome for the victor because he is still left with no one to recognize him – he is no closer to having his humanity recognized than he was before the battle. Thirdly, it can terminate when one of the combatants surrenders to the other and agrees to submit to a life of servitude rather than face the risk of violent death. 'The master is then satisfied', Fukuyama argues, 'because he has risked his life and received recognition for having done so from another human being.'[9]

It is important not to misunderstand this use of Hegel's account of the bloody battle at the dawn of history. Shadia B. Drury, for example, has argued that Fukuyama glorifies violence and that *The End of History and the Last Man* is animated by a desire to see the strong and the ruthless take their rightful place as the dominant members of society.

> Like Kojève, Fukuyama labours under the impression that to be a real man is to be animated with a desire to conquer and dominate others. The whole book is a subtle, but unmistakable, celebration of death and violence, on the ground that they are inseparable from masculine virility.[10]

It is hard to recognize the urbane Fukuyama in the picture which Drury draws here of a misguided and deluded follower of Kojève and Strauss who is fascinated by ideas of death and glory. Fukuyama does not claim that this violent battle ought to be recreated in modern society, any more than Hegel does; nor, unlike Hegel, does he claim that war is inherently desirable for the health and well-being of society.[11] What he does claim is that the desire to be recognized as a human being with dignity, worth and value in one's own right, is one of the major forces which led to the emergence of modern liberal democratic society. Far from seeking a return to a lost, ideal earlier warrior society, Fukuyama argues that modern, peaceful, liberal democratic society provides this recognition in a better way than any other possible society.

It is not entirely surprising that there has been misunderstanding of Fukuyama's use of recognition because it is far more complex than it first appears and in this context it is important to emphasize that recognition is double-edged. When considering the *rise* of democracy, the struggle of oppressed peoples to achieve freedom and dignity, recognition is a wholly positive force. When democracies have become fully established, however, Fukuyama is acutely aware that the continuing desire for recognition will pose significant problems. Nevertheless, far from seeing this as hope for the reintroduction of a more *machismo* culture, Fukuyama sees these as the most significant problems to be resolved, and he fears that the type of liberal democracy currently in the ascendant in the United States is ill-equipped to deal with the problem. The most frequent way of trying to come to terms with recognition is to trivialize it, to see it in the blandest possible terms, as we saw above. Such an approach is not merely irritating; it is extremely dangerous because it ignores the dark side which is always present in recognition. Fukuyama's understanding of these dangers is apparent in his discussion of the drug-dealing street gangs which are a dark feature of many American cities. Drury refers to this discussion as a further example of Fukuyama's glorification of aggression, picking up in particular on his comment that in some respect membership of such gangs creates a sense of greater humanity. But her criticisms miss the point which Fukuyama is making, and in doing so she again fails to grasp the depth of his insight. Fukuyama uses the example of the gangs not to extol their virtues but rather to point to a weakness of liberal democratic societies which fail to take the dangers inherent in *thymos* sufficiently seriously. He points out that such people are inevitably, and rightly, marginalized in the most progressive and advanced societies, but they also provide a terrible warning, for there is always the possibility that the cultured and civilized liberal democracies may give in to the darker side if it is not tamed. The question, then, is not how to return to such primitive barbarism but how to transform the power of recognition and harness it in such a dramatically different – and immeasurably better – society. That question, and the complex account of recognition which it embraces, lies at the heart of the book.

Because of this centrality which Fukuyama accords the concept of recognition he is not content with simply utilizing Hegel's discussion of it, powerful and suggestive as that is. He argues that it has a long tradition in Western philosophy, though often described in different words. He mentions Machiavelli's discussion of man's desire for glory, Hobbes's discussion of pride or vainglory as the well-spring of human action, Rousseau's *amour propre*, Hamilton's and Madison's emphasis on the love of fame, or ambition, and Nietzsche's approval of 'the beast with red cheeks'. This list is noticeable for including those, especially Hobbes, about whom Fukuyama has some misgivings. Again, it emphasizes the fact that recognition is double-edged.

The most important contribution to the understanding of the idea, after Hegel, is Plato's concept of *thymos*. In his *Republic*, Plato argued that there are three parts to the soul or, as Fukuyama puts it in contemporary terms, three elements in human psychology. The first of these is reason, which guides us well in most of our activities, when we will allow it to do so. The second is desire, the part of us which is controlled by such natural biological drives as hunger and thirst. Desire is important in its place but should always be subordinate to reason. The third element is *thymos*. A precise translation of the Greek word *thymos* is not easy to render. On some occasions, it is translated as 'spiritedness' at other times as dignity, courage, self-respect or honour. In the *Republic* Plato identified this as the part of character which should be particularly well developed in those who were charged with the defence of the just society. They were to be men and women who were sufficiently brave to be willing to risk their lives in the course of their duty.[12]

Fukuyama's use of the term focuses on his view that men and women are motivated not only by economic and material concerns, but also from a sense of their own dignity and worth, and a desire to have that recognized. It is this, he claims, which lies at the heart of the movement towards democracy.

> If human beings were nothing but reason and desire, they would be perfectly content to live in a South Korea under military dictatorship, or under the enlightened technocratic administration of a Francoist Spain, or in a Guomindang-led Taiwan, hell-bent on rapid economic growth. And yet, citizens of these countries are something more than desire and reason: they have a thymotic pride and belief in their own dignity, and want that dignity to be recognised, above all by the government of the country they live in.[13]

He makes the same point about the struggle for civil rights in the United States and the fight against apartheid in South Africa.

Fukuyama does not equate *thymos* with recognition. *Thymos* is a part of the soul which gives value and worth to oneself, and those things or persons which one values, whereas recognition seeks the agreement of others in that valuation. Nevertheless, the meanings are very close and they ultimately refer to the same phenomenon.

Megalothymia and the threat to liberal democracy

If there is a thymotic element in human nature then it may indeed help to explain the desire which many people do appear to have to have their inherent worth and dignity recognized by their governments. But the very power of *thymos* brings dangers with it, as Fukuyama acknowledges. One problem which he points to is that people may not only desire recognition as equals, but may come to desire it as a means to asserting their superiority. This could lead to attempts to dominate or even suppress groups in society which are regarded as inferior. There is also the opposite problem of an over-zealous attempt to impose complete conformity and to suppress all attempts to be different. Fukuyama regards these two tendencies to be so important that he coins new names for them. 'The desire to be recognised as superior to other people we will henceforth label with a new word with ancient Greek roots, *megalothymia*. . . . Its opposite is *isothymia*, the desire to be recognised as the equal of other people.'[14]

This is not a merely intellectual recognition of possible misuses of the thymotic element. Fukuyama sees two major political forces of the modern world as exemplifying these two dangers in virulent form and with catastrophic results.

The first of these is nationalism, which he sees as 'very much a manifestation of the desire for recognition, arising out of *thymos*'.[15] What the nationalist craves is not primarily economic well-being but recognition for his or her own nation as a nation among others. For this the nationalist will be willing to endure all manner of hardships, even the deathly struggle of war. In a powerful passage, Fukuyama compares the nationalist with the aristocratic master in Hegel's account of the first man:

> In a sense nationalism represents a transmutation of the *megalothymia* of earlier ages into a more modern and democratic form. Instead of individual princes struggling for personal glory, we now have entire nations demanding recognition of their nationhood. Like the aristocratic master, these nations have shown themselves willing to accept the risk of violent death for the sake of recognition.[16]

It is necessary to temper Fukuyama's comments with the fact that there are different kinds of nationalism, not all of which are aggressive.[17] But directed against many forms of nationalism of this century, current as well as past, the comment is perceptive and compelling.

Fukuyama makes an equally important criticism of what he takes to be representative of the other extreme misuse of *thymos*. He refers to this as 'the Marxist project', though in fact his criticisms apply not to all forms of Marxism but most specifically to the Soviet Union and those other countries which became communist in this century. Whereas nationalism is characterized by *megalothymia*, Marxism is distinguished by *isothymia*. It seeks to promote an extreme form of social equality at the expense of liberty, by eliminating what Fukuyama regards as natural inequalities.

> All future efforts to push social equality beyond the point of a 'middle class society' must contend with the failure of the Marxist project. For in order to eradicate those seemingly 'necessary and ineradicable' differences, it was necessary to create a monstrously powerful state.[18]

As with nationalism, Fukuyama's point about a certain variant of Marxism, which was very successful in forcing itself on large parts of the human race for a substantial part of the twentieth century, is an important one – the rulers of the Soviet Union and its ideological acolytes around the world did impose a monstrously oppressive state onto their subjects.

It might seem, from what has just been said, that Fukuyama's ideal is a liberal democratic society in which both *megalothymia* and *isothymia* have been abolished. That is an interpretation which has often been attributed to him, but it is a false one.

Such a society would, in fact, be the society of the last man and this brings us to Fukuyama's discussion of the last man who will emerge at the end of history. The thymotic element in man has always led him in the past to struggle against dangers and problems, and in doing so he gained the self-esteem which came through others' recognition of him. The person who wished to prove his own humanity, as the first man proved it in the primeval struggle to the death, could do so most emphatically by going to war. Hegel was not alone in thinking that wars were essential for the ongoing health of societies, when people could not only prove themselves as human beings but also identify all the more closely with their own society. Yet Fukuyama claims that at the end of history wars will cease. What will happen to men and women when they no longer have great challenges to stretch them?

One possibility is that the last man will lose an essential aspect of his humanity when he no longer needs to struggle. But there is also a different possibility, the danger that men who are no longer presented with great challenges – with great deeds to do – will become dissatisfied and restless. If that is so, perhaps liberal democracy will be overthrown by people seeking to prove themselves in something akin to the original battle for recognition. This is why it was emphasized earlier that recognition is both a very important and a positive factor in the rise of democracy, but may become potentially very dangerous once democracy has been established.

It has often been argued that Fukuyama's account of the last man is ambiguous. Part of the ambiguity, it has been claimed, is due to the fact that he is drawn in two directions simultaneously. One direction is towards Kojève's Marxist egalitarianism with its acceptance of the blandness of the last man and the world which will come at the end of history. In an important passage from his *Introduction to the Reading of Hegel* which Fukuyama quotes, Kojève accepts that the end of history will mean the disappearance of man as a free, creative being and will see him return to a purely animal life. Fukuyama's gloss on this captures the mood of the argument perfectly:

> A dog is content to sleep in the sun all day provided he is fed, because he is not dissatisfied with what he is. He does not worry that other dogs are doing better than him, or that his career as a dog has stagnated, or that dogs are being oppressed in other parts of the world. If man reaches a society in which he has succeeded in abolishing injustice, his life will come to resemble that of the dog.[19]

As Fukuyama points out, Kojève, believing that we had reached the end of history, gave up the academic life and became a senior member of 'that bureaucracy meant to supervise construction of the final home for the last man, the European Commission'.[20]

It is the chilling coldness of that last phrase which makes the other draw on Fukuyama's allegiance important. The most high-profile critic of the last man in *The End of History and the Last Man* is, of course, Nietzsche. Fukuyama clearly has great respect for Nietzsche, and claims that Nietzsche has many insights about the pitfalls of democratic society. But the most important influence at this point, as at so many others, is Leo Strauss.

For Strauss, as for Nietzsche, the last man represents not triumph but decay. Not the end of history in a positive sense but a false cul-de-sac. Strauss, and his followers like Alan Bloom, claim a commitment to liberal democracy, but it is a commitment to a liberal democracy which is very different from the semi-egalitarian and welfarist approach of Anglo-Saxon liberals such as John Rawls. It is this view, or something close to it, which underpins Fukuyama's view of liberal democracy, as we saw earlier.

It is at this point in our argument, when we have properly understood the nature and genuine depth of Fukuyama's commitment to liberal democracy, that we can appreciate the nature of his debt to Nietzsche. Fukuyama's reading of Nietzsche, like his reading of Hegel, is a complex and creative one but it is an understanding and use of Nietzsche which begins from a genuine commitment to liberal democracy, and which constantly subordinates Nietzsche's central ideas to the constraints of democratic theory.

Perhaps the most profound insight which Fukuyama claims to have derived from Nietzsche is the understanding that *megalothymia*, the desire to be recognized as greater than other people, is a necessary feature of the human condition. Very importantly, Fukuyama believes that the Anglo-Saxon concept of liberal democracy is deeply flawed in so far as it seeks to promote equality and completely suppress *megalothymia*. But Fukuyama also accepts that *megalothymia* poses the greatest threat to the long-term success of liberal democracy. This claim that there is such a threat to liberal democracy seems remarkable – how can there be a threat to liberal democracy at the end of history? Many critics have picked this point up and seen it as a prime example of inconsistency in Fukuyama. We will see in a while that it is no such thing and that Fukuyama is quite consistent in making this claim.

Isothymia – the desire that everyone should be given equal recognition and no more – by contrast, poses no great threat to liberal democratic societies because it is unnatural. This is one reason why Fukuyama thinks that communism was bound to fail in the long run. *Megalothymia* poses a threat to liberal democracy because, in Fukuyama's view, *megalothymia* is a necessary precondition for life itself. If liberal democracy simply tries to suppress *megalothymia*, the society will be torn apart by the stresses which will result. But although it is natural, *megalothymia* is also very dangerous – it is, after all, the force which led the first man to engage in a battle for pure prestige. Again, the twofold nature of the struggle for recognition is seen to be at the heart of Fukuyama's theory.

Wise and mature liberal democracies like the United States therefore provide outlets for *megalothymia*. 'Indeed', he argues, 'democracy's long-run health and stability can be seen to rest on the quantity and number of outlets for megalothymia that are available to its citizens. These outlets not only tap the energy latent in *thymos* and turns it to productive uses, but also serve as grounding wires that bleed off excess energy that would otherwise tear the community apart.'[21]

Spheres within which *megalothymia* is encouraged and regulated within liberal democratic societies include business, society, democratic politics and sport. Perhaps the most important, though, is the community. Most modern liberal democratic states are too large for most people to participate directly in government. Instead, the most tangible way of acting as citizens and gaining recognition through one's endeavours is through membership of civic associations.

> Recognition by the state is necessarily impersonal; community life, by contrast, involves a much more individual recognition from people who share one's interests, and often one's values, religion, ethnicity and the like. A member of a community is recognized not just on the basis of his or her universal 'personness,' but for a host of particular qualities that together make up one's being. One can take daily pride in being the member of a militant union, a community church, a temperance league, a women's rights organization, or an anti-cancer association, each of which 'recognizes' its members in a personal way.[22]

For Fukuyama, the importance of such associations cannot be over-emphasized. They provide 'democracy's best guarantee that its citizens do not turn into last men . . .'[23] Unlike Kojève, Fukuyama does not believe that the end of history will inevitably mean the coming of the last man.

Nevertheless, the communities which guarantee the health of liberal democracy are constantly under attack. And the attack comes not only from outside, from the states which remain in history, but from within. Most especially, it comes from the Anglo-Saxon tradition. This poses so great a threat because it plays down the importance of duty and emphasizes the notion of individual rights and as a consequence it encourages withdrawal into private life, rather than commitment to a community. The Anglo-Saxon tradition also plays down differences between the communities (for example, religion is acceptable as long as it is not taken too seriously, and especially if it does not claim that the members of its community are in some sense better than other members of the same state who are outside the religious community). By contrast, Fukuyama argues, that accepting the genuine and deep differences between communities has the effect of reinforcing the sense of identity which members of those communities have with each other and their mutual recognition of each other. It allows them to do noble and self-sacrificing deeds because, within the community to which they are committed, those deeds are properly recognized.

Another area in which *megalothymia* can be allowed relatively free rein in the contemporary world is in the sphere of international relations. While there are still aggressive states left in the historical world, there is scope for individuals to leave the democratic societies and find glory elsewhere. 'It is probably healthy for liberal democracies that the Third World exists to absorb the energies and ambitions of such people', Fukuyama writes, then adds, ruefully, 'whether it is good for the Third World is another matter'.[24] As we will see later, this is only a temporary condition. Fukuyama believes that as more and more states leave history and enter the post-historical world, a pacific union will develop which will gradually eliminate most, perhaps all, wars. Fukuyama's view of how international relations ought to be leans heavily on Kant's *Perpetual Peace* and rejects the view of Hegel, expressed in the *Philosophy of Right*, that wars are a permanent feature of international society.

This emphasis on the inevitability of *megalothymia* in a healthy society throws into a new light Fukuyama's claim that there is a long-term threat to liberal democracy even at the end of history. We said earlier that many critics have picked this point up and seen it as a prime example of inconsistency in Fukuyama. Now it becomes apparent why Fukuyama is consistent in making this claim.

Because *megalothymia* is such an important part of healthy social life it is impossible to have a liberal democracy in which *megalothymia* is absent. There are therefore two things which make the danger of falling back into history a very real one.

The first is that *megalothymia* might get out of hand. Even in a world in which liberal democracy had been so successful that tyranny and oppression had all but disappeared from the face of the Earth, there would still be those who, fired by *megalothymia*, would want to struggle to prove themselves. He cites as one example the French students who rebelled against De Gaulle's government in 1968. Although they were amongst the most privileged people in a free and wealthy society they fought against that society because they were driven by a misplaced *megalothymia*. A far graver example is to be found in one of the causes of the First World War, the outbreak of which Fukuyama attributes in part to the boredom of life in a safe liberal democracy.

> The pro-war demonstrations that took place in the different capitals of Europe in August 1914 can be seen in some measure as rebellions against that middle-class civilization with its security, prosperity, and lack of challenge. The growing *isothymia* of everyday life no longer seemed sufficient. On a mass scale *megalothymia* reappeared; not the *megalothymia* of individual princes, but of entire nations that sought recognition of their worth and dignity.[25]

This problem may be approached from a different angle, by looking again at the related concept of *thymos*. Plato's account of *thymos* in the *Republic* is by no means unproblematically positive. In his discussion of reason, desire and *thymos* in *Republic* Book IV, Plato claims that in the just man *thymos* will be the servant of reason, as the auxiliaries in the state are the servants of the philosopher rulers. But even here Plato allows that sometimes *thymos* might become more dominant than reason and lead to unjust actions. More significant, for our present purposes, is the fact that in the discussion of imperfect societies in Book VIII it is *thymos* which first leads people away from the just state. The timarchic man is precisely the man who has allowed *thymos* to predominate in his soul, with the consequence that reason has been dethroned.

The second danger is less dramatic, but perhaps more intriguing. If Anglo-Saxon political principles prevail over the more community-based ones which Fukuyama sees in the thought of Hegel and Tocqueville, democracy will be seriously weakened. It may even be the case that the overemphasis on individualism which is characteristic of the Anglo-Saxon tradition could lead to the collapse of liberal democracy.

Reference was made earlier, when discussing Fukuyama's account of the relationship between the two traditions of liberal democracy, to Marx's theory of the dictatorship of the proletariat at the end of pre-history. Marx believed that this would be a transition period between the collapse of the political and economic systems of capitalism and the emergence of a fully fledged communist society. He argued that in the most advanced societies the process of transition would be relatively short and painless, but that such a period was essential in order to put into place the structures required for communism to function properly. Despite his general optimism about the transition, there is a dark side to that concept, in that Marx conceded the possibility that the internal pressures which had built up in late capitalism would not be containable even once the proletariat had assumed power. In such circumstances there was the possibility that the move towards communism would falter and the whole attempt would collapse into tyranny. Such a possibility is also present in Fukuyama's account of the liberal democratic societies at the end of history. The pressures of unfulfilled *megalothymia* could force a violent return to a historical society, perhaps on the lines of the crisis within liberal democracies which preceded the First World War. Or the dominance of Anglo-Saxon ideas could precipitate the less obvious but still objectionable tyranny of the majority.

Of course, even if all the liberal democratic societies fell back into history that would not mean that the end of history had not come – there would still be no greater ideology to rival liberal democracy, even if no liberal democratic state now existed.

Fukuyama's acknowledgement of the ambiguous nature of *megalothymia*, and of recognition as such, and his fears about the dangers of the Anglo-Saxon tradition raise the question of how optimistic our assessment of the triumph of liberalism should be.

The single most important defence against the failure of liberal democracy, and the consequent plunging of the world back into the chaos of history is, in Fukuyama's view, the mechanism of modern technology and economic development and the enormous benefits which they bring.

Any setbacks would mean 'a break with this powerful and dynamic economic world, and an attempt to rupture the logic of technological development'.[26] He cites Japan and Germany in the 1930s and early 1940s as countries which for a time were driven by a desire for national recognition to wage wars in the attempt to secure their superiority over other states. But, very significantly, he argues that they were also driven by a desire to secure their economic future, and that 'subsequent experience' demonstrated 'that economic security was much more easily obtained through liberal free trade than through war, and that the path of military conquest was utterly destructive of economic values'.

There are two particular problems with this argument. The first problem is that Fukuyama is giving a confusing (and perhaps a confused) account of the relationship between economic progress and the desire for recognition. As we saw when discussing Fukuyama's account of the relationship between liberal democracy and capitalism, it is the desire for recognition which is most important and while economic progress may run parallel with the progress towards liberal democracy it cannot supersede it. Usually Fukuyama is clear that economic progress cannot guarantee progress towards liberal democracy. To the contrary, it is liberal democracy which ultimately guarantees economic progress. But there are times, as in the above examples of Germany and Japan, where this relationship comes close to being reversed.

This in effect brings us back to a slightly different formulation of the problem which we have just been discussing at length. If recognition has to be defined and understood separately from economic and scientific matters, what guarantee is there that the urge for recognition may not go off in different directions from those laid out by economic and scientific progress?

As we have seen, Fukuyama offers no cast-iron guarantee that this will not happen. We can underline this point through a comment on Fukuyama's relationship to Hegel and the Hegelian tradition. Hegel's answer to the question of what motivates the struggle for recognition, and makes of it something positive and creative but also directed towards an ultimate goal, is an answer at the metaphysical level – that spirit is at work through history, using human endeavours for its greater purposes. In Hegel's system, any idea of a permanent reversal of history is made impossible precisely because the whole process of empirically observable historical change is grounded in the meta-physical doctrine of spirit. Ultimately, observable historical progress is only the outer appearance of a more profound movement, which Hegel variously describes using such terms as the will of Providence or the rule of Reason. He makes the point explicitly in the *Introduction to the Philosophy of History*: '[t]he only thought which philosophy brings with it, in regard to history, is the simple thought of Reason – the thought that Reason rules the world, and that world history has therefore been rational in its course.'[27]

Because Fukuyama rejects the metaphysical account of Spirit, which he redefines in a highly reductionist way as 'universal human consciousness',[28] his view of the end of history is in a very important respect quite different from Hegel's. For Fukuyama, although the intellectual battle for liberal democracy has been won – no other ideology can ever possibly compete with it and win – the danger of falling back into history is always present.

Fukuyama's metaphysical position is, then, strikingly different from Hegel's, and this has very significant implications for his philosophy of history in general and his belief in the inevitability of progress in particular.

We shall make one last point, which owes more to the Marxist dialectic of history than to the Hegelian. Fukuyama does acknowledge that as more and more societies become liberal democratic the danger of falling back into history will grow less and less. This is particularly so as they come to embrace the higher form of liberal democracy embodied in Tocqueville's thought rather than in Locke's and permit the healthy development of *megalothymia*. But as the danger of falling back into history may grow less and less it may become apparent that new possibilities emerge which were hidden to the historical men. Marx believed that once communism had been achieved and prehistory had come to an end, human beings would take control of the dialectic of history and pass beyond communism to some yet higher form of society. That idea lies, I think, behind the otherwise highly inexplicable last paragraph of *The End of History and the Last Man*.

In the penultimate paragraph of the book Fukuyama compares the development of human history to a wagon train. The journey which it is embarked upon has been very dangerous and uncertain; some wagons are still held up on the way, others have been attacked by Indians and abandoned. Nevertheless, despite all the difficulties, most of the wagons will eventually arrive at their destination. When that happens, the apparent differences between the various wagons and their various occupants will come to be seen as no more than the result of their different positions on the road. Everyone will see that liberal democracy, properly understood, represents the true goal of mankind.

Thus far the argument is optimistic, but the last paragraph introduces a quite different note.

Alexandre Kojève believed that ultimately history itself would vindicate its own rationality. That is, enough wagons would pull into town such that any reasonable person looking at the situation would be forced to agree that there had been only one journey and one destination. It is doubtful that we are at that point now, for despite the recent worldwide liberal revolution, the evidence available to us now concerning the directions of the wagons' wanderings must remain provisionally inconclusive. Nor can we in the final analysis know, provided a majority of the wagons eventually reach the same town, whether their occupants, having looked around a bit at their new surroundings, will not find them inadequate and set their eyes on a new and more distant journey.[29]

There are two stages in Fukuyama's argument here. First he casts doubt on the claim that we have reached the end of history in a political sense – 'it is doubtful that we are at that point now . . . the evidence . . . remains provisionally inconclusive.' Then, secondly, he takes the much more radical step of suggesting that, when the end of history as Hegel and Kojève understood it is reached, it may well not signify the end of the journey after all, and that having rested from their journey the travellers may well 'set their eyes on a new and more distant journey'. Perhaps this is ultimately a far more optimistic view of history than that of Hegel or Kojève, for it does not rest content with a shape of life which has grown old and which we can understand only at dusk[30] but looks optimistically to the possibility of as yet unrealized new dawns. In this, as in other crucial places in his philosophy of history, Fukuyama is closer to the anti-metaphysical temper of Marx than he is to Hegel.

6 • Fukuyama III:
International Dimensions

Liberal democracy and international politics

The account of Fukuyama's political theory up to this point has concentrated on his view of progress, his emphasis on the Hegelian as opposed to the Anglo-Saxon concept of liberty, and his discussion of domestic politics. This leaves one central area as yet undiscussed, the area of political activity which Fukuyama is most familiar with and which first brought widespread attention to his work, the sphere of international politics. We must now turn to discuss this aspect of his thought, but doing so in the light of the earlier discussion will help to make his ideas in this area much clearer. It is only when we have understood his general political theory that we can fully appreciate his claims about the end of history on an international scale.

Fukuyama begins his account of international relations by arguing that the aggression in general and imperialism in particular, which have so often been a feature of the relationships between states, can be explained in terms of the struggle for recognition. As we saw in the last chapter, liberal democracy, uniquely, has the capacity to satisfy that desire and consequently the triumph of liberal democracy should lead to the end of aggression, and therefore the end of war.

It is important to emphasize again, as we have done earlier in different contexts, that Fukuyama's arguments are neither simplistic nor naïvely optimistic. Fukuyama does not claim that war is about to cease among all states and that we are about to enter a time of perpetual peace in international society. He is quite emphatic about this, and often berates his critics for misunderstanding him on this point.[1] Far from warfare being a thing of the past, it will remain in the world for the foreseeable future. This is because many states are still not liberal democracies, and are therefore still in history, and as such they are still liable to use violence as a major method of securing their international goals. It is very important to underline the point that Fukuyama acknowledges that some states may long remain in history and that some states which are currently democratic may lapse into non-democratic politics.

Despite this recognition of the difficulties Fukuyama maintains that there has recently been a marked increase in the number of liberal democratic states and he lists a large number of these. The list is eclectic to say the least. In addition to the obvious candidates, such as Britain, the United States, Canada and the other mature democracies, it includes some countries which have recently given up authoritarian governments but which are now firmly democratic, such as Spain and Portugal and the states of Eastern Europe such as Poland, Hungary and the then Czechoslovakia, along with the Baltic republics, which have thrown off communism and appear to be settling into democratic politics, and South American states such as Chile and Argentina, which have had a chequered career of moving between liberal democratic and authoritarian regimes. It is plausible to claim that all these countries are currently democratic and that most have a good chance of remaining so. However, the list also includes some states which are far less obviously democratic. Among these are some, such as Romania, which appear to have lapsed back into non-democratic forms of political life after breaking free of communism. More problematically, it also includes a number of south-east Asian states which appear to be moving towards democracy but about which there is considerable uncertainty. This last group is particularly problematic for Fukuyama because elsewhere he also places some of these states, particularly Singapore, outside the democratic camp altogether.[2]

Notwithstanding these problems, there is a good deal of plausibility in Fukuyama's general claim that the states which have fully passed into the post-historical world represent a clearly defined and recognizable group in contrast to the non-liberal democratic states which are still in history and that the growth of these states has significant implications for the practice of international relations. Members of this group include the United States, Canada and the United Kingdom. Stable and advanced liberal democratic states such as these do not go to war with each other, and often ally themselves together for mutual security against the 'historical states'. Such alliances, Fukuyama argues, are fundamentally defensive in nature and are not intended to promote some form of new imperialism.

The threat from history

Liberal democracies are not the only types of states, of course, and even if we accept Fukuyama's large list of newly democratic states that still leaves many which are undemocratic. Fukuyama divides such states into three categories.

The first comprises the states of the undeveloped world, particularly in Africa and parts of the Middle East, whose economic development lags so far behind that of the developed North that for the foreseeable future they will still be in history and subject to international conflict. He cites Iraq and Syria as clear examples of such historical states.

The states in this category could pose a military threat to liberal democracies, particularly if they were to come into possession of nuclear weapons. There may be occasions, such as the events which led up to the Gulf War, when liberal democracies need to resort to arms in order to protect themselves, and their interests, from such states. But despite the possibility of the serious economic and even military danger which they might pose, states of this type offer no ideological threat. No one either inside or outside these states who has the slightest understanding of how they function has any illusions they are anything other than violent police states whose policies are based on the self-interest of their rulers.

Nor do the states of the second category present a formidable threat to liberal democratic ideology. This category is made up of states which, although more advanced in many ways than the poor countries of the Third World, nevertheless harbour a deep resentment towards liberal democracies. They are the states of the Islamic world, some of which offer an alternative which is based on Islamic fundamentalism. Powerful as this is within the Moslem world, and much as it helps Moslems to regain their thymotic pride against the humiliations forced upon them by what they regard as the Christian paternalists of Europe and North America, it presents no threat to the ideological superiority of liberal democracy in liberal democratic societies. This might seem a cavalier attitude to take towards what is clearly a very powerful force in the modern world, but Fukuyama's criticism is rooted in his overall attitude towards religion. He does acknowledge that some forms of religion have had value at particular times in history – he refers particularly to the contribution of Calvinism to the growth of Western capitalism through its emphasis on the Protestant work ethic, and to the similar role played by *Jodo Shinshu* in Japan's economic development. However, these are rare examples, and Fukuyama claims that in the great majority of cases religion has acted as an obstacle to economic and political progress.[3]

Fukuyama's rejection of all claims that religious belief has intrinsic worth is total and forthright. Even those religions which once had instrumental value in the creation of capitalism no longer do so and we need to look elsewhere for the kind of stimulus they once provided. The influence of Nietzsche is at this point very deep, and Fukuyama takes over his account of Christianity as a slave ideology. Nietzsche thought that because Christianity propagated ideas which made men slaves, free men – or more specifically the supermen – should despise it. For all his genuine liberal tolerance – and his rejection of the idea of the superman – Fukuyama comes close to sharing this view of religion, which probably explains his dismissal of the possibility of Islam posing a serious threat to the ideological triumph of liberal democracy.

Fukuyama's claim that *Jodo Shinshu* once played the same formal role in the development of Japan as Calvinism did in the development of Western capitalism brings us to the last and most intriguing of the three categories, and the one which poses the most serious long-term threat to liberal democracy. This is the ideology of the capitalist states of East Asia which is especially dangerous because it is the ideology of 'those who are inordinately successful at the capitalist game'.[5] Fukuyama cites Japan and Singapore as particular examples. They are so prosperous that there is no possibility of them ceasing to be capitalist but their relationship to democracy is a complex one. Indeed they appear to offer a viable long-term alternative to liberal democracy, and thus to give substance to a fear which Fukuyama gives voice to on a number of occasions in the book that '. . . despite the apparent absence of systematic alternatives to liberal democracy at present, some new authoritarian alternatives, perhaps never before seen in history, may assert themselves in the future'.[6]

This is a remarkable statement from someone who has argued that the end of history has arrived among the liberal democratic states and that no other ideology can possibly provide an intellectually credible alternative. Fukuyama develops the argument through a close analysis of two of the most economically successful societies of East Asia: Japan and Singapore.

Although Japanese democracy is formally modelled on the American system, Fukuyama claims that in practice it is very different. Its political culture is far more deferential and paternalistic than those of the liberal democratic West. There is an acceptance of human rights and periodic elections, but very little change in those who wield real power. Although formally a multi-party system, in many important respects its form of government is that of a benevolent one-party dictatorship, though one to which the majority of the Japanese people have assented.[7]

Singapore presents an even more dramatic example of a successful capitalist society whose mode of government is very different from that of the West. It is an openly authoritarian society which, as Fukuyama points out, has an extremely illiberal record on human rights. Many of its leading politicians, including Lee Kuan Yew, its former prime minister, have nevertheless argued that what they refer to as its form of paternal authoritarianism is more conducive to a strong capitalist economy than is liberal democracy. This is because democracy encourages individualism and self-interest whereas paternal authoritarianism allows for far greater economic planning.

Joseph McCarney has argued that Fukuyama represents these states as providing a distinctly plausible alternative to Western liberal democracy, and that despite his own deep alarm at this prospect he has no effective means of establishing why they will not become the more effective and more dominant form of capitalist society. McCarney describes this threat in dramatic terms:

> . . . the spectre that haunts the latter part of the book is in its most chilling form the possibility that he has simply misidentified the end state, that the end of history thesis will stand provided that authoritarian is substituted for democratic capitalism as the final form of human society.[8]

The reason for this fear, in McCarney's interpretation of Fukuyama, is that liberal democracy is flawed by the radical individualism 'that corrodes the ties of community on which, ultimately, meaningful recognition and economic success alike depend'.[9]

If McCarney is right, the existence, and especially the prosperity, of these states does indeed pose a major ideological threat to liberal democracy, and hence to Fukuyama's claim that liberal democracy represents the end of history. However, when we look more closely at what Fukuyama has to say about these societies it becomes apparent that he does not perceive them to pose anything like so great a threat. The states of East Asia, and Japan in particular, are, he claims, 'at a particularly critical turning point with respect to world history'.[10]

They can choose to follow the road of Western liberalism, as Japan has made considerable strides in doing, or they can follow the Singapore model and reject liberal democracy entirely. If the capitalist economies of the West go into serious decline, or if major social problems such as the breakdown of the family are not adequately resolved, the Singapore model may be adopted.

However, even though this may be an option, it does not present an alternative path out of history – societies which choose this model will either remain in history, like Singapore, or fall back into history as Japan, perhaps presently wavering on the edge of the post-historical world, would do. Certainly Fukuyama is clear that such a model would present no more attractive an option for the West than would Islamic fundamentalism. Nor is it the best option even for the societies of East Asia, however much it may enhance their material prosperity. Fukuyama's characterization is almost brutal in its dismissiveness: 'The empire of deference that [the paternalist authoritarian model] represents may produce unprecedented prosperity, but it also means a prolonged childhood for most citizens . . .' And then he adds the conclusive reason for seeing such a model as inferior, that such a condition means 'an incompletely satisfied *thymos*'.[11] The clear inference is that although such forms of government may satisfy the material concerns of those they rule over, the fact that they can do so only at the expense of *thymos* means that eventually they are bound to fail. They too are part of history and, as such, are inferior to, and must at some time give way to, the post-historical politics of liberal democracy.

Although there are no true ideological challengers to liberal democracy, the three categories of states which we have just discussed do represent genuine political challenges. Liberal democracies may have to defend their interests against challenges from Third World states such as Iraq or Islamic fundamentalist states such as Iran. They may even have to fight rapacious non-democratic capitalist states. Such possibilities demonstrate the enormous complexity of international politics, and the realization of this informs Fukuyama's discussion of the problems facing liberal democratic states.

From this discussion, an important point re-emerges about Fukuyama's underlying thesis on the end of history. The end of history marks the end of all alternative ideologies to liberal democracy, but there are two important conditions to be attached to this claim.

The first is that within liberal democracy there is still a debate about certain specific issues, specifically in this case about the relationship between the individual and the community – in shorthand, between Locke's view and Tocqueville's view. In the context of this debate much can be learnt from the non-democratic societies of East Asia that is useful in improving both the theory and practice of liberal democracy. Joseph McCarney's comment that Singapore's emphasis on the importance of the community helps to point up the corrosive effect of radical individualism in the Western democracies provides a fine example of this, and one with which Fukuyama would agree. Nevertheless, recognizing that there are things to be learnt from observing such societies does not involve acknowledging the superiority of authoritarianism over liberal democracy. This debate among liberal democrats is a serious one, but it does not call into question the claim that liberal democracy has triumphed.

The second point is that although the liberal democracies of the West are stable and secure they are not perfect, not least because they are still evolving into their final form. An analogy may usefully be drawn here with Marx's account of the dictatorship of the proletariat. During this transitional phase between capitalism and communism, socialism will be firmly in control but there will still be a long period of adjustment during which both socialist thought and practice will have to be fine-tuned to take into account the new and developing situation. So it is with liberalism at the end of history. A final resolution of the differences between Anglo-Saxon liberalism and the liberalism of Tocqueville still has to be achieved, but the debate between them, in the post historical world, will take place in societies where liberalism is already secure.

The end of history and the new world order

Despite the measured tones in which Fukuyama usually presents his arguments in this area, some of his critics have dismissed his views about world affairs as being no more than an apology for American foreign policy. It must be said that some of Fukuyama's asides do appear to lend strength to this view. There is, for example, his rather ominous remark, referred to in the last chapter, that the Third World may offer opportunities for members of post-historical societies to find expression for their *megalothymia* thus offering a much needed safety-valve for those societies.

One such critic is Christopher Norris, who has written disparagingly of 'Francis Fukuyama's celebrated article on "The End of History?", written under the auspices of a US State Department think-tank and greeted as a major contribution to Bush's "New World Order" '.[12] Although Norris intends these comments to be taken ironically, and later in his book is very dismissive towards Fukuyama, they do help to bring us back to the point which was made at the very beginning of the discussion of Fukuyama. This is the claim that Fukuyama's dual role as a political actor and a political philosopher must be borne in mind when discussing his work.

President George Bush first used the phrase 'the New World Order' in the immediate aftermath of the Iraqi invasion of Kuwait. It was in part, of course, a piece of propaganda, a political rallying cry to those who opposed the invasion. The call to impose a New World Order to combat aggression and militarism was an appeal to the idealism and the optimism of those who had rejoiced at the fall of communism. But it would not be too naïve to say that there was among some of those who heard these words a genuine hope that a new order could be created, one in which moral values would come to play a larger part in world affairs than had hitherto been the case. There is no point in attempting to speculate what was actually going on in George Bush's mind, but the desire for a more moral approach to foreign policy is deeply embedded in American culture, and represents one aspect of a long debate between realists and idealists which has often been played out at the level of presidential politics.[13]

Fukuyama's views fit squarely into this long debate and his conclusions represent the standpoint of many in the post-Cold War world. His assessments have an added authority because of his one-time position as deputy director of the US State Department's Policy Planning Staff. Fukuyama has tended to play down the importance of his role in the State Department, partly because of his perfectly understandable exasperation at the way his ideas have sometimes been dismissed out of hand as the work of a government propagandist. In 'A Reply to my Critics' he pointed out that 'The End of History?' 'was conceived and written well before [he] had any intention of joining the State Department', that he was 'a relatively junior official with little impact on policy', and that the article had not even been read by many of his superiors.[14] Despite these rather self-effacing comments, both as a member of the State Department and the Rand Corporation Fukuyama has been an insider in the American foreign affairs community and much of what he says can be seen as an attempt to give an account of the New World Order from this perspective. For example, he justifies the Gulf War as a legitimate step in the establishment of a New World Order, even though, like many American foreign policy professionals, he is sceptical about the long-term value of the United Nations in its construction.

Norris's claim that Fukuyama's views reflect an important strand in mainstream American foreign policy analysis is therefore correct. However, the further suggestion that therefore he is not to be taken seriously does not follow at all. Even if Fukuyama were doing no more than defending the theoretical basis of American foreign policy from within that would not make his argument unimportant. Quite to the contrary, such a defence would be of great significance, given the importance of American power in the contemporary world. It may even be that such views happen to be true – such an account is at least as plausible as Marxism was as an analysis of international politics and deserves to be given due and careful consideration.

But criticisms based on the assumption that Fukuyama is simply defending the dominant view in the State Department are in fact misleading, because Fukuyama's views here, as in so many other places in *The End of History and the Last Man*, are more complex than they first appear. Most importantly, he is highly critical of realism, which is the dominant theory of the American foreign policy establishment.

Realism states that the fundamental element in foreign policy is, and always must be, the interest of the state. Power is the factor which is always decisive in analysing what a state ought to do and moral considerations ought not to figure in the statesman's calculations at all. Indeed, far from politicians having to weigh up moral considerations, they ought to ignore them altogether.

The idea that no moral judgements can be made about particular wars is an old one in Western culture. Fukuyama traces it back, as do all who discuss this issue, to the Ancient Greeks, and also discusses Machiavelli as one of its most important exponents in the early modern period. Realism became increasingly important in the thinking of foreign policy and defence analysts after the Second World War. Fukuyama discusses a number of the more important realist thinkers, including Hans Morgenthau, Reinhold Neibuhr,

George Kennan and Kenneth Waltz, but the real *bête noire* of his account is Henry Kissinger, who was secretary of state under presidents Nixon and Ford and whose influence, through his 'many students and protégés', continued 'long after Kissinger's departure from office'.[15] An influence which was still very strong, one might add, in the Bush State Department when Fukuyama was the deputy director of the Policy Planning Staff.

In the views of realist defence analysts, morality in foreign policy in general, and war in particular, is not only out of place but meaningless. When realists analyse wars they do so not in terms of the morality of the situation but in the context of the political and strategic advantage to their own states, even though they often seek to hide their true intentions under the cloak of moralistic language. Thus the United States justified its involvement in Vietnam – which, in fact, was concerned with matters of global strategy and international trade – in terms of defending the people of South Vietnam from a foreign, communist aggressor. In similar fashion, the Soviet Union justified its invasion of Afghanistan in terms of support for communism against reactionary and imperialist forces, although it is clear that its concerns were for its own security and the defence of its interests in the region.

Realism is therefore a highly influential theory amongst practitioners of foreign policy. It is not surprising that Fukuyama, who lays great emphasis on the importance of values in history, and who sees the end of history as involving the triumph of liberal democratic ideals, is highly critical of the realist approach. He offers two fundamental criticisms of realism.

The first is that realists have too simplistic a view of the states which make up the international system. Realists are uninterested in the internal affairs of states, preferring to see them, in a familiar analogy, as black boxes, with no internal life that has any bearing on their relationship with other states. The other metaphor that is most often used, and which Fukuyama himself utilizes in his account of realism, is that of billiard balls, whose behaviour on the billiard table is not governed by what is happening beneath their external shells. From such a perspective, it does not matter whether the internal politics of a particular state are democratic, communist or fascist. With regard to international affairs all states, whatever their form of government, act out of self-interest. This has led some realists to argue that it is possible to construct a science of international politics in a way that is analogous to the science of physics. In this view, the international system is governed by certain laws, similar in scope to the laws of physics, and states simply operate according to those laws. The most fundamental of these laws is held to be that states will seek to maximize their power, and that this will take precedence over all other considerations.

One very clear implication of this is that the intentions of the people within states, both the mass of people and individual powerful politicians, are largely irrelevant to the policies which their states are forced to follow. Fukuyama is strongly opposed to this view, arguing that the values and motivations of people within states fundamentally affect the policies of their states. The realist position, that the struggle for power is universal in space and time,[16] is, he says, simply untenable, and he gives a number of examples which he believes show that some other motivations are at work. 'The Greek colonels who yielded power to civilians in 1974, or the Argentine junta that stepped down in 1983 to face possible prosecution for crimes committed in office, could not reasonably be portrayed as "power maximisers".'[17] Yet such examples are not without difficulties. It might be plausibly argued by realists that the Greek colonels and the Argentine junta were faced with overwhelming forces arrayed against them – certainly both had just suffered catastrophic military defeats – the Greek colonels in Cyprus and the Argentine junta in the Falklands. However, Fukuyama gives another example which is more compelling. 'Britain in the last quarter of the nineteenth century devoted much of her national energy to the acquisition of new colonies, particularly in Africa, while after World War II it made an almost equal effort sloughing off its empire.'[18] One might add that the disengagement from empire after 1945 was not uncontroversial in Britain, and that it is highly unlikely that the Empire would have been dismantled so quickly if Churchill had been prime minister of a Conservative government rather than Attlee governing as head of a Labour government.

At the heart of Fukuyama's argument is his claim that legitimacy, rather than force, ought to be recognized as being the central category of political analysis. As we saw in the first chapter, claiming that the actions which the government of a state pursues are legitimate does not necessarily imply that the government is democratic. What it does mean is that all governments must respect the interests of those whose support they need to remain in power. Where states are liberal democratic, however, their legitimacy is in large part derived from the consent not just of political and economic élites but from the population as a whole. In those circumstances, the legitimacy of government action in foreign affairs is subject to the approval or disapproval of the electorate. The following passage deserves to be quoted at length because it makes the point very clearly.

> States . . . do not simply pursue power; they pursue a variety of ends that are dictated by concepts of legitimacy. Such concepts act as powerful constraints on the pursuit of power for its own sake . . . When Britain gave up India and other parts of the Empire after World War II, it did so in large measure because of its condition of victorious exhaustion. But it was also the case that many Britons came to believe that colonialism was inconsistent with the Atlantic Charter and the Universal Declaration of Human Rights, on which basis Britain had just concluded the war against Germany. If maximising its power position was its chief objective, Britain could plausibly have tried to hang on to its colonies as France did after the war, or to win them back when the nation recovered economically. That the latter course was inconceivable was due to the fact that Britain accepted the modern world's verdict that colonialism was an illegitimate form of domination.[19]

He also cites the disintegration of the Warsaw Pact as an example of the breakdown of legitimacy.

In emphasizing the importance of values in international relations, and rejecting the black-box model of international politics which realists often have at the basis of their thinking, Fukuyama is not claiming that power is unimportant as a factor in the relationships between states. What he does claim is that power is only one factor to be taken into account when considering how a state's foreign policy ought to develop.

This brings us to Fukuyama's second argument against realism, which is that 'it does not take account of history'.[20] By history here, he refers to the occurrence of events, not history in the more usual sense in which he uses the term. He develops this by saying that realism 'portrays international relations as isolated in a timeless vacuum, immune from the evolutionary processes taking place around it'. He means by these processes the growth of science and the development of liberal democracy.

With regard to science, it has had two important effects on the development of the international system. The first of these is that the increasing sophistication and expense of modern weapons has made wars not only far more costly in monetary terms but also so dangerous that using them can be counter-productive. Nuclear weapons obviously provide the most dramatic example of this.

The second argument raises more difficulties. This is the contention that the dramatic growth in material well-being that modern science has brought has eroded the need for wars of conquest: 'The tremendous increases in labor production which [the Industrial Revolution] permitted were far more significant and certain than any gains realized through territorial conquests.'[21] He acknowledges that the Iraqi invasion of Kuwait might be seen as contradicting this but rejects such an interpretation. 'The consequences of this invasion . . . are not likely to make this method of securing resources seem attractive in the future.' This seems a reasonable point. The next sentence is less convincing. 'Given the fact that access to these same resources can be obtained peacefully through a global system of free trade, war makes much less economic sense than it did two or three hundred years ago.'

This is a highly debatable point. While the capitalist economies of the North can certainly benefit from the consequences of the Industrial Revolution, and from their position of economic dominance in the world market, that is certainly not the case with the economies of Africa and, to a lesser extent, South America. At least so far as economic arguments are concerned, this seems to leave Fukuyama open to the charge that he is defending the unequal status quo which favours the rich North over the poor South. This in turn seems to re-open the charge that Fukuyama is a mouthpiece for the interests of the United States State Department.

Which brings us back to Christopher Norris, whose account of Fukuyama, which we referred to earlier, is unrelentingly hostile. The book in which he criticizes Fukuyama, *Uncritical Theory: Postmodernism, Intellectuals and the Gulf War*, is, as the title indicates, an attack on post-modernism and he treats Fukuyama as if he were a post-modernist. In particular, he attacks him as being a moral relativist in the mould of post-modernists such as Jean Baudrillard and Richard Rorty. This charge is misconceived, not least because the realism which dominated the Bush State Department shared with post-modernism a belief that transcultural values were of no relevance to the conduct of international relations (albeit for very different reasons). As we have just seen, Fukuyama is highly critical of realism because, among other reasons, it fails to take seriously the claim that there are universal moral principles.

Nevertheless, Fukuyama does appear to give some ammunition to his critics when he argues that while realism is inappropriate as a guide to the relationship between post-historical liberal democratic states it may be necessary for liberal democratic states to base their relationship with at least some historical states on power. This could be taken, on a cursory reading, to be no more than a defence of the dominance of the liberal democratic North over the rest of the world. And strength could be added to this argument when Fukuyama's sometimes rather triumphalist comments about the winning of the Cold War are taken into account.

Pacific unions and perpetual peace

Nevertheless, looked at more carefully his arguments take on a different hue. Central to Fukuyama's account of the international order at the end of history is the notion of a pacific union. The idea is explicitly Kantian, and Fukuyama's discussion draws heavily upon Kant's *Perpetual Peace* and *An Idea for a Universal History*.

In setting out his idea of a pacific union Fukuyama acknowledges, as we have seen, that the historical world will continue to present problems for the post-historical world for as long as there are historical states. He then seeks to address the problems which such a situation will give rise to.

The first of these problems is the one which gives most strength to Fukuyama's critics. It is the possible threat to the post-historical posed by the concentration of oil reserves and other vital natural resources in the historical world. This may on occasion lead to the necessity for armed intervention in the historical world. The second problem concerns immigration. The continuing disregard for human rights in the historical world coupled with the need for a supply of unskilled and semi-skilled workers in the liberal democratic countries provides a continuing impetus for immigration into the liberal democracies.[22] The third problem concerns what Fukuyama refers to as 'world order' questions, by which he means the need to restrict the transfer of technologies of mass destruction to historical states and also to ensure that their industrial practices do not harm the environment.

The pacific union of liberal states provides a just and equitable way of confronting these issues. The model Fukuyama takes is that of the League of Nations, whose founders he claims to have been heavily influenced by Kantian ideas, rather than the United Nations. Kant's argument required a league of republics (which Fukuyama interprets, not entirely accurately, as liberal democracies), which would act from a sense of justice. The problem with the United Nations is that it gave as much power to the Stalinist Soviet Union, which was a dictatorship of the most abysmal kind, as it did to the liberal democracies. The task of a pacific union would be to defend its members against dangers posed by the states of the historical world and also to seek, as far as possible, to extend the benefits of democracy to the members of the historical states. It would be expansionist in the sense that it would seek to encourage those states to become democratic and thus qualify themselves for membership of the union.

Fukuyama's solution to these issues might appear paternalistic, as if he is advocating on a global scale what he criticizes Singapore for doing on a national level. However, this is not so. Fukuyama is arguing for the exporting of liberal democratic values to non-democratic societies, and his argument does assume that these values are superior to the values which those societies are currently governed by. This is one very clear example of his rejection of cultural relativism. But it is not paternalistic because it has at its heart the belief that all people have a right to universal recognition. The pacific union is a union of free states. It also seeks to enshrine Kant's contention that justice within states is only possible once there is justice in the international order. Kant has often been criticized for making this claim because it seems to put the problem the wrong way round, how is it possible to have a just international order without first having justice within states? Fukuyama shows how in the current world situation, where there are already liberal democratic states which exhibit a great deal of internal justice, and which meet his three principal requirements of a liberal state, the existence of a powerful league of such states can have a profound effect on the international order and encourage the illiberal states to become liberal. The purpose of the pacific union is not imperialistic but idealistic, to extend justice, in the form of human rights and universal recognition, to all societies.

The last sentence will appear to some to contain a contradiction. The desire to extend justice, in the form of human rights and universal recognition, to all societies has been criticized by many multiculturalists as being no more than a disguised form of imperialism, and none the less a real form of imperialism for being primarily cultural. Fukuyama is aware of such criticisms, of course, but hardly takes them seriously. Indeed many of his criticisms of non-liberal democratic societies take on a new edge when seen in this light. Liberal democracy is not merely more efficient or more productive than other ideologies, it has the inestimable advantage of being true whereas all the others are false. Fukuyama has often been criticized for not taking Islamic fundamentalism at all seriously as a threat to liberal democracy. But, as we saw earlier, such criticisms miss the point. Such beliefs may well have played an important part in the development of human societies, and still do so in many con-temporary societies which are still in history – including the historical capitalist societies of East Asia, such as Singapore – but they are no longer relevant in the post-historical world. Islamic fundamentalism poses no ideological threat to the liberal democracies because liberal democrats can see that it is just superstition.

Such a claim brings to the fore again Fukuyama's frequently reiterated view that the end of history is to be understood primarily in terms of the triumph of the ideology of liberalism. Because of the ambiguity of the term 'ideology' it is possible to interpret him to be saying no more than that liberalism happens to have come out on top in the conflict between ideologies. Nothing could be further from his intention. He intends his claim that the theory of liberal democracy is true to be taken with the utmost seriousness. And it is to be taken in an exclusivist fashion. Because the theory of liberal democracy is true, all competing theories are false, or at the very most the truth within them can be subsumed into liberal democratic theory.

7 • Popper:
A Liberal Critic of the End of History

The attack upon the philosophy of history

We have tried to show in the last three chapters that Fukuyama's theories are far stronger and more coherent than many of his critics give him credit for. We have also argued that in many respects Fukuyama's position is not as far removed from his critics on the Left as they sometimes claim it is. Marxists, in particular, share many of the central themes of the end of history tradition with Fukuyama. There is, however, a very powerful line of criticism which is directed not just at Fukuyama but at the end of history tradition as such, and which explicitly identifies Hegel and Marx (though not Kant) as profoundly negative forces in Western culture. This criticism is to be found most forcefully and eloquently in the writings of Karl Popper.

The seriousness of the challenge to the idea of, the end of history which we will discuss in this chapter can be gauged from the fact that the doubts which they raise about Fukuyama's article and book concern not only the conclusions he comes to but also the very validity of the enterprise upon which he is engaged. Patrick Gardiner sums up the nature of this assault very well:

> The expression, 'philosophy of history,' has come to have various associations. By some it may be regarded as signifying a submarine monster, dredged from the deep waters of nineteenth century metaphysics, its jaws occasionally opening to emit prophecies in a dead (or at any rate foreign) tongue . . .[1]

The tongue is deemed to be foreign because it is Hegelian, and deemed to be dead because the type of activity to which it gives expression has been unmasked and shown to belong to the sphere of pseudo-knowledge like alchemy or astrology. Still, according to Gardiner, only 'some' have so regarded the philosophy of history. Others will have accepted that the philosophy of history has a worthier task than to 'emit prophecies in a dead language'.

William H. Dray distinguishes two very different activities which may both be called 'philosophy of history'. He calls the one 'speculative' and the other 'critical', and defines them as follows:

> The speculative seeks to discover in history, the course of events, a pattern or meaning which lies beyond the purview of the ordinary historian. The critical endeavours to make clear the nature of the historian's own inquiry, in order to 'locate' it, as it were, on the map of knowledge.[2]

It is the speculative variety of the philosophy of history that Gardiner calls a 'submarine monster'. Rather more prosaically, Dray says:

> It must be admitted, however, that the construction of speculative systems of history is also somewhat out of fashion. It was *Time* and *Life* magazines which received Toynbee's *Study of History* with enthusiasm; and Hegel's philosophy of history is nowadays usually regarded, even by those who have never read a word of it, as a paradigm of how not to theorize about the past.[3]

Historicism and the speculative philosophy of history

Most academic philosophers and historians of the second half of the twentieth century believed that speculative philosophy of history of the Hegelian (and every other) variety had been 'conclusively' exposed as vacuous and dangerous in mid-century by Karl Popper. Such was the respect accorded to his demolition of its intellectual respectability that the construction of a speculative philosophy of history has not been attempted for a generation since. Popper called the fatal flaw which vitiates so much speculative philosophy of history 'historicism'. In assessing *The End of History and the Last Man*, it is necessary to be aware of the major impact Popper has had on attitudes to speculative philosophy of history and to understand what Popper meant by 'historicism'.

Being clear about the Popperian idea is particularly important because Fukuyama himself employs the term 'historicist', but in an entirely different sense. Both Popper and Fukuyama call Hegel a historicist, but whereas that is a condemnatory epithet when employed by Popper, it is a commendatory one when applied by Fukuyama. Of Hegel, Fukuyama writes:

he was the first historicist philosopher — that is a philosopher who believed in the essential historical relativity of truth. Hegel maintained that all human consciousness was limited by the particular social and cultural conditions of man's surrounding environment — or as we say by 'the times.'[4]

Man is therefore constantly 'in the making' (as Sir Henry Jones used to say), and it is in this sense, which recognizes that human development is possible in history, that Fukuyama uses the term 'historicism'.

Both senses of historicism encapsulate a notion of patterns in history: those elusive entities which the historian H. A. L. Fisher famously failed to see in 1935 according to the preface to his *A History of Europe*.

> One intellectual excitement has, however, been denied me. Men wiser and more learned than I have discovered in history a plot, a rhythm, a predetermined pattern. These harmonies are concealed from me. I can see only one emergency following upon another as wave follows upon wave, only one great fact with respect to which, since it is unique, there can be no generalizations, only one safe rule for the historian: that he should recognize in the development of human destinies the play of the contingent and the unforeseen. This is not a doctrine of cynicism and despair. The fact of progress is written plain and large on the page of history; but progress is not a law of nature. The ground gained by one generation may be lost by the next. The thoughts of men may flow into the channels which lead to disaster and barbarism.[5]

Popper and Fukuyama were both aware of this preface by Fisher, the professional historian.[6] Popper saw a connection between the opening and closing sentences of Fisher's remarks, for he held that among those 'thoughts of men' that 'lead to disaster and barbarism' is the belief that there is discoverable in history 'a plot, a rhythm, a predetermined pattern'. He therefore set out to demonstrate that such a belief is both malignant and unwarranted. The malignancy of the belief that history has a predetermined pattern arises from its corollary, that by detecting and understanding it, predictions may be made regarding the future direction of society. Any approach to the social sciences which is based on such a view of history is labelled 'historicism' by Popper, which he defined as follows:

> . . . I mean by 'historicism' an approach to the social sciences which assumes that historical prediction is their principal aim, and which assumes that this aim is attainable by discovering the 'rhythms' or the 'patterns', the 'laws' or the 'trends' that underlie the evolution of history.[7]

Historical prediction, according to Popper, can be of either of two kinds. There is a type of (non-historicist) prediction, which he calls 'technological prediction',[8] which is really a hypothetical prediction, since it takes the form: '*if* you want to achieve x, then you will need to take steps ss.' The other type of prediction is historicist, and is labelled 'prophecy' by Popper. Unlike the first, this is a categorical or non-conditional prediction. It foretells a future state of affairs or events which we can do nothing to prevent. Historicists claim that there are 'inexorable laws of history', and that these laws are discoverable.

It might be thought that recognition of the inexorable nature of historical trends would have a paralysing effect, but historicists counter any temptation to fatalism by arguing that the great value of prophecy is that it enables us, having been thus forewarned, to take what steps we can to meet the future in a state of preparedness. As Marx said in the Preface to *Capital*:

> When a society has discovered the natural law that determines its own movement, even then it can neither overleap the natural phases of its evolution, nor shuffle them out of the world by a stroke of the pen. But this much it can do: it can shorten and lessen the birth pangs.[9]

Popper sees the confluence of historicism and activism as frighteningly potent, for few beliefs can provide greater inspiration than the conviction that one is working with history. Actions, otherwise unpalatable or repugnant, can be thought justified because they really shorten the labour pains of an inevitable birth. The interests of those who would resist may be quite conscientiously disregarded, since it is believed that they will be swept away by the tide of history anyway. It is to those whose interests were so dismissed that Popper dedicates *The Poverty of Historicism*.

In memory of the countless men and women
of all creeds or nations or races

who fell victims to the fascist and communist belief in
Inexorable Laws of Historical Destiny.

Historicism is a way of interpreting the past which gives nourishment
to totalitarianism. Popper launches a savage attack on Hegel because
he regards his variety of historicism as primarily responsible for the
atrocities of modern totalitarianism. 'Hegel's hysterical historicism is
still the fertiliser to which modern totalitarianism owes its rapid
growth.'[10] Historicism has features which exactly match the needs of
the apologists for totalitarian ideologies because historicism is
amoral, anti-individual and anti-egalitarian. For historicists, says
Popper, 'only *one* kind of "Judgement" can be passed on World
Historical deeds and events: their result, their success.'[11] As Hegel
himself said in *Philosophy of Right*, '. . . the history of the world . . .
is the world's court of judgement.'[12] In other words, what actually
happens in history is, for that very reason, what ought to have
happened.

Historicism can galvanize totalitarian convictions by suggesting
that the cause whose interest it seeks to promote will be judged by
future generations to have been right, for they will have the benefit of
seeing the outcome (now uncertain to all except those perceptive
leaders who see the direction in which history moves). Conviction
concerning its historical success is the justification and oxygen of
totalitarianism.

Historicism contributes to a climate favourable to totalitarianism
because the concern for, and the value of, individuals must fade in the
light of an historicist world view. Popper quotes Hegel's statement
that 'the History of the World occupies a higher ground than the
morality which is personal in character – the conscience of
individuals, their particular will and mode of action'.[13] In the notes to
chapter 12 of *The Open Society and its Enemies* Popper draws
attention to this statement of Hegel's in *Philosophy of Right*:

Justice and virtue, wrongdoing, power and vice, talents and their
achievements, passions strong and weak, guilt and innocence, grandeur
in individual and national life, autonomy, fortune and misfortune of
states and individuals, all these have their specific significance and
worth in the field of known actuality; therein they are judged and
therein they have their partial, though only partial justification. World-

history, however, is above the point of view from which these things matter.[14]

Since the dramatis personae of world history are not ordinary individuals but sovereign states, the true significance of the life and achievements of individuals can only be recognized from the perspective of a state's role in world history. Thus, speaking of the significance of courage in the individual citizen, Hegel said:

> The intrinsic worth of courage as a disposition of mind is to be found in the genuine, absolute, final end, the sovereignty of the state. The work of courage is to actualise this final end, and the means to this end is the sacrifice of personal actuality.[15]

The advent of mass or total war in modern times enables the true nature of war to be better appreciated, according to this viewpoint, because it is that much more impersonal than primitive warfare. Mass destruction serves historical necessities rather than personal animosities. Popper quotes Hegel again:

> The principle of the modern world – thought and the universal – has given courage a higher form, because its display now seems to be more mechanical, the act not of this particular person, but of a member of a whole. Moreover, it seems to be turned not against single persons, but against a hostile group, and hence personal bravery appears impersonal. It is for this reason that thought has invented the gun, and the invention of this weapon, which has changed the purely personal form of bravery into a more abstract one is no accident.[16]

Given the historicist premises that the judgements of history are always delivered in favour of the successful, and always in the interest of the mass over the individual, it is not surprising, according to Popper, that egalitarianism is not a moral value recognized by historicists. This is true both in respect of their views on the relations between states and the relations between citizens and their state. Hegel's historicism led him to dismiss the claims of less developed nations for equality of consideration by more developed predatory states: 'The civilised nation is conscious that the rights of barbarians are unequal to its own and treats their autonomy as only a formality.'[17]

Similarly, strong individuals, the great men of history, cannot be expected to abide by the undeveloped and restricted views of public opinion, according to Hegel. It was his view that the ability to detect and understand the needs of the age in the light of an understanding of the patterns of history is not vouchsafed to mankind in general.

> Public opinion contains all kinds of falsity and truth, but it takes a great man to find the truth in it. The great man of the age is the one who can put into words the will of his age, tell his age what its will is, and accomplish it. What he does is the heart and essence of his age, he actualises his age. The man who lacks sense enough to despise public opinion expressed in gossip will never do anything great.[18]

Historicism further provides totalitarianism with an alibi by making the great man of history sometimes the *unconscious* tool of inevitable historical progress. It is no proper criticism of a world historical figure that he is not motivated by the common weal of those over whom he exercises power.

> They are men, therefore, who appear to draw the impulse of their life from themselves; and whose deeds have produced a condition of things and a complex of historical relations which appear to be only *their* interest and *their* work.

> Such individuals had no consciousness of the general idea they were unfolding, while prosecuting those aims of theirs; on the contrary, they were practical, political men. But at the same time they were thinking men, who had an insight into the requirements of the time – *what was ripe for development.*[19]

The ripening, when it happens, is inevitable, of course, and individuals privileged to witness such momentous developments ought not to complain if they were ushered in at the expense of their individual interest and contrary to the moral norms governing the ordinary activities of men. Hegel gives such reservations short shrift indeed.

> In contemplating the fate which virtue, morality, even piety experience in history, we must not fall into the Litany of Lamentations, that the good and pious often – or for the most part – fare ill in the world, while the evil-disposed and wicked prosper.[20]

A World-historical individual is not so unwise as to indulge a variety of wishes to divide his regards. He is devoted to the One Aim, regardless of all else. It is even possible that such men may treat other great, even sacred interests, inconsiderately; conduct which is indeed obnoxious to moral reprehension. But so mighty a form must trample down many an innocent flower – crush to pieces many an object in its path.[21]

Popper's criticism of Hegel has been subjected to a great deal of criticism, though as we have argued in chapter 2, Hegel's account of the relationship between states is not as liberal as some of Popper's critics have claimed. What is most important at this stage in the argument, though, is to underline the way in which Popper sees historicism, as he defines the term, to be a powerful contribution to the emergence of totalitarianism.

Not only is historicism malignant in its outcome, says Popper, but its intellectual basis is completely flawed also. Historicism can be analysed into three basic constituent concepts, each of which has been borrowed from a field of study other than history. They are: evolutionism; essentialism; and holism.

Evolutionism, essentialism and holism

The theory of evolution has often been extended beyond its original application in biology in an attempt to apply it to the development of society. Marx, for example, was deeply impressed with the work of Darwin, and he found in his theory of evolution a vocabulary which would enable him to express his analysis of history. Popper is highly critical of such views and makes the point that since evolution is a concept which has its primary locus within the biological sciences, its application within the social sciences depends entirely upon the validity of the analogy drawn between history and the development of organisms.

The idea that the natural life-cycle of birth, growth, maturity, decline and death may be observed in societies as well as in individual organisms is one with a long pedigree. It is to be found in the works of, among others, Plato, Vico, Spengler and Toynbee. Popper quotes Toynbee's version of the analogy: 'Civilizations are not static conditions of society but dynamic movements of an evolutionary kind. They not only cannot stand still, but they cannot reverse their direction without breaking down their own law of motion . . .'[22]

The analogy is reinforced by a certain concept of continuity. In every change, it is argued, there must be some thing that undergoes change.[23] We could not speak of change at all unless we were able to specify what it was that had changed. There is, then, an underlying essence which preserves a changing thing's identity through change. This essence is the 'inner life' forming the connectedness of events which constitutes continuity and identity through history, comparable to the 'inner life' which constitutes the continuity between caterpillar, pupa and butterfly. The successive changes which are manifest in the subsequent life-cycle of what starts as a caterpillar are in their turn a realization of the potentialities which lay in its essence from the beginning. No actuality will emerge which was not at one time a potentiality within the essence. The essence, however, is never observed except in one or other of the realizations of its potentialities, therefore the essence can only be known through its changes. Detailed study of such changes with a view to penetrating the temporal appearances in order to reveal the underlying essence has become the chosen vocation of the historicist.

The discovery of this underlying essence demands of the investigators (be their investigation biological or historicist) an approach which is holistic. By 'holism' Popper means the view that demands that the entity under investigation be viewed in its totality. Thus, social groups must never be regarded as mere aggregates of persons.[24] Furthermore, groups *qua* groups may have a history of their own for they could have a continuity-of-life which transcends their members as individuals: 'It is even conceivable that a group may keep much of its original character even if all of its original members are replaced by others.'[25]

It is Popper's belief, however, that the whole biological/sociological analogy is based on a misunderstanding of the nature and methods of the natural sciences, and he proceeds to examine in turn the evolutionist, essentialist and holist features of historicism.

Even in biology there could not be such a thing as a *law* of evolution, for the simple reason that the evolution of life on earth is a unique historical process. If we are confined to the observation of one unique example, we are denied the possibility of ever establishing a universal law. Popper says of the evolutionary hypothesis in biology: 'This hypothesis is not a universal law, even though certain laws of nature, such as laws of heredity, segregation, and mutation, enter into the explanation. It has, rather, the character of a particular (singular or specific) historical statement.'[26] This is reminiscent of H. A. L. Fisher's characterization of human history as a single and unique process when he said in the Preface to his *History of Europe*: 'I see . . . only one great fact with respect to which, since it is unique, there can be no generalizations.'

It may be argued that even in a unique process trends or tendencies may be detected, and that a hypothesis setting this out could be tested. A prime example might be the success of predictions made in astronomy on the basis of observations of the solar system. But this is no counter-argument, says Popper, because predictions are made in astronomy on the basis of the solar system's static nature. Laws are formulatable within astronomy, and predictions are founded upon them, precisely because (in the relevant respects) there is no change.[27] The theory of evolution, however, is an account of change.

Nevertheless, even if no laws can be formulated on the basis of observations of a unique developing process, might it not be possible to detect trends within the process? Popper claims that even if this were possible, it would not help the historicist. Trends, unlike laws, could not form the basis of a prediction, for trends may cease. There is an important reason for this, namely, that laws and trends are different in kind. A trend is not a mild form of law. A statement to the effect that a certain trend has been observed makes an existential claim, but the statement of a universal law does not.[28]

Furthermore, says Popper, trends could not apply universally to 'history', only to aspects of it. There is no central essence or main series of facts which constitute history, although that is a common opinion. In *The Open Society and its Enemies* he asks:

> How do most people come to use the term 'history'? . . . They see what is treated in the books under the name 'history of the world' or 'the history of mankind', and they get used to looking upon it as a more or less definite series of facts.[29]

Accounting for the prevalence of this common opinion, Popper writes with passion about the way 'history' has been hijacked.

> There is no history of mankind, there is only an indefinite number of histories of all kinds of aspects of human life. And one of these is the history of political power. This is elevated into the history of the world. But this, I hold, is an offence against every decent conception of

mankind. It is hardly better than to treat the history of embezzlement or of robbery or of poisoning as the history of mankind. For *the history of power politics is nothing but the history of international crime and mass murder* (including, it is true, some of the attempts to suppress them). This history is taught in schools, and some of the greatest criminals are extolled as its heroes.[30]

There are reasons why it is the history of power politics that is regarded as the connecting thread or essence of history rather than the history of art, or of language, or of eating habits or of typhus fever. The most obvious reason is that the whole of humankind, in all its various societies, is affected by power politics. Art affects far fewer people. Also, people are inclined to worship power, a trait much regretted by Popper. This unfortunate trait is reinforced by those who wield power, since their activities may be pursued all the more conveniently where those over whom it is exercised are predisposed to respect it. Thus, many historians wrote under the supervision of the powerful. But this does not lend any validity to the identification of the essence of history with the history of power politics, neither does it establish that there actually is such an essence.

> But is there really no such thing as a universal history in the sense of a concrete history of mankind? There can be none . . . A concrete history of mankind, if there were any, would have to be the history of all men . . . For there is no one man more important than any other. Clearly this history cannot be written.[31]

Essentialism is closely intertwined with holism. Popper believes that those who advocate the holistic approach to the study of history base their view on a misunderstanding of scientific method, arising, in this case, out of a fundamental ambiguity in the use of the concept of wholeness. The word 'whole', says Popper, is used in two different senses:

> . . . to denote (a) the totality of all the properties or aspects of a thing, and especially of all the relations holding between its constituent parts, and (b) certain special properties or aspects of the thing in question, namely those which make it appear an organized structure rather than a 'mere heap'.[32]

A study of the wholeness of anything in sense (b) is both possible and proper, but this is taken by holists to justify study in sense (a) also, a view which is derived from Gestalt theory in psychology. Popper thinks that holists have erroneously interpreted the theory as if it stipulated that complex entities should be studied as totalities. But that is not what the theory maintains; indeed, such a study would be logically impossible to undertake. What is both possible and proper is the study of some aspect or aspects of a thing which account for its cohesion as one whole, but not the study of every aspect of a whole thing, nor even the whole piece of a thing. It is necessary to be selective.

'All scientific descriptions of facts are highly selective', says Popper,[33] and he differentiates between what he calls 'the bucket theory of the mind' and 'the searchlight theory of science'. The bucket theory is the naïve view which holds that scientific descriptions are based upon the totality of amassed information; the searchlight theory holds that scientific descriptions are based upon our interests, which are as a rule connected with the theory or hypothesis we wish to test, just as what the searchlight makes visible will depend upon its position, direction, intensity and colour among many other factors.

> Like the natural sciences, history must be selective unless it is to be choked by a flood of poor and unrelated material . . .The only way out of this difficulty is, I believe, consciously to introduce a preconceived selective point of view into one's history; that is, to write that history which interests us.[34]

Of course, some points of view will be deemed more commendable than others on grounds of explanatory fecundity and utility. No point of view, however, has the distinction of providing the historian with the 'objective facts' of his discipline, and rarely will it provide a theory in the scientific sense.

The reason for this is the unfalsifiability of so much historical explanation. This is very important for Popper. As a philosopher of science, he held that a theory is confirmed only to the extent that it stands up to attempts to overthrow its predictions: numerous confirmations by themselves are valueless as verification.[35] What the rational study of history produces is not theory but historical interpretation.

Interpretations should not be viewed as unconfirmed or weak theories. History is enriched by a plurality of interpretations, even when they are incompatible (as they often are), in a way that science could not be enriched by accommodating incompatible theories. In history, opposed interpretations may well be seen as complementary to each other, 'as would be two views of the same landscape seen from two different points'. One of the cardinal errors of historicism is that it mistakes these interpretations for theories. The students of history are the gainers when they are invited to interpret events as an aspect of the class struggle, or of the competitiveness of nations, or of the evolution of democracy, but they lose sight of history if they are persuaded that 'all history is the history of class struggle' – or of any other single feature whatever. This is not to say that all interpretations are of equal merit, for clearly some interpretations have a deeper or/and wider explanatory power than others.

The inability of history to generate theories (in the scientific sense) about the past in no way diminishes its great importance, however:

> for there is indeed a pressing need to be answered. We want to know how our troubles are related to the past, and we want to see the line along which we may progress towards the solution of what we feel, and what we choose, to be our main tasks. It is this need which, if not answered by rational and fair means, produces historicist interpretations. Under its pressure the historicist substitutes for the rational question: 'What are we to choose as our most urgent problems, how did they arise, and along what roads may we proceed to solve them?' the irrational and apparently factual question: 'Which way are we going? What in essence, is the part that history has destined us to play?'[36]

Historicism, in Popper's view, leads us to seek after a type of fact which does not exist, facts about the direction of the march of history, which once discovered will enable us to walk in step with it. But there is nothing with which to walk in step; we merely walk the course we have set ourselves. For that reason, the discovery of the *possibilities* that are open to us becomes a pressing urgency. Historical facts (or facts of physics or chemistry) do not have an in-built end or value; 'facts as such have no meaning.'[37] Since, therefore, it is we who determine what our values shall be, we must also decide how best to realize such values, and we need to be able to make such decisions in the light of what can be discovered about values and practices of earlier times. The more information society has of this type, the better equipped it will be to mould a future for itself.

Historicism, Popper believes, is an attempt to overcome the fact/value divide by utilizing the concepts of inevitability and certainty.

It believes that true values are discovered rather than chosen. Popper has a much less deterministic approach which would replace historicist concepts with moral concepts like choice and responsibility. In his understanding of history there is a place for hope. For him it is an assault on human dignity to seek to transfer our responsibility as persons on to 'history' and 'powers beyond ourselves'. We ought not seek to distil the values we would adopt for our age from the 'facts of history', but rather struggle to ensure that the future course of history is given direction by values which we have freely chosen.

> History has no meaning, I contend. But this contention does not imply that all we can do about it is to look aghast at the history of political power, or that we must look on it as a cruel joke . . . Although history has no ends, we can impose these ends of ours upon it; and although history has no meaning, we can give it a meaning.[38]

There seems to be an acknowledgement here that it is at least possible that a speculative philosophy of history could be written which was non-historicist. It would have to see itself as an alternative 'picture' of the world which viewers might find satisfying but not demonstrably true. It is not surprising that there has not been a torrent of speculative philosophies of history written on those terms. Marxist historians and philosophers, of course, have not seen historicism as a flaw to be avoided. Liberals like Fukuyama, however, have not hitherto been inclined to produce speculative philosophies of history.

Fukuyama could well argue that his thesis is not as historicist (in Popper's sense) as might appear at first, for although he claims to detect a pattern in history (rather than imposing one upon it in the approved Popperian manner), his view is neither straightforwardly evolutionist nor essentialist nor holistic.

In speaking of the 'end' of history, Fukuyama is not drawing any analogy with biological or evolutionary life-cycles. For him, the 'end' signifies fulfilment and completion rather than decline and death. He points to the scientific method as the paradigm of the notion of historical direction:

> Discovery of the scientific method created a fundamental, non-cyclical division of historical time into periods before and after. And once discovered, the progressive and continuous unfolding of modern

natural science has provided a directional Mechanism for explaining many aspects of subsequent historical development.[39]

This highlights one striking similarity between Fukuyama's account of the end of history and Popper's criticism of historicism, which is that both writers have a high regard for the achievements of modern natural science. For Fukuyama, it is the progressive economic development unleashed by the adaptation of natural science to production that defines the contemporary period and for Popper it is the methods of natural science that characterize human rationality. One of the main guarantees, as Fukuyama understands it, that the human race will not regress from its present high standards of civilization is that the insights and knowledge achieved by science cannot entirely be forgotten. Having once discovered how to divide the atom, the human race, no matter how reduced by unforeseen future events, will not be at a loss as to how to rediscover this secret. And even if individuals are indifferent to the high standards of life afforded by the application of science in industry, they will never be indifferent to greater levels of security and greater effectiveness of defence afforded by the application of science to the production of weapons. For all these reasons Fukuyama believes science is an ineradicable achievement of the human race.

Popper is, as we have seen, if anything, even more positive about natural science. Not only in *The Poverty of Historicism* and *The Open Society and Its Enemies*, but also in his major work in the theory of knowledge, *The Logic of Scientific Discovery*, he is concerned to establish a reliable method for the human acquisition of knowledge and he argues there that a successful model for all knowledge can be derived from the procedures and practices of natural science.

Nevertheless, these similarities between Popper and Fukuyama are less deep than they first appear, and Popper would not have been impressed with the use Fukuyama makes of progress in science as an indicator of the direction in which history moves. Popper sees in the way that scientific knowledge grows 'the refutation of historicism'.[40] Here are three propositions taken from a slightly longer sequence which constitutes the 'refutation':

(1) The course of human history is strongly influenced by the growth of human knowledge.

(2) We cannot predict, by rational or scientific methods, the future growth of our scientific knowledge.

(3) We cannot, therefore, predict the future course of human history.

Thus, even though Fukuyama has not drawn an illicit analogy with evolution in arguing his thesis, Popper would have rejected the appeal he makes to the example of progress in scientific knowledge as a paradigm of progress which might have any wider significance for the study of history.

But how far would this rejection be justified? Fukuyama is certainly not a straightforward essentialist in Popper's sense. At the heart of his theory we do not find a claim that there is in history an underlying mystical essence, the 'thing' that persists through all change giving successive ages continuity. In this respect he differs sharply from Popper's understanding of what a follower of Hegel must be, and indeed from Hegel himself. For Fukuyama, the continuity is provided by an examinable human nature, and a sense of progress is derived from the concept of recognition. Popper's position, however, commits him to a rejection of any trans-historical (to use Fukuyama's term) basis for historical continuity which is in any way substantive.

What would particularly concern Popper about Fukuyama's views on the end of history is their holistic nature. Popper would argue that Fukuyama shares this holism with Hegel. Popper thinks that our knowledge advances best by attempting to account for the particular. The problem with a totalizing account such as that of Fukuyama is that it is extraordinarily difficult to disprove. In Popper's view, a plausible theory of society should be formulated in such a way that it makes itself open to disproof. In other words, from the general propositions upon which the theory is based it should always be possible to draw out individual propositions which can be tested against the facts. To demonstrate its worth, a general theory of society should lead to small-scale individual predictions with which we can test the theory.

It is difficult to see precisely what this might imply in terms of Fukuyama's end of history thesis. Fukuyama's thesis is supposed both to be factually correct and normatively appealing. In other words, we are both supposed to agree that history is at an end and we are supposed to think that it is a good thing. Fukuyama attempts to demonstrate the truth of his theory in terms of the development of past events. He believes, for instance, that his thesis explains very well the collapse of communism, it also tells us a great deal about the past course of events in the Far East. In general sense, also, Fukuyama thinks his theory will tell us a great deal about the future. For example, we might expect on the basis of his theory that more and more states will turn to liberal democracy and capitalism. But Fukuyama avoids specifying which states and eschews making any particular predictions.

Popper would find this quite exasperating. Fukuyama appears to be advancing a theory of society which applies to the whole of the human species and which has no time limit on its possible realization. At root it is doubtful that someone of a Popperian disposition might regard this theory as any more persuasive or structured at all differently from religious theories about the human species. Popper would not be the least surprised that Fukuyama's theory derives from an internal critique of the Hegelian and Marxian outlooks since Fukuyama's thinking bears upon it all the hallmarks of their philosophical project. Fukuyama, like Hegel and Marx, is seemingly attempting to realize a prophecy. Just as Hegel and Marx are seen by Popperians as giving news of the world as it is about to be, subject in Hegel's case to spirit and in Marx's case to the development of the working-class movement, so Fukuyama is seen as predicting the end of history on the basis of the world-wide spread of liberal democracy and capitalism. Undoubtedly Popper would be a good deal more sympathetic to Fukuyama's political goals than he would be to those of Hegel and Marx, but Popper cannot from the standpoint of his theory of knowledge and philosophy of the social sciences condone Fukuyama's approach.

But again this would be to dismiss Fukuyama's views too easily. Despite his interest in Universal History, Fukuyama is not a holist in the sense that he aspires to grasp a total history.

A Universal History of mankind is not the same thing as a history of the universe. That is, it is not an encyclopaedic catalogue of everything that is known about humanity, but rather an attempt to find a meaningful pattern in the overall development of human societies generally.[41]

Holism in the sense of a search for the unifying principle which makes a thing an entity rather than a collection of disparate elements was acceptable to Popper, but a quest for a pattern in the overall development of such entities would probably be deemed illegitimate by him. He would, however, have approved of Fukuyama's adoption of the 'searchlight' rather than the 'bucket' approach.

> For 'history' is not a given, not merely a catalogue of everything that happened in the past, but a deliberate effort of abstraction in which we separate out important from unimportant events. The standards on which this abstraction are based are variable.[42]

But although Fukuyama is not a simple historicist in Popper's sense of the term, he does have a view of history which ultimately sets him apart from Popper. Fukuyama works from his idea of the whole of human history inwards to an idea of what a specific society might be experiencing. His theory is based on a grand idea which is intended to capture the public's imagination and to depict the nature of our age. Popper's critique of historicism implies that such ambitious thinking is bound to be misleading. In Popper's opinion, it is by definition impossible to account for any whole in its entirety. All theorizing involves abstraction, so our idea of the whole has always to be less than the concrete totality. In Popper's view, it would be impossible to cite an instance of anyone having successfully presented an account of a society as a whole. No matter how small the whole is, it is always made up of discrete parts which have to be explained in a distinctive way. Consequently, no overarching philosophy of history is possible:

> for history, like any other kind of enquiry, can only deal with selected aspects of the object in which it is interested. It is a mistake to believe that there can be a history in the holistic sense, a history of 'States of Society' which represent the 'whole social organism' or 'all the social and historical events of an epoch'. This idea derives from an intuitive view of a *history of mankind* as a vast and comprehensive stream of development. But such a history cannot be written. Every written history is a history of a certain narrow aspect of this 'total' development, and is anyhow a very incomplete history even of the particular incomplete aspect chosen.[43]

It is clear from these words that Popper could not accept Fukuyama's global account of history. At best Fukuyama could only be reporting a local picture depicting certain trends that had become apparent in recent years. Fukuyama might be seen as having in mind in particular the consequences of the collapse of communism in Europe and the response in the United States to this. From Popper's point of view, there would be no justification in extrapolating these trends outside Europe. Popper might not be surprised that the Middle East fits only with difficulty into Fukuyama's picture since to try to extend a hypothesis derived from the study of one society to another can at best be illuminating and at worst entirely misplaced. From this point of view, Fukuyama's theory contains too much that is uncommon and too little that is genuinely similar.

Conclusion: two theories of liberalism

The depth of the disagreement between Fukuyama and Popper seems all the more surprising because politically they appear to be very close. The two principal modern targets of Popper's attack on historicism, Hegel and Marx, are attacked in large part because they are opposed to liberalism. Fukuyama, by contrast, is avowedly liberal and shares many specific political principles with Popper. Moreover, Fukuyama is as thoroughly anti-communist as Popper, and the triumphalism at the victory of liberal democracy over communism which many readers have detected in 'The End of History?' is something which the author of *The Open Society and Its Enemies* would have found very congenial.

Why, then, does there appear to be such a gulf between them? Part of the answer lies in a possible misunderstanding which might make the gap between them seem greater than it actually is. In particular, as we have seen above, Fukuyama is not straightforwardly historicist, and he actually rejects some of the central theses which Popper attributes to historicists. But that is not the whole explanation, because as we have just seen, there are still very significant differences between the two, especially over the question of explaining wholes, as opposed to specific events.

We should not try to minimize the differences, for they reflect genuine conflicts within the liberal traditions, disagreements which in Fukuyama's view need to be resolved before liberal democratic societies can finally resolve their internal problems. In particular, Fukuyama points to the dangers inherent in what he describes as the Anglo Saxon strand of liberalism, which are due to its excessive individualism. By contrast, Fukuyama emphasizes the need for community and a sense of belonging.[44] Popper is a major theorist within the Anglo-Saxon tradition and the differences between the two highlight Fukuyama's argument.

Fukuyama would claim that Popper's rejection of the idea that there could be any recognizable pattern in history contributes to an excessive individualism, for without the idea of community and of belonging which such patterns bring we are forced back on the idea of solitary individuals seeking their own destiny in isolation from their fellows, and often in conflict with them. In this respect, Popper's philosophy of history represents a serious departure from the more communitarian liberal democracy which Fukuyama seeks to defend.

What draws Fukuyama and Popper together politically is their hostility to totalitarianism. Neither would countenance a political order in which freedom of thought and expression were undermined and in which all social initiatives were confined to all-embracing political movements. Popper's opposition to totalitarianism pushes him towards an emphasis upon the individual which strongly resembles Kant's ideas on personal moral responsibility. Because of this he rejects the tendency of communitarians to place considerable faith in the interests of the community. Judgement always has to be reserved on any developing social trend and its value assessed in terms of the extent to which it contributes to the greater freedom of individual members of society. By contrast, Fukuyama places great hope in certain types of community because he believes that the right kind of communal life is (among other things) helpful in developing and maintaining an anti-totalitarian spirit. And Fukuyama believes that in some important senses the progress towards the end of history is intimately connected with the development of such communities. From a liberal perspective, both these views contain important truths, and Popper's caution may offer an important restraining influence on some of Fukuyama's more excessively optimistic ideas. There is, for example, a danger that with the proliferation of certain types of economic choices a great deal of spiritual autonomy might be lost.

When we consider Popper's and Fukuyama's anti-totalitarianism in its entirety a further critical relation emerges. Both thinkers seek to identify fascism and communism in their general rejection of centralization and dictatorship but can both doctrines and their representatives be equally morally culpable? There were certainly great evils in Stalin's Soviet Union which may place it at the same level as Hitler's Germany, but we would argue that in many crucial respects central European communism and central European fascism were decidedly different.

In the first place, central European communism (once liberated from the Soviet empire) *abolished itself*, whereas central European fascism had to be torn down from the outside by military force. Secondly, the conflict between the two systems cannot be overlooked. Despite the similarities detected by liberals such as Popper and Fukuyama, communists felt themselves to be totally at odds with fascism. This suggests that something might be rescued from the communist tradition which is compatible with the central aims of liberal society. But how could this be? How is it possible to reconcile the Gulags and the show trials of Stalinist rule with the liberal emphasis on human freedom and dignity? The answer is that no such complete reconciliation is possible, but we might justly argue that not all communists have been Stalinists. Even within central European communism during the Soviet era, alternatives were put forward which offered a significant internal criticism of communism. Most prominent among these was the attempt during the 'Prague Spring' of 1968 to oppose the stultifying post-Stalinist ideology of the Soviet government with a more humanistic Marxism based on a rediscovery of the early writings of Marx himself, such as the Paris Manuscripts. Moreover, the demise of the old communist system in central Europe has not led to the complete disappearance of communist (or Marxist) ideas from that area. Indeed in a number of these countries revitalized and revisionist communist parties have been voted back into power. This is not altogether surprising given the pressures built up by the rapid changes towards a market economy introduced by the first post-communist governments, to which the communist parties offered a slower and seemingly more communitarian alternative.

The suggestion that something might be rescued from the communist tradition which is compatible with the central aims of liberal society does not, then, seem quite so outrageous. It might be more constructive for the weaker societies of eastern Europe to rebuild in a spirit of thoroughgoing anti-fascism rather than in a spirit of thoroughgoing anti-communism. The complete rejection of fascism implies the rejection of totalitarianism – which was an integral part both of fascism and Soviet communism – so what Popper and Fukuyama both rightly despise would be decisively rejected by any new synthesis. Such a synthesis would also have to look back beyond the totalitarian brands of communism which have been so influential in the twentieth century, in countries such as China, North Korea and Cambodia, as well as the Soviet Union, and rediscover the writings of Marx himself. In attempting to perform this far from easy task they would be greatly assisted by placing Marx firmly in the tradition of those who have written on the end of history. Such a process would at least have the merit of potentially including those people outside of western Europe who have lived for the majority of their lives outside democratic systems. In becoming liberal democrats such people need not see themselves as entirely abandoning their past.

8 • Religion and the End of History

The idea that history has an end does not have its origin in Western philosophy but, as Fukuyama acknowledges, in Western religion. As we saw in earlier chapters, Kant and Hegel regarded their writings on history as being compatible with Christianity, and Hegel, in particular, frequently referred to progress towards the end of history as the outworking of providence. The first major break with religion from within the end of history tradition came with Marx, who saw religion as offering a false view of the world which actually hindered the coming of the end of the present age of capitalism. Fukuyama shares Marx's secular view of history and it is helpful in assessing the end of history tradition, and Fukuyama's place within it, to see how deeply the religious ideas with which it began remain an important part of any coherent account of the theory. If they are very deeply embedded in the theory Fukuyama's position may come to appear untenable from within the end of history tradition itself.

We might best approach the influence of religious thought on the idea of the end of history by contrasting it with the philosophical and scientific thought of the ancient Greeks, the other main well-spring of Western culture. According to R. G. Collingwood,[1] Greek thought, as opposed to biblical thought, had an anti-historical tendency. This developed as a consequence of working with a concept of knowledge which required permanence of its objects. The objects of knowledge were deemed to be real, true and certain. Thus, because numbers have eternal qualities, and because mathematical propositions are universally true, the study of mathematics was very highly esteemed. In contrast, history was seen as the study of the contingent and particular.

As the objects of historical study were thought to have neither permanence nor universality, the possibility of there being such a thing as historical knowledge (or science) was ruled out. Aristotle thought that poetry was possessed of greater universality than history.

a poet's object is not to tell what actually happened but what could and would happen either probably or inevitably. The difference between a historian and a poet is not that one writes in prose and the other in verse – indeed the writings of Herodotus could be put into verse and yet would still be a kind of history, whether written in meter or not. The real difference is this, that one tells what happened and the other what might happen. For this reason poetry is something more scientific and serious than history, because poetry tends to give general truths while history gives particular facts.[2]

Yet, the Greeks did not entirely discount the value of thought which was not scientific and which therefore did not qualify as knowledge in the strict sense. Quasi-knowledge of non-permanent and non-universal particulars could have some value. Clearly, being well informed about non-eternal facts was useful for the conduct of life. This was because the changes observable in the world of impermanence display certain patterns. Even history then, as a mere account of what actually happened, could yield something of value – a view expressed by Collingwood in these words:

> Thus history has value; its teachings are useful for human life; simply because the rhythm of its changes is likely to repeat itself, similar antecedents leading to similar consequents; the history of notable events is worth remembering in order to serve as a basis for prognostic judgements, not demonstrable but probable, laying down not what will happen but what is likely to happen, indicating the points of danger in rhythms now going on.[3]

This view of history, as a rhythm that repeats itself, was held by the Stoics, who went so far as to believe that such a repeated rhythm transcended the destruction of the world and its subsequent regeneration. Chrysipus, a Stoic who taught at Athens in the late third century BC said,

> It is not at all impossible that after our death, after the passage of many periods of time, we shall be re-established in the precise form which we now have . . . There will again be a Socrates, a Plato, and each man with the same friends and same fellow citizens, and this restoration will not take place once but many times; or rather all, all things will be restored eternally.[4]

Such a cyclical view of history has no place for a concept of an ultimate end of history, or indeed of an ultimate beginning.

The Hebrew approach to history was very different.[5] It was entirely governed by beliefs held about *the nature of God*. Whatever the origins of the belief in Jehovah, the Hebrews came to hold a view of him as a completely transcendent God. They believed that the whole of creation was brought into existence through his divine fiat, and that it is entirely dependent upon him for its continued existence. God, for them, stands outside history, which is an aspect of his own creation. Transcendent though they believed him to be, however, the Hebrews saw God as active in history, and able to intervene in it, though essentially separate from it.

The doctrine of creation entailed that history at least had a beginning, and this in itself made acceptance of a cyclical interpretation of history along the lines developed by the Greeks impossible for Judaism. Nevertheless, despite these great differences a number of Jewish scholars attempted to engage sympathetically and constructively with Greek thought. Philosophically the most significant of these was the Jewish philosopher Philo of Alexandria (*c.*25BC–*c.*40AD) who believed that Judaism and Greek philosophy contained the same truths, but expressed them in different forms. Indeed, Philo went so far as to claim that the Hebrew Scriptures conveyed philosophical doctrines in an allegorical mode. Nevertheless, even he condemned the cyclical interpretation of history because the termination of each cycle in conflagration was inconsistent with the nature of God. He specifically attacks Chrysippus's view that the consuming fire is the seed of the succeeding world:

> Still further, a good point I think is made by the investigators of truth when they say that if the world is destroyed, it will be destroyed either by some other cause or by God. Nothing else at all will cause it to undergo dissolution. For there is nothing which it does not encompass, and what is encompassed and dominated is surely weaker than what encompasses and therefore also dominates it. On the other hand, to say that it is destroyed by God is the worst of profanities. For those who hold the true creed acknowledge Him to be the cause, not of disorder, disharmony and destruction, but of order and harmony and life and all that is most excellent.[6]

Philo ultimately condemns the cyclical view because the repeated destruction of the world is inconsistent with God's nature, which is beneficent. But cyclical theories need not entail the periodic destruction of the world; the cycles could be a feature of human societies uniquely. Such a view may indeed be found in the Bible:

> One generation passeth away, and another generation cometh: but the earth abideth for ever . . .The thing that hath been, it is that which shall be; and that which is done is that which shall be done: and there is no new thing under the sun.[7]

Indeed, the biblical historian who wrote the account of the settlement of the Israelites in Canaan following the exodus clearly interprets that phase of Hebrew history in terms of a cyclical theory. The account in the Book of Judges is punctuated by a recurring formula, along the lines, '. . . and the children of Israel again did evil in the sight of the Lord . . . and the Lord sold them into the hands of . . . and when the children of Israel cried unto the Lord, the Lord raised up a deliverer to the children of Israel . . . and the land had rest forty years'.[8]

Such a view of history sees its events as resulting from both human and divine intentions, with the latter ultimately triumphant. The history that unfolds in the Bible is a story of the interplay between mankind's freedom and God's will. Jehovah, transcendent and omnipotent, stands over and above his creation, but he has a purpose for it. He has the power to intervene in human events to bring his purpose about. Thus it is that history has a goal. Whatever cycles may be discerned in history, they will not be endlessly repeated, for God has an ultimate purpose, and that will be eventually realized. That is the end of history. If history is teleological, with its events determined by its goal, it can be more appropriately described as being linear rather than cyclical. Some of the Hebrew authors have a deep sense of history's line of direction, seeing it as leading to 'the time of the end'.[9]

A theme in Hebrew historical writings which is just as central as the view that history is linear is the view that God has a human instrument which he employs to fulfil his purpose, namely, his Chosen People. The book of Genesis begins with stories which belong to universal history like the Fall, the Flood, the Tower of Babel, but soon concentrates on the history of the descendants of Abraham to the almost complete exclusion of all other people, except in so far as they impinge upon the life of the 'seed of Abraham'. There is here the germ of a very potent concept, that history has a line of development, and that that development is brought to fruition in and by the activity of a nation.

God's chosen instrument is no robot, however, and frequently acts contrary to his will. By intervening in the course of events, God is able to adjust and correct the direction from time to time. And although he is so often disappointed by his people's unwillingness to abide by his plan, he does not irrevocably abandon them. They will not be finally abandoned: they will in the end be saved. Indeed, biblical history can be understood as the story of God's efforts to save his people, a theological theme taken up by Christian theologians who have coined a technical term for it, *Heilsgeschichte* (Salvation History).

Christianity: the end of history and the coming of the Kingdom

Christianity inherited from Judaism the idea of a God who is transcendent yet intervenes in history, and whose purpose is to save his people. These ideas, however, underwent something of a metamorphosis in two important respects: in Christianity, God's people are not a single nation, and God's final act of salvation has already occurred. This latter concept made the Patristic authors reject all cyclical interpretations of history as incompatible with the doctrine of the Atonement. The point is made concisely by Augustine:

> Heaven forbid, I repeat, that we should believe this (the cyclical theory). For 'Christ died once for all for our sins'; and 'in rising from the dead he is never to die again: he is no longer under the sway of death' . . . The following verse I think suits our (cyclical) theorists very neatly, 'The ungodly will walk in a circle'; not because their life is going to come round again in the course of those revolutions which they believe in, but because the way of their error, the way of false doctrine, goes round in circles.[10]

Christ's death was a never-to-be-repeated act of cosmic significance, therefore, argued Augustine, since there cannot be any parallel or repeated atonements, history must be a single linear progression. On the same grounds, it might be argued also that the end of history has already arrived. Two interpretations of Augustine are possible. He sometimes writes as if the present age (that is, the time since Christ's death and Resurrection) is no more than the final tidying up of loose ends: 'the drama has reached its peak; now we have but to finish the last act.'[11]

But he can equally easily be understood as seeing the present age as the prelude to a climax yet to come. Augustine's ambivalence is brought out in a passage like the following, where he describes the ages of history in terms of the days of Creation.

> As therefore God made man in His own image on the sixth day: thus we find that our Lord Jesus Christ came into the sixth age, that man might be formed anew after the image of God. For the first period, as the first day, was from Adam to Noah; the second, as the second day, from Noah unto Abraham; the third, as the third day, from Abraham unto David; the fourth, as the fourth day, from David unto the removal to Babylon; the fifth period, as the fifth day, from the removal to Babylon unto the preaching of John. The sixth day beginneth from the preaching of John, and lasteth unto the end; and after the end of the sixth day, we reach our rest. The sixth day, therefore, is even now passing.[12]

It is an ambivalence which is reflected in the different theological interpretations given to one of the most central Christian concepts, that of the Kingdom of God. Is the Kingdom already established, or is it yet to come? Jews for many generations before Christ looked forward to a period when God would exert his power on earth and assert his authority as its king. When Jesus launched his mission with the words 'The time has come; the kingdom of God is upon you',[13] he could be interpreted as saying that the time of waiting was over. Yet, the prayer he taught his followers includes the petition, 'Thy kingdom come', as if the coming of the kingdom is yet to happen. Sometimes in the gospels one is presented within a few verses with evidence for both interpretations. Here is an example from Luke:

> The Pharisees asked him, 'When will the kingdom of God come?' He said, 'You cannot tell by observation when the kingdom of God comes. There will be no saying, "Look, here it is!" or "there it is!"; for in fact the kingdom of God is among you.'

> He said to the disciples, 'The time will come when you will long to see one of the days of the Son of Man, but you will not see it. They will say to you, "Look! There!" and "Look! Here!" Do not go running off in pursuit. For like the lightning-flash that lights up the earth from end to end, will the Son of Man be when his day comes.'[14]

There have been various attempts at reconciling these seemingly contradictory views. All concur that the Kingdom of God is a concept with its own peculiar dynamic: the Kingdom is here, and it is to come. There has thus issued from the work of Christian theologians the notion of realized eschatology, that is, the final phase, the end of history, has come and is even now running its course.

Christian theology is able to handle such seemingly internally unstable concepts as realized eschatology because its concept of time has been enriched by the Greek of the New Testament. Greek has two words for time – *chronos* and *kairos*. *Chronos* means time in the sense of temporal sequence, whereas *kairos* means time in the sense of a significant moment. Thus, the coming of Christ was an event which happened in *chronos*, but it marked a *kairos* in history. Paul Tillich elaborated upon *kairos* in this sense as follows:

> *Kairos*, for the biblical writers, is fulfilled time, the time in which the appearance of the Christ was possible because, in spite of actual rejection, all the conditions of His reception were prepared. The one real *kairos* is the moment of history in which the preparatory period of history comes to an end because that for which it was a preparation has become historical reality.[15]

The 'one real *kairos*' is sometimes called by Tillich 'the central event' or the 'centre' of history. This presupposes a sequence of prelude, central pivot and sequel. The beginning is the Jewish expectation of the Kingdom of God, within which there are in fact several lesser *kairoi*; then comes the major and decisive *kairos* with the coming of Christ, the event which gives significance to the pattern of history, past, present and future; and, finally, there follows the period of fulfilment of the kingdom, which also has within it several lesser *kairoi*. The lesser *kairoi* can only be judged to be so in the light of the central *kairos*. It seems paradoxical, but according to this view, the end of history is really in its centre. Those of us who live in the AD era could therefore be said to be living after the end of history, but prior to its final consummation.

For Christianity, the crucial point is that God has already triumphed in history. The future has nothing in store for which the climax already achieved will be found inadequate. This being so, the future can be faced with optimism by the People of God. Judaism also was (and is) optimistic in outlook, but for another reason. Its optimism is derived from the belief that in history God always kept his covenants, and that he will do so again in the future. Christian optimism, however, is based on a belief that God has already fulfilled the final covenant. This is an optimism shared by those who believe that the end of history has already arrived (in the sense that the final saving act has taken place) and those who believe that the end is yet to come (in the sense that all the consequences of the final saving act are yet to be realized).

This optimism has been critically discussed by both Christian and non-Christian philosophers. Karl Popper's criticism, for example, is based on a rejection of all theories which hold that history contains a 'meaning' – the Christian view being just one such theory. In *The Open Society and Its Enemies* he writes:

> . . . although there is hardly anything in the New Testament to support this doctrine, it is often considered a part of the Christian dogma that God reveals Himself in history; that history has meaning; and that its meaning is the purpose of God. . . . I contend that this view is pure idolatry and superstition, not only from the point of view of a rationalist or humanist but from the Christian point of view itself . . . it looks upon history – political history – as a . . . kind of lengthy Shakespearean play . . . Then they ask, 'Who has written this play ?' And they think that they give a pious answer when they reply, 'God'. But they are mistaken.[16]

Christian optimism is rooted in the conviction that even though the play is not performed according to the script, the plot cannot be overturned. But this, says Popper, is incompatible with the Christian virtue of hope.[17] Whether the end of history is achieved by a dialectical law or by direct divine intervention, the effect is to eliminate the possibility that the future is still ultimately open-ended, to deny the reality of human freedom, and to render hope and faith redundant.

The operation of dialectical laws in history must place limits on the possibilities it might contain. It is because he wished to secure the authenticity of the exercise of freedom that Kierkegaard denied that history could contain any in-built necessities.

> If necessity could gain a foothold at a single point, there would no longer be any distinguishing between the past and the future. To

assume to predict the future (prophesy) and to assume to understand the necessity of the past, is one and the same thing, and only the fashion makes the one seem more plausible than the other to a given generation. The past has come into being; becoming is a change in actuality brought about by freedom.[18]

For Kierkegaard, there is nothing to choose between those who would identify a pattern in history and those who would predict the course of the future. He calls anyone who would apprehend the past in the 'historico-philosophus' mode, 'a prophet in retrospect'.[19] Retrospective prophets often claim to detect necessities of history, but, says Kierkegaard, knowledge of the past does not confer necessity upon it, for 'no knowledge and no apprehension has anything of its own to give'.[20] Indeed, the farther we are removed in time from what we are looking at, the more likely it is that our view will be distorted.

Distance in time tends to promote an intellectual illusion, just as distance in space provokes a sensory illusion. A contemporary does not perceive the necessity of what comes into being, but when centuries intervene between the event and the beholder he perceives the necessity, just as distance makes the square tower seem round.[21]

The religious interpreter of history is not likely to be deflected by such considerations, however, for in the final analysis the Judaeo-Christian teleological interpretation of history is based not so much upon reflection on events in the past as upon an understanding of the nature of God, and particularly upon an understanding of his relationship as creator to his own creation. Any view of the end of history which arises from an understanding of the nature of God as creator will also have a 'flip side', namely, the view which arises from an understanding of the nature of human beings as creatures of God. It is this 'flip side' of the Christian theology of creation which was one of the springs of Western humanism. In *The Humanist Tradition in the West* Alan Bullock argues that

As a rough generalization, Western thought has treated man and the cosmos in three distinct modes. The first, the supernatural or transcendental, has focused on God, treating man as a part of the Divine Creation. A second, the natural or the scientific, has focused on Nature and treats man as part of the natural order like other organisms. The third, the humanistic, has focused on Man, and on human experience as the starting point for man's knowledge of himself, of God and of Nature.[22]

Bullock makes the point that these elements are three tendencies which have been combined in a variety of ways – not hard and fast lines of demarcation. Not every humanist interpretation has felt a need to incorporate all three elements. So, although the view that history has an end is rooted historically in a certain understanding of the nature of God, it is just as likely to arise from certain views concerning the nature of man, with or without a corresponding theology.

Fukuyama's view of history is just such an example of this. Although his discussion begins with an account of the international political developments of the recent past, he recognizes at the end of Part Two of his book that the answer to questions concerning the end of history will not be found by amassing empirical facts about historical events, but by a clearer understanding of human nature.

> It seems inevitable . . . that we must move from a discussion of history to a discussion of nature if we are to address seriously the question of the end of history.[23]

> We would look not simply at *empirical* evidence . . . Rather, we would appeal to an understanding of human nature, those permanent though not consistently visible attributes of man as man . . .[24]

Fukuyama himself draws attention to the religious context in which the concept of a universal human nature was conceived: '. . . it was Christianity that first introduced the concept of the equality of all men in the sight of God . . . what mattered was the redemption of man as man, an event that would constitute the working out of God's will on earth.'[25]

He is here referring to both sides of the same coin, the Christian view of human nature and of the divine nature. It is because God has a purpose for all men (not just the Jews) that it becomes possible to speak of man as man. It was this vision that made possible the writing of universal history, and since such a history would incorporate a teleology (God's purpose) it would have a built-in concept of the end of history.

> All nations were but branches of a more general humanity, whose fate could be understood in terms of God's plan for mankind. Christianity

moreover introduced the concept of a history that was finite in time, beginning with God's creation of man and ending with his final salvation. For Christians, the end of earthly history would be marked by the day of judgement that would usher in the kingdom of heaven, at which point the earth and earthly events would literally cease to exist. As the Christian account of history makes clear, an 'end of history' is implicit in the writing of all Universal Histories. The particular events of history can become meaningful only with respect to some larger end or goal, the achievement of which necessarily brings the historical process to a close. This final end of man is what makes all particular events potentially intelligible.[26]

What Fukuyama has missed, and it is a very serious oversight indeed, is the Christian conviction that there is a sense in which the end of history has already arrived. It is precisely because the Messiah has arrived that Christian universalism is able to supersede the obsolete exclusivism of Judaism. Fukuyama does not discuss realized eschatology. He thinks that it is a doctrine of Christianity that when the Kingdom of Heaven is ushered in (as he puts it), the earth will literally cease to exist.

As we have seen, the Christian doctrine of the kingdom has a complex dynamism – it has come, and is to come. It is perhaps significant that Fukuyama uses the expression 'Kingdom of Heaven' rather than 'Kingdom of God'. The former expression was in fact employed by the author of the gospel of Matthew where the other three evangelists would use the latter expression. Clearly, Fukuyama thinks that the Christian heaven belongs to some future state of affairs. He is therefore seriously misled on the nature of the Christian involvement in history. Following a decidedly Young Hegelian interpretation of Hegel,[27] he says:

> The problem with Christianity . . . is that it remains just another slave ideology, that is, it is untrue in certain crucial respects. Christianity posits the realization of human freedom not here on earth but only in the Kingdom of Heaven. Christianity . . . had the right concept of freedom, but ended up reconciling real-world slaves to their lack of freedom by telling them not to expect liberation in this life.[28]

Such an interpretation of the Christian view of liberation is not borne out by the record, of course. If Fukuyama was right on this point, then

Christianity would not have had any impact on politics, economics or social life; the history of Christianity would be a story of quietism. While quietism has indeed been an element in Christianity, and remains so, it has nevertheless contributed massively and actively to this-world affairs. To take just one, contemporary example, the proponents of the Theology of Liberation have shown that the politics of the Kingdom of God can have a decidedly unsettling effect on the politics of the 'kingdoms' of the world. For these theologians, the Kingdom of God seeks to bring about liberation here and now. This quotation from Gutierrez makes the point unambiguously.

> . . . liberation theology as we understand it here involves a direct and specific relationship with historical praxis; and historical praxis is a liberation praxis. It implies identification with oppressed human beings and social classes and solidarity with their interest and struggles. It involves immersion in the political process of revolution, so that from there we may proclaim and live Christ's gratuitous and liberative love. That love goes to the very root of all exploitation and injustice: the breakup of friendship with God and other people. That love enables human beings to see themselves as children of their Father and brothers and sisters to each other.[29]

Gutierrez, like so many Christian social and political reformers before him, has to contend with those who believe that the Gospel brings liberation 'of the spirit' or only in the hereafter, rather than also within history. Those who, like him, feel a Christian vocation to establish God's kingdom on earth will nevertheless agree with their critics that God's final purpose is not achieved within history. That could not be so, since history itself is finite.

Fukuyama rightly sees that the concept of the end of history has its roots in the Christian idea that mankind's common sonship of the same Father makes all men equally participants in the unfolding of a divine purpose. What he has failed to fully appreciate is that this concept was first espoused by a Christianity which taught that the end of history is already upon us. For the past two thousand years millions of people have believed that the end of history has arrived, and they have understood their own times in the light of that religious conviction.

This lack of understanding points also to a deeper weakness in Fukuyama's argument. He shares Marx's, and Nietzsche's, view that religion offers a false view of the world and, very significantly, for him, Hegel's concept of *Geist* has no divine aspect: it is supremely human consciousness.

Fukuyama points to natural science as the basis for his hope in historical progress, but in doing this he offers no compelling reason to suppose that his solution is any more tenable than Marx's as a means of avoiding the problems of historical relativism. For all the difficulties which have been recognized by the numerous critics of liberation theology, Gutierrez and others have at least understood the need to ground their political and social programmes for change in a universalist basis (however much the Marxist nature of the pro-gramme has come into repeated conflict with the theological base).

In this respect, Richard Brookhiser's comment that 'Straussians typically handle theology with tongs, unless they can portray it as a mask for secret skepticism',[30] actually points to a significant element in Strauss's thought which Fukuyama ignores. Strauss acknowledged that in seeking universal truth, philosophy (as he understood it) would always be in conflict with religion. Yet this conflict did not lead to the simple, straightforward rejection of religion; rather it required a sophisticated displacement of religious belief by metaphysical knowledge.[31] Such knowledge would really only be available to the few, and between that élite and the masses there would always be conflict.[32]

Fukuyama is an unusually democratic Straussian. Central to his conviction that we are at the end of history is the belief in the triumph of liberal democracy over all other ideologies (including all religions). But for democracy to reach its full potential it must be much more communally based than the Anglo-Saxon version stemming from Locke.[33] It must allow, and indeed encourage, every citizen to participate fully in the life of his or her own community.

In a striking way, this account of liberal democracy appears very much like a secular analogue of the Kingdom of God. Liberal democracy has, on Fukuyama's account, already triumphed – a triumph which, it must be recalled, came not lately, at the fall of the Berlin Wall, but more than two centuries ago with the liberation of the American Colonies and the Revolutionary overthrow of the *ancien régime* in France. And yet, as Fukuyama continuously stresses, liberal democracy has constantly to be realized and made over again by its members living their lives as members of a liberal democratic society.

That is not all. The very depth of this allegiance is something which requires a commitment which goes beyond the coldly cerebral. Indeed, Fukuyama acknowledges that in early New England the communities which became such an important model for the democratic practices of the later United States were based on profoundly religious convictions. Yet in one of his lengthiest comments on this phenomenon he displays a peculiar evasiveness.

> The Pilgrims and other Puritan communities that settled New England were all bound together by a common interest not in their own material well-being, but in the glorification of God. Americans like to trace their love of liberty to these non-conformist sects escaping religious persecution in seventeenth-century Europe. But while these religious communities were highly independent in temper, they were in no way liberal as the generation that made the Revolution understood liberalism. They sought the freedom to practice *their* religion, not freedom of religion per se. We could, and often do, regard them today as groups of intolerant and close-minded fanatics.[34]

Dismissing the early colonists as religious fanatics is, of course, easier than engaging in constructive debate with their ideas. But there is a price to be paid for such unreflective rejection. If Fukuyama is right in stressing the immense importance of commitment to the community in the bringing about and sustaining of mature democratic societies, he must take seriously the language and imagery of the people who played a key part in laying the foundations of such communities in the United States. And he ought to acknowledge that commitment to such values is not restricted to early colonial America. In many ways he is far too selective in his use of this material, as if, not being used to handling the tongs, he is uncomfortable with the feel of them. It is certainly true that a number of the leaders of 'the generation of the Revolution' were liberal-minded (in Fukuyama's sense) Deists. Thomas Jefferson is perhaps the most prominent of these, and his championing of a non-confessional polity fits exactly the image which Fukuyama is seeking to convey. But Jefferson was not typical of his generation of Americans, many of whom were devoutly Christian in their theology and who saw the success of the revolution as a vindication of their Puritan reliance on God's particular providence. Nor did such views die out shortly after the Revolution – they remained a central part of American public life throughout the nineteenth and twentieth centuries.[35]

To make these points is not the same as saying that the idea of the end of history has to have a religious content, but it is to claim that religious metaphors and ideas, especially those drawn from Christianity, have had and continue to exert a profound influence on the development of the tradition. In rejecting religion in the way that he does, Fukuyama is failing to engage with these metaphors at a sufficiently complex level. In this respect he has perhaps strayed too far from Hegel and been unduly influenced by Marx. There is an irony here. The liberal democrat who prides himself on being a Hegelian has underestimated a source of potentially great enrichment for his account of democracy. And he has done so under the influence of the one writer whose work he claims led to some of the most anti-democratic regimes of the twentieth century, and whose influence Fukuyama has come to bury for ever.

Conclusion

Fukuyama's thesis of the end of history is, as we have seen, far from original. It is, as *The End of History and the Last Man* itself makes abundantly clear, the product of a long and distinguished tradition which includes three of the most influential modern philosophers – Kant, Hegel and Marx. Situating Fukuyama precisely within this tradition, as we have tried to do, is of the greatest importance in understanding the significance of his work. This is all the more necessary because Fukuyama speaks very directly to many of the preoccupations which dominate our thinking at the end of the twentieth century. It is doubtful that *The End of History and the Last Man* will become a philosophical classic like Kant's three *Critiques* or Hegel's *Philosophy of Right* but it may none the less come to be seen as having played a pivotal role in the history of the ideas of the late twentieth and early twenty-first centuries. For all the criticisms levelled against his work, both in its detailed arguments and the broad sweep of its conclusions, Fukuyama has produced an extraordinarily timely and accessible work. Testimony to its timeliness and accessibility is to be found in the great interest which the book has aroused in many different parts of the world, from the United States and Great Britain to Germany and Eastern Europe to the Far East. *The End of History and the Last Man* is a speculative piece for our times, perhaps marking a watershed period in world history and in the development of relations among states. The book's appearance both marks the passing of the Cold War and offers some stimulating reflections on the social and political order of the future.

One of Fukuyama's most important achievements is to have almost single-handedly revived philosophical debate about the nature of history. In doing so, he has given a new lease of life to the philosophy of history, a branch of philosophy that has too often been neglected in the past as being peripheral to the central issues of the discipline. Such neglect has had unfortunate consequences, not least because a philosophy of history has deep implications for the more obviously central areas such as ethics and politics. These implications are very apparent in the past works in the philosophy of history upon which Fukuyama draws. As we have seen, Fukuyama situates himself in the Kantian-Hegelian tradition, deriving his ideas expressly from leading interpreters of Hegel such as Alexandre Kojève. If nothing else, Fukuyama draws attention to the substantial qualities of this tradition. He also demonstrates, because of the closeness of Marx to the ideas of this tradition, that Marx's theories cannot be wholly consigned (in a phrase made memorable by Marxists themselves) 'to the scrap heap of history'. In reviewing these classical debates in the philosophy of history, and in taking them in a new direction, Fukuyama has made a valuable contribution to contemporary thought.

Bringing the philosophy of history back to the centre of attention is also important in another way. The broad view we take of our historical context often represents the key vantage point from which present social and political enquiries are undertaken. Often the historical underpinnings of political and social arguments are not made explicit, but they are nevertheless present. Fukuyama has made explicit one theoretical underpinning for a free enterprise society. Fukuyama's account of history presents a general case for the progress towards free markets and liberal democracy. Moreover, by exploring so fully the consequences of his own views he challenges those who are sceptical about his diagnosis to demonstrate a plausible alternative. Clearly there are alternatives to Fukuyama's liberal capitalist account – such as democratic varieties of socialism, and nationalist conservatism – but such views have to be spelt out in considerable detail if they are to stand as viable alternatives to Fukuyama's position.

Of course, Fukuyama's work has not been without its critics! We have discussed two of these at some length because they represent formidable alternatives to Fukuyama's work from positions which he would recognize as being of significance. Karl Popper, for all that he rejects any attempt to find a meaning in history, shares with Fukuyama a passionate commitment to the truth claims of liberal democracy and the freedoms which they both believe that such a political and economic system offers. Equally, although Fukuyama rejects traditional religious accounts of the meaning of history, he does share the theist's belief that history has a meaning. Indeed, as we argued in the previous chapter, there is a real sense in which Fukuyama's position arises from within a theistic framework, although it is a framework which he seeks to abolish.

There is, though, a quite different line of criticism to which we now turn. This is the objection which is offered to the whole end of history idea, and even to the very notion that history as a whole has any decipherable meaning or purpose at all. It is the challenge of post-modernism. The differences of outlook which separate Fukuyama from post-modernism are profound, but a short discussion of them is of great importance in evaluating Fukuyama's contribution to contemporary thought. In particular, such an analysis will underline his enormous importance in reinvigorating the end of history tradition as a living alternative to post-modernism.

Fukuyama accepts the power of reasoned argument to arrive at least at a semblance of the truth, so Plato can be as illuminating, and as relevant to our current situation, as a modern philosopher such as Hegel or, indeed, as a contemporary writer. In this respect Fukuyama is very much a modernist, as opposed to a post-modernist, thinker.

Modernity is often defined in terms of the project of the eighteenth-century Enlightenment. This included a belief in the power of reason to solve problems, the importance of empirical methods, the secularization of knowledge and society, and a faith in progress. All these were interlinked, and the one thing which provided the rationale for them, in the eyes of many Enlightenment *philosophes*, was the triumphant success of the natural sciences. Fukuyama shares all of these ideals, and, as we have seen, the role of science as one of the chief vehicles for human progress provides a central theme of *The End of History and the Last Man*.

Post-modernity strikes at the heart of the Enlightenment project. Most crucially it rejects foundationalism – the view that there are certain truths about the nature of the world which can be discovered and which are capable of providing a yardstick by which all our other beliefs can be tested. The moderns of the Enlightenment claimed, following John Locke, that anything which can be learned or tested through the senses can provide us with just such a foundation. Locke expressed it with great confidence and certainty in a passage much quoted and admired by his eighteenth-century followers:

Let us then suppose the Mind to be, as we say, white Paper, void of all Characters, without any *Ideas*; How comes it to be furnished? Whence comes it by that vast store, which the busy and boundless Fancy of Man has painted on it, with an almost endless variety? Whence has it all the materials of Reason and Knowledge? To this I answer, in one word, From *Experience*: In that, all our Knowledge is founded; and from that it ultimately derives it self.[1]

Such an argument might appear to lead to a very narrow view of knowledge, as many of Locke's critics at the time, and later critics of the Enlightenment, were keen to claim. But it had one great advantage, which appeared to its supporters to outweigh all other considerations: it seemed to provide an unimpeachable justification for the methods of the natural sciences.

It is precisely this that the post-modernist rejects. For the post-modernist there is no absolute foundation which can be discovered, and therefore no such thing as absolute truth. Locke's immense confidence in the power of scientific method to present the truth about reality is flawed not only in its details but in its very nature. Science, like all other human activity, is a 'discourse', a way of seeking to make sense of phenomena which has its own internal rules and method but which is no more absolutely 'true' than was Ptolemaic astronomy or, for that matter, medieval astrology.

There is a clear sense in which Fukuyama's work is out of step with the post-modernist perspective. But the relationship between Fukuyama and post-modernism is rather more complex than is apparent from what has been said so far. The term 'post-modern' implies that the modern has been left behind, that we are now in a post-modern world in the same way that Marxists believed we would one day live in a post-capitalist world. In such a view we could describe post-modernism as having 'transcended' or 'overcome' or 'improved upon' modernism. Some writers indeed refer to it in this way. David Lyon puts the idea succinctly when he argues that '[t]he postmodern . . . refers above all to the exhaustion of modernity'.[2]

But there is something distinctly unsettling about characterizing post-modernity in this way. Post-modernism disclaims any belief in truth, so how can it be said that the post-modern condition is better than the modern? All talk of the modern being transcended or improved upon by the post-modern implies some means of testing one against the other, some absolute criteria such as the reason or empirical methods of the moderns.

One of the most influential of post-modernist writers, Jean-François Lyotard, has acknowledged that the 'post' in post-modern can be misleading in precisely this way, and he has suggested that a new term be used. The term he proposes is 'rewriting modernity'.[3]

Addressing himself to the problem of comparing two disparate historical periods, he argues that '. . . neither modernity nor so called postmodernity can be identified and defined as clearly circumscribed historical entities, of which the latter would always come after the former'.[4] Instead we should see that the post-modern is always implied in the modern. He means by this claim that the project of modernity will always find itself going beyond the boundaries which it imagined were there in front of it. Once the moderns used reason to attack the settled world view of the Middle Ages, they discovered that they had opened the door to relativism. Modernity posits a world of rational, scientific order. Such a world does not exist but it needed the destructive power of modernity to take us to the point where the relativity of knowledge could be realized. 'Modernity', he writes, 'is constitutionally and ceaselessly pregnant with its postmodernity'.[5]

Lyotard is careful to warn against understanding 'rewriting' as meaning discovering the ultimate truth, in the way that, to use his own analogy, a detective solves a crime. 'If we understand "rewriting modernity" in this way, like seeking out, designating and naming the hidden facts that one imagines to be the source of the ills that ail one, i.e., as a simple process of remembering, one cannot fail to perpetuate the crime, and perpetuate it anew instead of putting an end to it.'[6] He cites Marx and Nietzsche as examples of moderns who have fallen into precisely this trap.

Nor is post-modernism an alternative theory of the way the world is to be understood, which might be ranked alongside, and in competition with Marxism or Christianity or some other world view, 'on the market of competing ideologies'.[7]

> Postmodernity is not a new age, but the rewriting of some of the features claimed by modernity, and first of all of modernity's claim to ground its legitimacy on the project of liberating humanity as a whole through science and technology. But, as I have said, that rewriting has been at work for a long time now, in modernity itself.[8]

Lyotard's argument is that we can do no more than display the multiple possibilities in modernity – there is no 'way out', the most that can be hoped for is to show that some of the possibilities have failed to achieve their ends, as he claims to do with Marxism. Now this is clearly at odds with Fukuyama, who most certainly does want to argue for modernity's legitimacy – its overriding, complete and exclusive legitimacy – in large part on precisely the ground which Lyotard rejects, 'the project of liberating humanity as a whole through science and technology'. If it were simply a matter of there being two rival ideologies, Fukuyama could reject post-modernism and rest content with modernism. But Lyotard's programme of rewriting modernity is far too subtle to be dismissed so easily. Indeed Fukuyama shares with Lyotard and others some of the ideas that are often understood as being distinguishing marks of the post-modernist, such as a belief in the profound importance of images and iconography in the modern world, and the sense of the importance of globalization.

So how can Fukuyama avoid being sucked into what he would regard as the deadly whirlpool of rewriting modernity?

Is a universal history possible?

A striking aspect of Fukuyama's end of history thesis, and the one which most helped to bring his ideas to international prominence, is its applicability and relevance to the present condition of the United States. Fukuyama writes as an American citizen, and, despite his protestations that he has been at most only a comparatively junior member of the Foreign Service, as an American citizen who has acted in an advisory capacity to his own government. Many of the examples he draws upon and the issues he deals with arise directly from the experience of the people of the United States in the Cold War and post-Cold War era. Two of the central themes of *The End of History and the Last Man*, those of capitalist economic growth and liberal democracy, are themselves prominent features of United States society. Because of this, Fukuyama's liberal aspirations for the rest of the world appear to some critics to be vulnerable to the charge that they do little more than mirror the strategic and political interests of the society of which he is part. Fukuyama, it is alleged, is guilty of being ethnocentric in his approach. Inhabitants of South America, East Asia or Africa might find it difficult to identify their experience and aspirations with those of Fukuyama. In particular, individuals in these non-Western societies might have their own view of what a better future might look like, which might not necessarily involve this blend of individual freedom and capitalist enterprise. Fukuyama's favoured ethic is a product of European – mainly Protestant –

thinking, and on the face of it there must be strong doubts about its universal applicability. Fukuyama, they say, has to show that the secularized Protestant ethic he commends is not only taking root in the non-Western world but is positively demanded by non-Western individuals.

Of course, as we have seen, Fukuyama does offer a robust defence of his claim that liberal democracy and capitalism are superior to all other political and economic systems. He also goes into considerable detail to explain why he believes that the introduction of these systems into other areas of the world is in the interests of the inhabitants of these regions. But his disagreement with post-modernism is even more fundamental than this. Not only is Fukuyama's argument universalist in the sense of arguing that there is one universally true set of moral and political principles; he also argues there is one universally true form of rationality which underpins these principles. He argues this way because he shares the same Enlightenment picture of the world as his key predecessors Kant, Hegel and Marx. Fukuyama tells us that 'the modern notion of progress had its origins in the success of modern natural science, and allowed Francis Bacon to assert the superiority of modernity to antiquity on the basis of inventions like the compass, printing press and gunpowder'. According to Fukuyama, this 'concept of progress as the cumulative and endless acquisition of knowledge was stated most clearly by Bernard Le Bovier de Fontenelle'.[9] Fukuyama sees this view of progress, which culminated in the work of Enlightenment figures like Voltaire, Turgot and Condorcet, as chiming in with his own view of progress first systematically developed by Kant. It is at this point that his disagreement with post-modernism is most acute. Post-modernists regard the model of objective thinking pursued and cherished by modern philosophers as a myth. In their view, the particular, the subjective and the cultural can never be exorcized from anyone's thought. The post-modernist argues that there is no privileged position in time and space from 'which to view an argument or a way of life. Indeed the supposition of such a possible objective standpoint is itself a culturally specific view. As Pauline Marie Rosenau has written,

> Post-modernists have developed a unique counterintuitive view of time, geography or space, all of which are redefined and reconstituted in a mutually reinforcing, if not entirely unified, perspective. They

question almost all that is taken for granted about these concepts: a knowledge of history is essential for comprehending the present; time is linear; and space is fixed, constant, measurable. Post-modernism reverses the priority accorded to these terms by calling for more attention to time and space and less to history. [10]

This is the reason why post-modernists are especially harsh on the notion of 'metahistorical narrative' which might provide a context from which to view human society. They regard it as a particular trait of modernity that individuals seek to be guided by a notion of general human development which will give meaning and significance to their actions. Fukuyama, by contrast, does not want to give up the Enlightenment search for a metanarrative to account for our present condition. To the contrary, he argues that we should all agree that there is only one possible metanarrative which can make sense of things.

The idea of progress

One important element in this narrative is the idea of progress. Here, as elsewhere, Fukuyama is situated centrally in the Enlightenment/modernist tradition. Universal history supposes there is one common humankind whose vast multiplicity of activities, achievements and aspirations can be woven into one continuous whole. Fukuyama's supposition, like Kant's, Hegel's and Marx's is that there is one story that can be told about the human race, and this story on the whole a positive one. Whatever one holds of this supposition, it has to be conceded that there is an extraordinary process of aggregation and synthesis taking place. Need there be a pattern to the endless diversity of human experience? Post-modernists think not. At most there can be particular stories, involving individuals and groups of individuals, sometimes demonstrating improvement, sometimes not. Such is the variety of human taste and notions of fulfilment that it is not difficult to imagine circumstances that from one person's point of view might represent improvement being taken by another to represent a worsening. Post-modernists would argue that it is a modernist supposition that we have to agree as to what is progressive and what is not. How does Fukuyama rise to this challenge? It has to be said that he does not present a conclusive argument for presupposing a cumulative view of history. Rather he makes the negative point that those who believe that history may not be progressive will in the end be proved misguided. As he puts it, 'it is possible that if events continue to unfold as they have done over the past few decades, that the idea of a directional history leading up to liberal democracy may become more plausible to people, and that the relativist impasse of modern [sic] thought will in a sense solve itself'.[11]

There is on this point a considerable difference of opinion amongst the various advocates of the end of history thesis who, from Kant onwards, have disagreed on what sort of justification is possible for the claim that there is universal human improvement. Kant himself argued that such a justification could not be established on the basis of empirical evidence and that the argument for progress has to be a moral one, motivated by considerations of human virtue and good taste. Here Fukuyama disagrees. He believes a factual case can be made for human improvement, and that these facts are both political and economic. There are two aspects to his account.

First, Fukuyama believes that we can demonstrate a tendency for more and more states to develop into liberal democracies over time. This is because this form of society is very effective at satisfying the desire for recognition. As the desire for recognition is the most fundamental force in history we would expect more and more societies to be driven towards this type of system. Indeed, Fukuyama claims, there is abundant evidence that this is in fact happening around the world, and he offers many examples of the ways in which erstwhile illiberal and undemocratic states have become liberal and democratic, starting, most famously, with the states of the old Soviet empire. Following many earlier writers in the perpetual peace tradition, he also suggests that as a consequence of this move to liberal democracy war amongst states will cease to become an acceptable means of resolving disputes. Kant had indeed postulated this as a moral imperative, but Fukuyama believes that there is sound factual evidence to suggest that the peoples and governments of liberal democratic societies are gradually learning to obey the imperative.

The second strand in his justification is the argument that economic and scientific developments increasingly show that capitalism and Western science are far more successful than any of their rivals, and that they are actually delivering the goods. Just as he points to the success of liberal democracy so he refers to the empirical evidence which he believes establishes the undoubted success of capitalism and science. In arguing in this way, Fukuyama is diametrically opposed to Kant but he is strikingly close to Marx. We said earlier in this chapter that one of the consequences of Fukuyama having revived the end of history tradition is that Marx's theories cannot be wholly consigned 'to the scrap heap of history'. There is a rich irony in this because when 'The End of History?' was first published it was applauded by some and lambasted by others as an anti-Marxist tract. But Fukuyama's relationship to Marx is far more complex, and correspondingly more interesting, than this.

Fukuyama is, of course, highly critical of Marx, and even more so of Marxism. When he attacks Marx from within the end of history tradition Fukuyama turns him on his head, which from the standpoint of a Hegelian means turning him the right way up. Having thus asserted that ideas (in the form of the quest for recognition) play the dominant role in history, Fukuyama can then utilize Marx's insights that economic and scientific progress play a very important part in historical development, and that this progress can be empirically proven.

There is an important distinction to be made between the factual accuracy of Fukuyama's account of what the end of history looks like and the intellectual coherence of putting forward such an account in the first place. Even if the facts which he adduces do not on closer analysis fit the picture which he is trying to portray, this does not rule out the viability of the project in which he is engaged. There is nothing prima facie illogical in supposing that human history at a global level might be progressive; rather it is a conjecture which others can explore, seek to deny, modify or ignore in whatever way they wish. The most important point of conflict between Fukuyama and the post-modernists comes precisely when he attempts to present his interpretation as the only correct one. Of course, this is enormously ambitious and at one level bound to fail. The sphere of human history is so diffuse and variable that events may not fit with the conjecture and certainly contrary interpretations of the same events are always possible. But that is not to reject the end of history thesis as such – it may well be reasonable to modify the details of the conjecture, but not to reject it altogether.

Identity and the end of history

One of Fukuyama's most important contributions has been to revive
and to bring to public attention once again some of the central
questions of philosophy: What can I know?; What ought I to do?;
What may I hope for?

Since biblical times the question of the end of history is one that
has concerned people's identity. The story related of the Jews in the
Old Testament deals with their advance from a subjugated people in
Egypt to their eventual return to their homeland in Israel. Yet the
story did not end there with this longed-for return. Rather more was
promised to the Jewish people. At the millennium their entire history
would be vindicated by the coming of the Messiah. In having this
millennialist story about themselves the Jews were probably amongst
the first people to forge for themselves a notion of their subjectivity
which not only extended deeply into the past but also unendingly
into the future. The biblical story of the end of history in the coming
of the Messiah allowed Jewish people to know who they were and
where they might be going. To have a sense of direction and purpose
is to be somebody. One can also be known by others in relation to this
tale. Being somebody in a world which is seemingly in a process of
endless change and not always receptive to human interests is an
achievement.

We can see this link between the notion of the end of history and
identity in the thinking of the three classical figures we have focused
upon. Kant, Hegel and Marx were all concerned to establish who we
are and where we might be going. The fascinating thing is that all
three see the 'we' in a different sense. In looking briefly at how these
three thinkers identify their dramatis personae in their accounts of
history, we can put into perspective Fukuyama's attempt to turn an
old story in a new direction.

It is perhaps most difficult with Kant to establish who precisely he
sees standing at the centre of his account of history. Partly this is
because he is so universalistic in his approach. He welcomes any sign
of improvement wherever it might be. Prussia and the European states
(especially France) are naturally his main focus but he also pays
attention to those who were not regarded as civilized by many of his
Western contemporaries, such as the Negroes and the Indians of
North America. Kant seems to want to avoid particularizing in his
account of possible improvement. Most people (perhaps excluding

women and minors) stand a good chance of being heroes in his account. Even the anti-heroes (those with evil intentions in politics and life) can play a role in the upward march of humanity. This is not because of their bad intentions, but despite them. If we are lucky, nature and providence can blend the immoral actions of individuals and political leaders into a generally progressive story. The clash of immoral concerns can lead to beneficial side-effects. But such people figure positively in Kant's story against their wills. Kant's true heroes are to be found elsewhere.

To find who Kant places at the centre of his story of potential human improvement we have to look outside his philosophy of history to his wider philosophy. The best place to look is in his moral philosophy which constitutes part of the branch of philosophy which for Kant has the greatest objective reality: practical philosophy. As Kant sees it, practical philosophy is best suited to rise to the challenge of realizing reason. In its theoretical aspect philosophy unavoidably runs into insoluble contradictions when it seeks to give reality to reason. We can never know with certainty that the demands of reason are met by the objects of observation. Within its own limits scientific knowledge is satisfactory but it cannot provide the finality which reason seeks. In contrast practical philosophy does provide reason with an object for its realization. In the human will we have something which is objectively real and which can seek to determine the world. Because of the capacity of human individuals to act according to principles they set themselves, Kant sees them as unique beings. They are unique because they possess the potential to be free.

Thus, the sole candidate for the central role in Kant's account of progress is the individual and, in particular, the autonomous human individual who alone possesses a good will. A person with a good will is one who is motivated in acting solely by the motive of duty which in turn prompts him or her to act in such a manner as always to take into account the interests of humankind as a whole by seeking to treat others never solely as means but always also as ends. It is a striking feature of Kant's philosophy of history, and his account of the end or purpose of history, that everyone can play a part. Political leaders can seek to play a part by ensuring that their policies are not contrary to right and morality, and their subjects or citizens can play a part by ensuring their actions conform with law and morality. In Kant's philosophy of history there is a mutual interdependence between the story of progress – which is necessary in providing motivation for us to act morally – and behaving morally – which is necessary if there is to *be* progress.

If with Kant it is the human individual that stands at the centre of history, for Hegel, the philosophical idealist, it is *Spirit*. Spirit is a translation of the German term *Geist* which can variously mean mind, spirit or intellect. With the term, Hegel tries to convey the intellectuality that he sees at the centre of our experience and history. As Hegel sees it, nothing stands outside Spirit. Once something is named it is already intellectual. Hegel's notion of Spirit stands close to the Christian (particularly the Protestant) notion of God. Indeed Hegel would not wish to see his idea of Spirit as at all antithetical to the Christian God, rather he would wish to present it as a higher synthesis of the underlying Christian ideal. Spirit for Hegel represents the possibility of the human individual being at one with the universe.

Hegel's philosophy of history has to do with the way in which this at-oneness or reconciliation does not occur immediately. Spirit unfolds itself over time. In political terms it is the story of the realization of human freedom. Although there is just the one spiritual identity at the centre of Hegel's account of history there are several carriers of this identity. Spirit realizes itself progressively in the Oriental, Greek, Roman and Germanic worlds. At certain times one nation or group of peoples may stand at the centre of this onward process of development. Clearly, in the Greek world the Athenian people and the people of Sparta played a pre-eminent role in the advancement of human culture and society. The people of one city, Rome, subsequently stood at the centre of world civilization and played their part in the unfolding of freedom. Just as some people play more important parts than others so certain individuals can figure prominently in the unfolding story of Spirit. These are world-historical individuals like Julius Caesar and Napoleon Bonaparte. But they are not the self-conscious agents of the Spirit of the world. Rather, such world-historical individuals have immediate ambitions of their own, but in realizing these personal ambitions they inadvertently serve to advance world Spirit.

Following Hegel's account of world history we should now be looking for the present-day bearers of Spirit in its onward course. In his own time Hegel believed that the Protestant peoples of Northern Europe represented in their culture and politics the furthest point of advance of Spirit. Their identity was therefore at one with that of Spirit. But Hegel also hints that the Germanic world can expand further West to North America, and he speculates that the people of the United States might hold the future in their hands. The implication of his view is that freedom may enter a more advanced phase in the New World. But although the geographical and political location of the identity which lies at the heart of world history may change, Spirit itself does not change. For Hegel it is the one Spirit which goes through the process of continual metamorphosis from one age to the next. *Geist* is the identity which lies at the heart of world history.

As a Left Young Hegelian Marx rejected the story of Spirit. His early philosophical development, marked by such works as *German Ideology* and *The Holy Family*, show him struggling with the problems of finding an alternative to the Hegelian vision. Perhaps it was Marx's encounter with French socialism in 1844 in Paris which provided him with the stimulus to see beyond the Hegelian account of history to another form of identity which would realize the historical process. Marx was strongly influenced by the view, developed in Hegel's *Philosophy of Right*, that the proper ordering of society depended on the mediating and steering activity of a universal class. Hegel had depicted this universal class as the estate of civil servants and intellectuals found in modern bourgeois society. Marx was highly dissatisfied with this view, believing that Hegel was encouraging the bureaucratization of politics and society. Marx therefore sought an alternative to the Hegelian vision of the universal class.

Marx found that alternative in the modern working class. The members of this class were to be the bearers of the historical project and also the true realization of the ideal of a universal class. What is most remarkable about Marx's vision of history is its extraordinary romanticism. Marx believed himself to have found in the modern proletariat the answer to the problems of politics and history. For Marx, the modern proletariat was the class of the outsider in modern society. The worker belonged to civil society but still was not properly part of it. Compared with all previous forms of social association, bourgeois society was extraordinarily productive and wealthy. But this wealth seemed somehow to bypass its creators. Marx regarded modern proletarians as alienated from society. The more wealth they generated, the poorer they appeared to become. Indeed the more productive society was, the greater the profusion of commodities it supplied, the more precarious became the life of the direct producer. Under capitalism the worker could only lose. The worker was threatened on all sides by poverty, unemployment and degrading labour.

The identity that lies at the heart of Marx's vision is the identity of the modern working class. But he does not see this as an isolated form of identity, nor exclusive to one group or race. Marx believes that as modern capitalist society advances more and more people will become workers or employees. Barriers of race, nationality, gender and geography will all be broken down by the worldwide spread of the capitalist economy. So, in connecting his story of history with the emancipation of the working class, Marx sees himself as dealing with the universal emancipation of the human race. In a strange way Marx's vision brings us back to Kant's focus upon the individual, because Marx sees himself as concerned with the development of a true or authentic human individuality. The focus upon the working class is not one that he chooses. Rather, Marx believes that it is one forced upon him by history. It is the natural, unplanned development of human society which will ultimately turn the majority into employed producers, dependent upon others for their livelihood and prosperity. Thus, for Marx the realization of our true humanity and freedom is not a process separate from the emancipation of the working class but is, in fact, one and the same process.

In Fukuyama's approach to the end of history there is a worldwide focus and concern which is also reminiscent of Kant's universalism. Fukuyama attempts to show how the human race has become more homogeneous in its political structures, culture, interests and tastes. Fukuyama is anxious that no one is left behind in the conflictual, ultimately stagnant world of history. But the most fascinating part of Fukuyama's work, and the aspect which deservedly gained for him the great attention he enjoys, is the centrality it gives to the American people in its historical tale. Fukuyama writes about the end of history as a concerned and active American citizen. His major interest is the direction the United States should follow now that the Cold War has ended. His view appears to be that the United States should head further in the direction towards which it is already going. The pursuit of the end of history should continue so that eventually the whole of humankind is brought into its purview.

The United States and other liberal democracies will have to come to grips with the fact that, with the collapse of the communist world, the world in which they live is less and less the old one of geopolitics, and that the rules and methods of the historical world are not appropriate to the historical one. For the latter, the major issues will be economic ones like promoting competitiveness and innovation, managing internal and external deficits, maintaining full employment, dealing cooperatively with grave environmental problems, and the like. They must, in other words, come to terms with the fact that they are the heirs of the bourgeois revolution started over four hundred years ago. The post-historical world is one in which the desire for comfortable self-preservation has been elevated over the desire to risk one's life in a battle for pure prestige, and in which universal and rational recognition has replaced the struggle for domination.[12]

The reference to 'other liberal democracies' seems to be a mere afterthought. What is primarily meant is the United States. Fukuyama seems to be arguing that the United States has to take a less crusading attitude to politics and that there is no longer the need for the leaders of the United States to try to set the agenda in international affairs. What its leaders have rather to do is to accept the agenda that already exists. This existing agenda is the unfolding of the capitalist revolutions of modern times which have brought the middle class to power. Here Fukuyama is in danger of sounding rather too much like Marx, who also believed that the rise of the middle class to power had set the agenda for modern times. For Marx this was not an agenda the bourgeoisie could control, and eventually they would come to realize that in seeking to control capitalism they were holding a tiger by the tail. The working masses brought into being by capitalist methods of production would overthrow the system for their own benefit. Of course, Fukuyama does not accept this picture. The history of the United States demonstrates in his view that it is possible to have mass equality without an overthrow of capitalism. Indeed Fukuyama would probably argue that United States' capitalism brought about greater actual equality than any of the communist states created in response to Marx's ideal of history.

Despite this generally optimistic perspective, Fukuyama is by no means at ease with every aspect of modern American society. In particular, he wants the people of the United States to have a greater confidence in the values that underlie their social and political institutions. This unease is most apparent in the qualms which he has about 'the last man' that emerges at the end of history. In particular, he is concerned by the lack of challenge that may be experienced by individuals who live in material plenty and political security. In the end he dismisses those qualms as taking us too far down the path of Nietzsche's philosophy,[13] but the threat remains a real one. Liberal tolerance and physical plenty do bring their own problems, but we in the West have to rise to the challenge. We should neither go down the right-wing path of excessively privileging the individual nor the left-wing path of excessively privileging minority groups. Essentially Fukuyama believes that the people of the United States have to come to terms with their achievements, and to recognize the inherent superiority of Western liberal democratic capitalist values over all alternatives.

These last considerations lead Fukuyama to reject Samuel Huntington's argument that the world is moving into a period in which the major conflicts will not be between different ideologies, as they were during the Cold War, but between different civilizations.[14] Fukuyama accepts that 'cultural differences will loom larger from now on',[15] but he dismisses the notion that they will necessarily be the source of conflict. 'On the contrary, the rivalry arising from the interaction of different cultures can frequently lead to creative change, and there are numerous cases of such cultural cross-stimulation.'[16] Fukuyama's prime example of a creative change is highly revealing. He cites the opening up of Japan to the West after the arrival of Commodore Perry's 'black ships' in 1853, which 'paved the way for the Meiji Restoration and Japan's subsequent industrialization'.[17] That the Japanese-American Fukuyama should regard the Westernization of Japan as a largely unalloyed benefit is not altogether surprising, but it points to a more general conclusion that is sharply at odds with Huntington. For Fukuyama, the culture of the United States is potentially the culture of the world and in the light of this claim, Huntington's notion of a potential future clash of civilizations appear to be a particularly unfortunate one. Huntington's vision that 'in the post-Cold War world, the ideological conflict between communism and democracy will no longer exist, conflicts between ethnic, religious, and national groups will predominate, and the conflict between Western and non-Western civilisations will hold centre stage'[18] seems to be willing trouble on the world. Huntington's premises seem to be the deterministic ones that future armed conflicts are unavoidable and we have now to hunt around for the most plausible causes. Huntington stresses, like Fukuyama, that democratic states have a tendency to live in peace with one another, but since very many states still cannot be recognized as democratic we have no right to expect that conflict will not occur. The morality of democratic societies cannot easily be transferred to non-Western civilizations. We have to prepare ourselves for the worst. But in preparing ourselves for the likely outbreak of conflict, may we not play a part in precipitating such conflict? In expecting bad behaviour from non-Western civilizations we are likely to create a barrier between ourselves and the people of those civilizations which may very well prevent peaceful relations from developing.

Fukuyama's optimism about the West is much to be preferred to the gloomy prognosis of Huntington because it does at least encourage us to expect more of those societies which lie outside the advanced Western world. Fukuyama demands more involvement from the American people in the fate of people who for him still lie within history in the non-Western world. From Fukuyama's perspective, we should sympathize with the efforts of such people to remove themselves from history. Arguably all that Huntington's argument demands of us in relation to non-Western people is that we should be wary of them. Huntington seems not to want the people of the United States to relax their guard in relation, for example, to Islamic people or the people of China. In contrast, Fukuyama perceives fewer external threats and seems at times to be more concerned with internal tendencies in the West which might plunge us 'back into history'.

Although neither Fukuyama nor Huntington explicitly say so, both are concerned with the identity of the people of the United States in outlining their visions of world history. Fukuyama's notion of the identity of the United States' people is essentially secular and materialistic. The people of the United States are concerned with their material comfort and their individual well-being. They are self-absorbed and intent on acquiring the latest gadgets and responding to the latest fashions. They see themselves as acquiring and consuming individuals who are entitled to rights which facilitate their development and progress. Potentially they share such characteristics with the whole of humankind and Fukuyama sees no barriers of race and culture that can ultimately withstand the lure of such freedom. In contrast, Huntington's vision is less secular and less expansive. There are boundaries to the kind of civilization which the people of the United States enjoy. According to Huntington, 'the Velvet Curtain of culture has replaced the Iron Curtain of ideology as the most significant dividing line in Europe'.[19] And he leaves no doubt as to which side of the line of culture the United States belongs. The people of the United States belong to the Protestant and Catholic tradition of Western Europe. They have 'shared the common experiences of European history – feudalism, the Renaissance, the Reformation, the Enlightenment, the French Revolution, the Industrial Revolution'.[20] There seems little place in Huntington's view of United States' identity for the connection with Asia or Africa. In short, he seems to reject Fukuyama's universalism.

As partial outsiders we cannot enter fully into this debate about American identity. But we can express concern about the potential narrowness of Huntington's vision and commend what is outward-looking in Fukuyama's approach. In the American century we cannot show indifference to the debate since it matters very much to Europeans what direction the people of the United States take. As the debate about the end of history shows, the question of the identity of the people of the United States is tied very closely to the future of the world. The burden of being, in Hegelian terms, a 'historical nation' is that the people of the United States will take the rest of the world with them in whatever direction they may choose to go.

Notes

Introduction

1   For an example of Fukuyama's work in this field see Francis Fukuyama 'Military aspects of the U.S. – Soviet competition in the Third World' in Marshall D. Shulman (ed.), *East–West Tensions in the Third World* (New York, W. W. Norton, 1986), pp.181–211.

2   In an early response to his critics following the publication of 'The End of History?' Fukuyama complained that many of those who most vociferously attacked his ideas had not read the article.

1 Kant: History and the Moral Imperative

1   L. W. Beck, *Kant Selections* (New York, Macmillan, 2nd edn., 1988) (henceforth Beck), pp.415–25; Kant, *Gesammelte Schriften, Akademie-ausgabe* (Berlin, 1902–68) (henceforth AA), VIII, pp.17–31.

2   Beck, p.417; AA, p.19.

3   Beck, p.418; AA, p.121.

4   Beck, p.421; AA, p.25.

5   Beck, p.423; AA, p.28.

6   Beck, p.350; AA, p.434.

7   Beck, p.436; AA, p.354.

8   Immanuel Kant, *Metaphysic of Morals* (trans. M. Gregor) (Cambridge, Cambridge University Press, 1991), p.125; AA, p.313.

9   See Francis Fukuyama, *The End of History and the Last Man* (London, Hamish Hamilton, 1992), chapter 26, 'Towards a Pacific Union', especially p.83.

10   AA, VIII, p.123; L. W. Beck, *Kant on History* (New York, Bobbs-Merrill, 1963), p.68.

11   The essay appears in AA, VII, pp.1–116.

12   H. Reiss, *Kant's Political Writings* (Cambridge, Cambridge University Press, 1991), p.177.

13   Ibid., p.177.

14   Ibid., p.180.

15   Ibid., pp.226–7.

[16]   Ibid., p.234.
[17]   Ibid., p.180.
[18]   Ibid.
[19]   Ibid., p.181.
[20]   Ibid., p.179.
[21]   Ibid., p.180.
[22]   Yirmiahu Yovel, *Kant and the Philosophy of History* (Princeton, N.J., Princeton University Press), 1980.
[23]   Ibid., p.29. Some of this material is drawn from the *Bulletin of the Hegel Society of Great Britain*, 'Y. Yovel, Kant and the Philosophy of History', No.4, Autumn/Winter 1981, pp. 46–50. We are grateful to the editor for permission to reprint it here.
[24]   Ibid., p.70.
[25]   Ibid., p.165.
[26]   This is discussed in ibid., chapter 4.
[27]   Ibid., pp.188–9.
[28]   Immanuel Kant, *Religion within the Limits of Reason Alone*, p.5 (trans. T. M. Greene and H. M. Hudson) (New York, Harper, 1960), p.114.
[29]   Yovel, *Kant and the Philosophy of History*, p.202.
[30]   Ibid., p.238.
[31]   Ibid., p.302.
[32]   Karl Popper, *The Poverty of Historicism* (London, Routledge, 1957), pp.v–vii.

2 Hegel: Spirit and State

[1]   Hugh Brogan, 'Hegel in blue jeans', *History Today*, 42 (December 1992), 58.
[2]   Gertrude Himmelfarb, 'Reply to Fukuyama', *National Interest* (Summer 1989), 24–6 and Irving Kristol, 'Reply to Fukuyama', *National Interest* (Summer 1989), 26–8. The quotation from Kristol is on 28.
[3]   Kristol, 'Reply to Fukuyama', 28.
[4]   G. W. F. Hegel, *The Phenomenology of Spirit* (trans. A. V. Miller) (Oxford University Press, 1977), p.443.
[5]   Compare L. P. Hinchman, *Hegel's Critique of the Enlightenment* (Tampa/Gainsville, University of Florida Press, 1984), pp.63–9 with S. Houlgate, *Freedom, Truth and History* (London, Routledge, 1991), pp.15–16. For a helpful discussion of the contemporary theological background to Hegel's concept of Geist see Alan M. Olson, *Hegel and the Spirit: Philosophy as Pneumatology*, New Jersey, Princeton University Press, 1992.
[6]   See Fukuyama, *The End of History and the Last Man*, p.60.

7   G. W. F. Hegel, *Werke in Zwanzig Bänden* (Frankfurt, Suhrkamp, 1971),
    vol. 20, p.460; G. W. F. Hegel, *Hegel Selections* (ed. M. Inwood) (New
    York, Macmillan, 1989), p.441.
8   G. W. F. Hegel, *Philosophy of History* (transl. J. Sibree) (London, Dover,
    1956), p.457; *Werke in Zwanzig Bänden*, 12, p.540.
9   Hegel, *Philosophy of History*, p. 56.
10 Ibid., p. 57.
11 Ibid., p. 99.
12 Ibid., p. 107.
13 Ibid., p. 20.
14 Ibid., p. 25.
15 Ibid., p. 439.
16 G. W. F. Hegel, *Philosophy of Right* (trans. T. M. Knox) (London, Oxford
    University Press, 1942), p.189.
17 Ibid., 236.
18 Ibid., 238.
19 Ibid., 273.
20 Ibid.
21 Shlomo Avineri, *Hegel and the Modern State* (London, Cambridge
    University Press, 1972), p.188.
22 Fukuyama, *The End of History and the Last Man*, p.60.
23 Ibid., p.61.
24 Fukuyama, 'The End of History?', 18.
25 Fukuyama, *The End of History and the Last Man*, p.329.
26 Hegel, *Philosophy of Right*, p.324.
27 Ibid., p.324.
28 Ibid., p.268.
29 Alexandre Kojève, *Introduction to the Reading of Hegel*, 2nd edn., 1947
    (translated by James H. Nichols and edited by Alan Bloom) (Ithaca,
    Cornell University Press, 1969.)
30 Andrew Vincent, 'The Hegelian state and international politics', *Review
    of International Studies*, 9 (1983), 191–205.
31 Hegel, *Philosophy of Right*, p.324A.
32 Fred R. Dallmayr, *G. W. F. Hegel – Modernity and Politics* (London and
    New York, Sage, 1993), p.159.
33 Shlomo Avineri, 'The Problem of War in Hegel's Thought', *Journal of
    the History of Ideas*, 22 (1961), and *Hegel and the Modern State*
    (Cambridge University Press, 1972).
34 Many recent books on Hegel's political thought, such as Dallmayr's
    G. W. F. Hegel – Modernity and Politics, largely endorse Avineri's
    discussion of Hegel's view of war – see Dallmayr, pp. 156–8.
35 Hegel, *Philosophy of Right*, p.324A.
36 Avineri, *Hegel and the Modern State*, p.196.

[37] Hegel, *Philosophy of Right*, p.334.

[38] Avineri, *Hegel and the Modern State*, p.196.

[39] Stephen Walt, 'Hegel on war: another look', *History of Political Thought*, X (1) (Spring 1989), 118.

[40] Avineri, *Hegel and the Modern State*, p.198.

[41] Hegel, *Philosophy of Right*, p.279.

[42] Ibid., p.331.

[43] Ibid., p.334.

[44] See, for example, Michael Inwood, *A Hegel Dictionary* (Oxford, Blackwell, 1992), p.308.

[45] Walt, 'Hegel on war', 113–24.

[46] Hegel, *Philosophy of Right*, p.322R.

[47] Vincent, 'The Hegelian state and international politics', 202.

[48] Ibid., p.194.

[49] Ibid., pp.194-5.

[50] See, for example, his comments on the native peoples of North and South America in Hegel, *The Philosophy of History*, pp.82–3.

[51] Hegel, *Philosophy of Right*, p.338.

[52] Ibid., p.338A.

[53] Ibid., p.339A.

[54] Ibid., p.340.

[55] Fukuyama, *The End of History and the Last Man*, p.389.

[56] See *The End of History and the Last Man*, p.64 and pp.332–3. Fukuyama's view of the dangers of relativism, and the way in which Nietzsche's thought has been used by modern relativists, is close to that of Alan Bloom in *The Closing of the American Mind*.

3 Marx: Communism and the End of Prehistory

[1] Ludwig Feuerbach, *The Essence of Christianity* (New York, Harper, 1957).

[2] Karl Marx, *The Holy Family* (1843) (London, Lawrence and Wishart, 1957).

[3] Karl Marx, *The German Ideology* (1845–6) (London, Lawrence and Wishart, 1970).

[4] Karl Marx, *Theses on Feuerbach* in *The German Ideology*, Appendix, p.121.

[5] For Marx's use of the term 'prehistory' see *Preface to a Contribution to the Critique of Political Economy* in *Early Writings* (Harmondsworth, Penguin, 1974), p.426. Also in *Selected Works in One Volume* (London, Lawrence and Wishart, 1971).

[6] Karl Marx, *Economic and Philosophic Manuscripts of 1844* (London, Lawrence and Wishart, 1970), p.135.

7   Marx, *The German Ideology*, p.56.

8   Ibid., p.59.

9   Marx, *Economic and Philosophic Manuscripts of 1844*, p.145.

10   Marx, *The German Ideology*, p.42.

11   Fukuyama, *The End of History and the Last Man*, pp.64–5.

12   Ibid., p.65.

13   Marx, *Economic and Philosophic Manuscripts of 1844*, p.146.

14   *Contribution to the Critique of Political Economy* in K. Marx and F. Engels, *Selected Works in One Volume*, p.21.

15   *Contribution to the Critique of Political Economy*, pp.21–2.

16   Karl Marx, *Critique of the Gotha Programme* in *Selected Works in One Volume*, pp.324–5.

17   Karl Marx, *The Eighteenth Brumaire of Louis Bonaparte* in *Selected Works in One Volume*, p.97.

18   Karl Marx, *Capital*, Preface to the first German edition (London, Lawrence and Wishart, 1962), pp.8 and 10.

19   *Contribution to the Critique of Political Economy*, p.21.

20   On this, see David McLellan, *Karl Marx: His Life and Thought* (London, Macmillan, 1973), pp.217ff.

21   *The Class Struggles in France: 1848 to 1850* in Karl Marx, *Surveys from Exile* (edited by David Fernbach) (Penguin, Harmondsworth, 1973), p.72. He also makes similarly caustic comments about the lumpenproletariat – what contemporary sociologists would refer to as the underclass – describing them as 'thieves and criminals . . . living off the garbage of society' (p.52).

22   Karl Marx, 'A contribution to the critique of Hegel's *Philosophy of Right*', in *Critique of Hegel's Philosophy of Right* (Cambridge, Cambridge University Press, 1970), p.141.

23   Marx, *Capital*, Volume I (1863) (London, Lawrence and Wishart, 1970), p.763.

4 Fukuyama I: Reinventing Optimism

1   See, for example, Stephen Holmes, ' "The Scowl of Minerva", a review essay on *The End of History and the Last Man*', in *New Republic*, 206 (12) (March 23, 1992), 27–32; John Dunn 'In the Glare of Recognition', *Times Literary Supplement* (April 24, 1992), 6; and, in a somewhat more sympathetic vein, Joseph McCarney, 'Reflections on Fukuyama', *New Left Review*, 202 (November–December 1993).

2   See, for example, Francis Fukuyama, 'The beginning of foreign policy', *New Republic*, 207 (8–9) (1992), and 'Against the new pessimism', *Commentary*, 97 (2) (February 1994).

3   See, for example, H. S. Harris, 'The end of history in Hegel', *Bulletin of the Hegel Society of Great Britain*, 23/24 (1991), 1–14.

4   Alexandre Kojève, *Introduction to the Reading of Hegel: Lectures on the Phenomenology of Spirit* (assembled by Raymond Queneau, edited by Allan Bloom, translated by James H. Nichols, Jr.) (Ithaca, Cornell University Press, 1969). First published in French, 1947.

5   Fukuyama, *The End of History and the Last Man*, p.66.

6   Ibid., p.144.

7   Ibid., p.66. The quotation from Kojève concerning the alignment of the provinces is from *Introduction to the Reading of Hegel*, p.436.

8   Ibid., p.351, note 32 to p.66.

9   Stephen Holmes, 'The Scowl of Minerva'.

10 *Introduction to the Reading of Hegel*, p.161, footnote.

11 Francis Fukuyama, 'The End of History?' in *The National Interest*, 16 (Summer 1989), 3–18.

12 Fukuyama, *The End of History and the Last Man*, p.3.

13 See especially *The End of History and the Last Man*, chapters 2 and 3.

14 Ibid., p.17.

15 Ibid., p.xi.

16 Ibid.

17 Fukuyama, 'The End of History?', p.3.

18 Fukuyama, *The End of History and the Last Man*, pp.42–3.

19 Fukuyama, 'The End of History?', p.5.

20 Fukuyama, *The End of History and the Last Man*, p.43.

21 Ibid., p.43.

22 See Isaiah Berlin, 'Two concepts of liberty' in *Four Essays on Liberty* (Oxford, Oxford University Press, 1969), pp.118–72.

23 Fukuyama, 'The End of History?', p. 3.

24 Ibid., p.6.

25 Ibid.

26 Ibid., p.18.

27 Ibid.

28 Francis Fukuyama, 'A reply to my critics', *The National Interest*, 18 (Winter 1989/90), 21–8.

29 Ibid., p.28.

30 Ibid.

31 Ibid.

32 Ibid., pp.26, 27.

33 Ibid., p.26.

5 Fukuyama II: Recognition and Liberal Democracy

1   Francis Fukuyama, *The End of History and the Last Man* (London, Hamish Hamilton, 1992), p.109.

2   Ibid., p.145.

3   John Locke, *Two Treatises of Civil Government* (1689). The definitive modern edition is that of Peter Laslett.

4   Fukuyama, *The End of History and the Last Man*, pp.214–15.

5   See *The End of History and the Last Man*, chapter 20 for Fukuyama's discussion of Nietzsche's theory of the state. For Nietzsche's own account of the state in these terms, see *Thus Spoke Zarathustra*, pp.75–8, 'Of the New Idol'.

6   Fukuyama, *The End of History and the Last Man*, p.215.

7   Ibid., p.121.

8   Ibid., p.303.

9   Ibid., p.147. In Hegel's own account in *The Phenomenology of Spirit* there is one further stage to the dialectical process. He claims that ultimately the one who yields in fact has the greatest potential for freedom – see the discussion in chapter 3 above.

10 Shadia B. Drury, *Alexandre Kojève: The Roots of Postmodern Politics* (London, Macmillan, 1994), p.196.

11 For this aspect of Hegel's view of war, see *The Philosophy of Right*, section 324.

12 See *Republic*, iv 434 D–441 C. Fukuyama has been accused of misunderstanding or misrepresenting Plato, but, as with his relationship to Hegel, we shall not pursue that argument here – the point is that he is using the concept of *thymos* to explore problems in contemporary thought and practice, not as an exercise in the interpretation of ancient philosophy. For an important modern discussion of Plato's meaning – and a recognition of the ambiguity of the concept – see Julia Annas *An Introduction to Plato's Republic* (Oxford, Clarendon Press, 1981), chapter 5.

13 Fukuyama, *The End of History and the Last Man*, p.206.

14 Ibid., p.182.

15 Ibid., p.201.

16 Ibid.

17 One important distinction in the discussion of nationalism is that between the liberally oriented *risorgimento* nationalism of people such as Mazzini and Gandhi and the integral nationalism which lies at the heart of many fascist movements. Fukuyama's arguments are more relevant to the second than to the first. For an influential discussion of this distinction, see Peter Alter, *Nationalism* (London, Edward Arnold, 1989).

18 Fukuyama, *The End of History and the Last Man*, p.293.

19 Ibid., p.311.

20 Ibid.

21 Ibid., p.315.

22 Ibid., p.323.

23   Ibid., p.323.
24   Ibid., p.318.
25   Ibid., p.331–2.
26   Ibid., p.336.
27   See *Philosophy of Right*, 341–60 and *Introduction to the Philosophy of History*. The quotation is from *Introduction to the Philosophy of History*, p.12.
28   Fukuyama, *The End of History and the Last Man*, p.60.
29   Ibid., p.339.
30   See Hegel, *The Philosophy of Right*, Preface, p.23.

6 Fukuyama III: International Dimensions

1   See, for example, Francis Fukuyama, 'Reflections on the end of history, five years later', p.29, in T. Burne, (ed.), *After History: Francis Fukuyama and his Critics* (Lanham, Maryland and London, Rowman and Littlefield, 1994), p.239.
2   The list is set out in a table in Fukuyama, *The End of History and the Last Man*, pp.49–50.
3   See Fukuyama, *The End of History and the Last Man*, pp.226–9.
4   Richard Brookhiser, ' "Fresh Air?" a review of Thomas L. Pangle *The Ennobling of Democracy*', in *National Review*, 44 (5) (1992), 44.
5   Fukuyama, *The End of History and the Last Man*, p.235.
6   Ibid., p.235.
7   Fukuyama's analysis of the Japanese political system may have to be reviewed in the light of events which have taken place since the publication of *The End of History and the Last Man*. For a stimulating account of modern Japanese political and economic developments, which includes a detailed discussion of Fukuyama, see David Williams, *Japan: Beyond the End of History* (London: Routledge, 1994), especially chapter 13.
8   Joseph McCarney, 'Reflections on Fukuyama', *New Left Review*, 202 (November–December 1993), 47.
9   Ibid., 46.
10   Fukuyama, *The End of History and the Last Man*, p.242.
11   Ibid., pp.243–4.
12   Christopher Norris, *Uncritical Theory: Postmodernism, Intellectuals and the Gulf War* (London, Lawrence and Wishart, 1992), p.137.
13   The debate between what were later called idealists and realists goes back to the founding of the Republic and can be seen in the contrasting attitudes of Jefferson and Hamilton, for example. In the twentieth century the most important idealist president was Woodrow Wilson and the most clearly realist was Richard Nixon.

[14] Fukuyama, 'A reply to my critics', p.23.
[15] Fukuyama, *The End of History and the Last Man*, p.264.
[16] Quoting Hans Morgenthau, *The End of History and the Last Man*, p.256.
[17] Ibid., p.256.
[18] Ibid.
[19] Ibid., p.258.
[20] Ibid.
[21] Ibid., p.262.
[22] Fukuyama argues in *The End of History and the Last Man* that post-historical countries 'have had difficulty formulating any just principle of excluding foreigners that does not seem racist or nationalist, thereby violating those universal principles of right to which they as liberal democracies are committed' (p.278). Since the publication of *The End of History and the Last Man* he has contributed to the increasingly acrimonious debate in the United States about immigration and has continued to take an open-handed approach to the question – see, for example Peter Brimelow and Francis Fukuyama, 'Are immigrants a threat to American values and culture?', *National Review* (22 June 1993).

7 Popper: A Liberal Critic of the End of History

[1] Patrick Gardiner, *The Nature of Historical Explanation* (London, Oxford University Press, 1952), p.ix, quoted in William H. Dray, *Philosophy of History* (Englewood Cliffs, NJ, Prentice-Hall, 1964), p.67.
[2] Ibid., p.1.
[3] Ibid., p.2.
[4] Fukuyama, *The End of History and the Last Man*, p.62.
[5] H. A. L. Fisher, *A History of Europe* (London, Edward Arnold, 1935), Preface to 1936 edition, p.v.
[6] Karl R. Popper, *The Poverty of Historicism* (London, Routledge and Kegan Paul, 1957), p.109; Fukuyama, *The End of History and the Last Man*, p.5.
[7] Popper, *The Poverty of Historicism*, p.3.
[8] Ibid., p.43.
[9] Quoted in ibid., p.51.
[10] Karl R. Popper, *The Open Society and Its Enemies* (London, Routledge, 1945), vol.2, p.59.
[11] Ibid., p.66 (Popper's italics).
[12] See *The Philosophy of Right*, p.340.
[13] Popper, *The Open Society and Its Enemies*, vol.2, p.67.
[14] Hegel, *The Philosophy of Right*, section 345.
[15] Ibid., section 328.

[16] Ibid., section 328R.
[17] Ibid., section 351.
[18] Ibid., section 318A.
[19] Hegel, *The Philosophy of History* (transl. J. Sibree) (New York, Dover Publications, 1956), p.30.
[20] Ibid., p.34.
[21] Ibid., p.32.
[22] Quoted in *The Poverty of Historicism*, p.112.
[23] Ibid., p.33.
[24] Ibid., p.17.
[25] Ibid.
[26] Ibid., pp.106–7.
[27] Ibid., p.113.
[28] Ibid., p.61.
[29] Popper, *The Open Society and Its Enemies*, vol.2, p.269.
[30] Ibid., vol.2, p.270.
[31] Ibid.
[32] Popper, *The Poverty of Historicism*, p.76.
[33] Popper, *The Open Society and Its Enemies*, vol.2, p.260.
[34] Popper, *The Poverty of Historicism*, p.150.
[35] Popper, *The Open Society and Its Enemies*, vol.2, p.260.
[36] Ibid., vol.2, p.268.
[37] Ibid.
[38] Ibid., vol.2, p.270.
[39] Fukuyama, *The End of History and the Last Man*, p.73.
[40] Popper, *The Poverty of Historicism*, p.v.
[41] Fukuyama, *The End of History and the Last Man*, p.55.
[42] Ibid., p.138.
[43] Popper, *The Poverty of Historicism*, p.81.
[44] See chapter 5 above.

8 Religion and the End of History

[1] R. G. Collingwood, *The Idea of History* (London, Oxford University Press, 1946), p.20.
[2] Aristotle, *The Poetics*, IX (London, Heinemann,1927), p.35.
[3] Collingwood, *The Idea of History*, p.23.
[4] Quoted in F. E. Manuel, *The Shapes of Philosophical History* (London, Allen and Unwin, 1965), p.9.
[5] This is the conventional view of the distinction between Greek and Hebrew thought. For a discussion of the views of history adopted by ancient Hebrew authors which is critical of the conventional account see

Giovanni Garbini, *History and Ideology in Ancient Israel* (London, SCM, 1988), especially chapter 14. For a discussion of Christian views of history, see David Bebbington, *Patterns in History: A Christian Perspective on Historical Thought* (Leicester, Apollo, 1990).

6   Philo, *The Eternity of the World* (transl. F. H. Colson) (London, Heinemann, 1941), I.i., p.259.

7   Ecclesiastes 1:4, 9.

8   See Book of Judges.

9   Daniel 13:4.

10 Augustine, *The City of God* (transl. Henry Bettensen) (Harmondsworth, Penguin, 1972), XII, 14, p.488.

11 On this see Vernon J. Bourke, *The Essential Augustine* (Indianapolis, Hackett, 1964), p.221.

12 Augustine, 'On the value of believing', quoted in Bourke, *The Essential Augustine*, p.224.

13 Mark 1:15 (New English Bible).

14 Luke 17:20–4 (New English Bible).

15 M. Halverson and A. Cohen (eds.), *A Handbook of Christian Theology* (London and Glasgow, Collins (Fontana Books), 1960), p.198. See also P. Tillich, *The Interpretation of History* (New York and London, Charles Scribner's Sons, 1936).

16 Karl Popper, *The Open Society and Its Enemies*, vol.2, p.271.

17 Ibid, p.273.

18 Søren Kierkegaard, *Philosophical Fragments* (transl. David Swenson) Princeton, NJ, Princeton University Press, 1936), p.63.

19 Ibid., p.65.

20 Ibid.

21 Ibid.

22 Alan Bullock, *The Humanist Tradition in the West* (New York and London, W. W. Norton & Co., 1985), p.16.

23 Fukuyama, *The End of History and the Last Man*, p.139.

24 Ibid., p.138.

25 Ibid., p.56.

26 Ibid.

27 And a view which also shows the influence of Nietzsche on his thinking at this point.

28 *The End of History and the Last Man*, p.197.

29 Gustavo Gutierrez in Rosino Gibellini (ed.), *Frontiers of Theology in Latin America* (Maryknoll, 1979 and London, 1980, SCM), p.24.

30 Richard Brookhiser, ' "Fresh Air?" a review of Thomas L. Pangle, *The Ennobling of Democracy*', in *National Review*, 44 (5) (1992), 44. This phrase is quoted and discussed at greater length in chapter 6 above.

31 See Leo Strauss, *The City and Man* and *Studies in Platonic Philosophy*.

[32] Alan Bloom makes this point very clearly in his commentary on the Myth of the Cave in his edition of the *Republic*. See Alan Bloom, *The Republic of Plato* (New York, Basic Books, 2nd edn., 1991), pp.403ff. Bloom acknowledges his debt to Strauss, acknowledging that his interpretative essay 'relies heavily on Leo Strauss' authoritative discussion of the *Republic* . . .', p.xxiv.

[33] See above, chapter 6.

[34] Fukuyama, *The End of History and the Last Man*, p.326.

[35] For an excellent discussion of the continuing centrality of religion in American public life from the colonial period to the present, see Gary Willis, *Under God: Religion and American Politics* (New York, Simon and Schuster, 1990).

Conclusion

[1] John Locke, *An Essay on Human Understanding* (1689) (edited with an Introduction by Peter H. Nidditch) (Oxford, Clarendon Press, 1975), Book II, Chapter 1, section 1, p.104.

[2] David Lyon, *Postmodernity* (Buckingham, The Open University Press, 1994), p.6.

[3] Jean-Francois Lyotard, *The Inhuman* (London, Polity Press, 1991). See Chapter 2, 'Rewriting Modernity'.

[4] Ibid., p.25.

[5] Ibid.

[6] Ibid., p.28.

[7] Ibid., p.34.

[8] Ibid.

[9] Fukuyama, *The End of History and the Last Man*, p.57.

[10] Pauline Marie Rosenau, *Post-Modernism and the Social Sciences* (Princeton, NJ, Princeton University Press, 1992), p.62.

[11] Fukuyama, *The End of History and the Last Man*, p. 338.

[12] Ibid., p.283.

[13] Ibid., p.313.

[14] See Samuel P. Huntington, 'The clash of civilizations?', *Foreign Affairs*, 72 (1993) and 'Political conflict after the Cold War', in A. M. Melzer, J. Weinberger and M. R. Zinmen (eds.), *History and the Idea of Progress* (Ithaca, Cornell University Press, 1995).

[15] Francis Fukuyama, *Trust: The Social Virtues and the Creation of Prosperity* (London, Hamish Hamilton, 1995), p.5.

[16] Ibid., p.6.

[17] Ibid.

[18] Huntington, 'Political Conflict after the Cold War' , p.154.

[19] Ibid., p.149.

[20] Ibid.

Bibliography

Allison, Henry E., *Kant's Transcendental Idealism: An Interpretation and Defence* (London, Yale University Press, 1984).

Alter, Peter, *Nationalism* (London, Edward Arnold, 1989).

Althusser, Louis, *Politics and History: Montesquieu, Rousseau, Hegel and Marx* (tr. Ben Brewster) (London, New Left Books,1972).

Annas, Julia, *An Introduction to Plato's Republic* (Oxford, Clarendon Press, 1981).

Arendt, Hannah, *Between Past and Future* (New York and Harmondsworth, Penguin, 1993).

Augustine, *The City of God* (tr. Henry Bettensen) (Harmondsworth, Penguin, 1972).

Avineri, Shlomo, 'The problem of war in Hegel's thought', *Journal of the History of Ideas*, 22 (1961).

―― *Hegel and the Modern State* (London, Cambridge University Press, 1972).

Bebbington, David, *Patterns in History: A Christian Perspective on Historical Thought* (Leicester, Apollo, 1990).

Beck, L W. (ed.), *Kant Selections* (New York, Macmillan, 2nd edn., 1988).

Beiner, R., and Booth, W. J. (eds.), *Kant and Political Philosophy: The Contemporary Legacy* (New Haven, Yale University Press, 1993)

Berlin, Isaiah, 'Two concepts of liberty', in *Four Essays on Liberty* (Oxford, Oxford University Press, 1969).

Berry, C. J., *Hume, Hegel and Human Nature* (The Hague, Martinus Nijhoff, 1982).

Bloom, Alan, 'Response to Fukuyama', *The National Interest*, 19 (Summer 1989), 19–21.

―― *The Closing of the American Mind* (New York, Simon & Schuster, 1990).

Bourke, Vernon J., *The Essential Augustine* (Indianapolis, Hackett, 1964).

Brogan, Hugh, 'Hegel in blue jeans', *History Today*, 42 (December 1992).

Brookhiser, Richard, ' "Fresh Air?" a review of Thomas L. Pangle, *The Ennobling of Democracy*', in *National Review*, 44 (5) (1992), 44.

Carlnaes, Walter, *The Concept of Ideology and Political Analysis: A Critical Examination of its Usage by Marx, Lenin and Mannheim* (London, Greenwood Press, 1981).

Cohen, G. A., *Karl Marx's Theory of History – A Defence* (Oxford, Clarendon Press, 1978).

Cohen, G. A., *History, Labour and Freedom: Themes from Marx* (Oxford, Clarendon Press, 1988).

Collingwood, R. G., *The Idea of History* (London, Oxford University Press, 1946).

Cooper, Barry, *The End of History: An Essay on Modern Hegelianism* (Toronto, Toronto University Press, 1984).

Derrida, Jacques, *Writing and Difference* (Chicago, University of Chicago Press, 1978).

—— *Margins of Philosophy* (Chicago, University of Chicago Press, 1982).

Dray, W. H., *Philosophy of History* (Englewood Cliffs, NJ, Prentice-Hall, 1964).

Drury, Shadia B., *Alexandre Kojève: The Roots of Postmodern Politics* (London, Macmillan, 1994).

Dunn, John, 'In the glare of recognition', *Times Literary Supplement*, 24 April 1992, p.6.

Federn, Karl, *The Materialist Conception of History: A Critical Analysis* (London, Macmillan and Company, 1939).

Feuerbach, Ludwig, *The Essence of Christianity* (New York, Harper, 1957).

Fisher, H. A. L., *A History of Europe* (London, Fontana, 1935).

Foucault, M., *The Order of Things* (New York, Vintage Books, 1973).

Friedrich, Carl, *The Philosophy of Hegel* (New York, Random House, 1953).

Fukuyama, Francis, 'Military aspects of the US–Soviet competition in the Third World', in Marshall D. Shulman (ed.), *East–West Tensions in the Third World* (New York, W. W. Norton, 1986), pp.181–211.

—— 'The End of History?', *The National Interest*, 16 (Summer 1989), 3–18.

—— 'A reply to my critics', *The National Interest*, 18 (Winter 1989/90), 21–8.

—— *The End of History and the Last Man* (London: Hamish Hamilton, 1992).

—— 'The beginning of foreign policy', *New Republic*, 207 (8–9) (1992).

—— 'Against the new pessimism', *Commentary*, 97 (2) (February 1994), 25–30.

—— 'Reflections on the end of history, five years later', in T. Burns (ed.), *After History: Francis Fukuyama and his Critics* (Lanham, Maryland/London, Rowman & Littlefield, 1994).

—— *Trust: The Social Virtues and the Creation of Prosperity* (London, Hamish Hamilton, 1995).

—— and Brimelow, Peter, 'Are immigrants a threat to American values and culture?', *National Review*, 22 June 1993.

Galston, William, *Kant and the Problem of History* (Chicago, University of Chicago Press, 1975).

—— *Liberal Purposes* (New York, Cambridge University Press, 1992).

Garbini, Giovanni, *History and Ideology in Ancient Israel* (London, SCM, 1988).

Gardiner, Patrick, *The Nature of Historical Explanation* (London, Oxford University Press, 1952).

Gellner, Ernest, *Nations and Nationalism* (Oxford, Blackwell, 1983).

Goldman, Lucien, *Lukacs and Heidegger* (London and Boston, Routledge & Kegan Paul, 1977).

Gutierrez, Gustavo, in Rosino Gibellini (ed.), *Frontiers of Theology in Latin America* (Maryknoll, 1979, London, 1980, SCM).

Habermas, J., *The Philosophical Discourse of Modernity* (Cambridge, MIT Press, 1987).

Halverson, M., and Cohen, A. (eds.), *A Handbook of Christian Theology* (London and Glasgow, Collins (Fontana Books), 1960).

Harris, H. S., 'The end of history in Hegel', *Bulletin of the Hegel Society of Great Britain*, 23/24 (1991), 1–14.

Hassner, Pierre, 'Response to Fukuyama', *The National Interest*, 19 (Summer 1989), 22–4.

Hegel, G. W. F., *The Philosophy of Right* (tr. T. M. Knox) (London, Oxford University Press, 1942).

—— *Philosophy of History* (tr. J. Sibree) (London, Dover, 1956).

—— *Werke in Zwanzig Bänden* (Frankfurt, Suhrkamp Verlag, 1971).

—— *Phenomenology of Spirit* (tr. A. V. Miller) (New York, Oxford University Press, 1977).

—— *Selections* (ed. M. Inwood) (New York, Macmillan, 1989).

—— *Elements of the Philosophy of Right* (ed. Alan Wood and tr. H. B. Nisbet) (Cambridge, Cambridge University Press, 1991).

Himmelfarb, Gertrude, 'Response to Fukuyama', *The National Interest*, 19 (Summer 1989), 24–6.

Hinchman, L. P., *Hegel's Critique of the Enlightenment* (Tampa/Gainsville, University of Florida Press, 1984).

Hobsbawm, E. J., *Nations and Nationalism since 1780*, 2nd edn. (Cambridge, Cambridge University Press, 1992).

Holmes, Stephen, ' "The Scowl of Minerva", a review essay on *The End of History and the Last Man*', in *New Republic*, 206 (12) (23 March 1992), 27–32.

Houlgate, S., *Freedom, Truth and History* (London, Routledge, 1991).

Huntington, Samuel P., 'The clash of civilizations?', *Foreign Affairs*, 72 (1993).

—— — 'Political conflict after the Cold War', in A. M. Melzer, J. Weinberger and M. R. Zinmen (eds.), *History and the Idea of Progress* (Ithaca, Cornell University Press, 1995).

Inwood, Michael, *A Hegel Dictionary* (Oxford, Blackwell, 1992).

Kant, Immanuel, *Gesammelte Schriften* (Berlin, Akademieausgabe, 1902–68).

—— *Religion within the Limits of Reason Alone* (tr. T. M. Greene and H. M. Hudson) (New York, Harper, 1960).

—— *Metaphysic of Morals* (tr. M. Gregor) (Cambridge, Cambridge University Press, 1991).

—— *Political Writings* (ed. Hans Reiss and tr. H. B. Nisbett) (Cambridge, Cambridge University Press, 2nd edn., 1991).

Kierkegaard, Søren, *Philosophical Fragments* (tr. David Swenson) (Princeton, NJ, Princeton University Press, 1936).

Kojève, Alexandre, *Introduction to the Reading of Hegel: Lectures on the Phenomenology of Spirit* (assembled by Raymond Queneau, ed. Allan Bloom, tr. James H. Nichols Jr.) (Ithaca, Cornell University Press, 1969).

Kristol, Irving, 'Response to Fukuyama', *The National Interest*, 19 (Summer 1989), 26–8.

Lamb, David, *Hegel and Modern Philosophy* (London, Croom Helm, 1987).

Locke, John, *An Essay on Human Understanding* (1689) (ed. with an introduction by Peter H. Nidditch) (Oxford, Clarendon Press, 1975).

—— *Two Treatises of Government* (1689) (edited by Peter Laslett) (Cambridge, Cambridge University Press, 3rd edn., 1988).

Lyon, David, *Postmodernity* (Buckingham, Open University Press, 1994).

Lyotard, Jean-François, *The Post Modern Condition* (Minneapolis, University of Minnesota Press, 1984).

—— *The Inhuman* (London, Polity Press, 1991).

McCarney, Joseph, 'Reflections on Fukuyama', *New Left Review*, 202 (November–December 1993).

McLellan, David, *Karl Marx: His Life and Thought* (London, Macmillan, 1973).

Manuel, F. E., *Shapes of Philosophical History* (London, Allen & Unwin, 1965).

Markus, R. A., *Saeculum: History and Society in the Theology of St Augustine* (Cambridge, Cambridge University Press, 1970).

Marx, Karl, *The Holy Family* (London, Lawrence and Wishart, 1957).

—— *Capital*, Volume I (London, Lawrence and Wishart, 1962).

—— *Critique of Hegel's Philosophy of Right* (Cambridge, Cambridge University Press, 1970).

—— *Economic and Philosophic Manuscripts of 1844* (London, Lawrence and Wishart, 1970).

—— *The German Ideology* (London, Lawrence and Wishart, 1970).

—— *Selected Works in One Volume* (London, Lawrence and Wishart, 1971).

—— *Surveys from Exile* (ed. David Fernbach) (Harmondsworth, Penguin, 1973).

—— *Early Writings* (Harmondsworth, Penguin, 1974).

Matthews, E. Gwynn, *Hegel* (Dinbych, Gwasg Gee, 1984).

Moynihan, Daniel Patrick, 'Response to Fukuyama', *The National Interest*, 19 (Summer 1989), 28–30.

Niethammer, Lutz (with D. van Laak), *Posthistoire – Has History Come to an End?* (tr. P. Camiller) (London, Verso, 1992).

Neitzsche, Friedrich, *Thus Spoke Zarathustra* (Harmondsworth, Penguin, 1966).

—— *The Genealogy of Morals* (ed. Keith Ansell-Pearson and tr. Carol Diethe) (Cambridge, Cambridge University Press, 1994).

Norris, Christopher, *Uncritical Theory: Postmodernism, Intellectuals and the Gulf War* (London, Lawrence & Wishart, 1992).

Olson, Alan M., *Hegel and the Spirit: Philosophy as Pneumatology* (Princeton, NJ, Princeton University Press, 1992).

O'Neill, Onora, *Constructions of Reason – Explorations of Kant's Practical Philosophy* (Cambridge, Cambridge University Press, 1989).

Pangle, Thomas, *The Ennobling of Democracy: The Challenge of the Postmodern Era* (Baltimore, Johns Hopkins University Press, 1992).

Pelczynski, Z. A. (ed.), *Hegel's Political Writings* (Cambridge, Cambridge University Press, 1964).

—— (ed.), *The State and Civil Society: Studies in Hegel's Political Philosophy* (Cambridge, Cambridge University Press, 1984).

Philo, *The Eternity of the World* (tr. F. H. Colson) (London, Heinemann, 1941).

Pippin, R. B., *Hegel's Idealism – The Satisfaction of Self-consciousness* (Cambridge, Cambridge University Press, 1989).

Plato, *Republic* (tr. Alan Bloom) (New York, Basic Books, 2nd edn. 1991).

—— *Republic* (tr. Robin Waterfield) (Oxford, Oxford University Press, 1993).

Popper, Karl, *The Poverty of Historicism* (London, Routledge, 1957).

—— *The Open Society and Its Enemies*, Volumes I and II (London, Routledge, 5th edn., 1966).

Rawls, John, *A Theory of Justice* (Cambridge, Harvard University Press, 1971).

Rosenau, Pauline Marie, *Post-Modernism and the Social Sciences* (Princeton, NJ, Princeton University Press, 1992).

Siedentop, Larry, *Tocqueville* (Oxford, Oxford University Press, 1994).

Smith, S. B., *Hegel's Criticism of Liberalism* (Chicago, University of Chicago Press, 1989).

Strauss, Leo, *Natural Right and History* (Chicago, University of Chicago Press, 1953).

—— *The City and Man* (Chicago, Rand McNally, 1964).

—— *Studies in Platonic Political Philosophy* (Chicago, University of Chicago Press, 1967).

—— *On Tyranny: Revised and Expanded Edition* (ed. V. Gourevitch and M. Roth) (New York, Free Press, 1991).

Sullivan, David (ed.), *Nation and Community*, Coleg Harlech Occasional Papers (Harlech, Coleg Harlech, 1994).

—— 'Fukuyama and the idea of progress', in Patrick Dunleavy and Jeffrey Stanyer (eds.), *Contemporary Political Studies, 1994* (London, Political Studies Association, 1994), vol.1, pp.383–94.

—— 'Hegel on war and international order', in Ian Hampsher-Monk and Jeffrey Stanyer (eds.), *Contemporary Political Studies, 1996* (London, Political Studies Association/Blackwells, 1996).

Tocqueville, Alexis de, *Democracy in America* (introduction by Alan Ryan) (London, Dent, 1994).

Vincent, Andrew, 'The Hegelian state and international politics', *Review of International Studies*, 9 (1983), 191–205.

Wilkins, B. T., *Hegel's Philosophy of History* (Ithaca, Cornell University Press, 1974).

Williams, David, *Japan: Beyond the End of History* (London, Routledge, 1993).

Williams, Howard, *Marx* (Dinbych, Gwasg Gee, 1980).

—— *Kant's Political Philosophy* (New York, St Martin's Press, 1983).

—— *Concepts of Ideology* (Brighton, Wheatsheaf Press, 1988).

—— *Hegel, Heraclitus and Marx* (New York, St Martin's Press, 1989).

—— *Essays on Kant's Political Philosophy* (Cardiff, University of Wales Press, 1992).

—— *International Relations in Political Theory* (Milton Keynes, Open University Press, 1992).

—— *International Relations and the Limits of Political Theory* (New York, St Martin's Press, 1996).

Willis, Gary, *Under God: Religion and American Politics* (New York, Simon & Schuster, 1990).

Yovel, Yirmiahu, *Kant and the Philosophy of History* (Princeton, NJ, Princeton University Press, 1980).

Index